THE
KOREAN
SINGER
OF TALES

HARVARD-
YENCHING
INSTITUTE
MONOGRAPH
SERIES, 37

PUBLISHED BY THE

COUNCIL ON EAST ASIAN STUDIES

HARVARD UNIVERSITY

AND THE HARVARD-YENCHING INSTITUTE

DISTRIBUTED BY

HARVARD UNIVERSITY PRESS

CAMBRIDGE, MASSACHUSETTS

AND LONDON

 1994

THE
KOREAN
SINGER
OF TALES

MARSHALL R. PIHL

The Harvard-Yenching Institute, founded in 1928 and headquartered at Harvard University, is a foundation dedicated to the advancement of higher education in the humanities and social sciences in East and Southeast Asia. The Institute supports advanced research at Harvard by faculty members of certain Asian universities, and doctoral studies at Harvard and other universities by junior faculty at the same universities. It also supports East Asian studies at Harvard through contributions to the Harvard-Yenching Library and publication of the *Harvard Journal of Asiatic Studies* and books on premodern East Asian history and literature.

Woodcut illustrations from Yi Hae-jo, *Kangsangnyŏn*, 1912, appear on the following pages: "The lamentably fated Blindman Shim and his sagacious wife, Kwak-ssi" (ff. 1:1a–3b), title page; "How hungry Father will be!" (ff. 1:13a–b), p. 1; "At the Crystal Palace, mother and daughter meet again" (ff. 2:11a–12b), p. 13; "On the road with Ppaengdŏk-ŏmi (ff. 2:21b–2:22a), p. 55; "Will he come or not?" (ff. 2:32b–33b), p. 112; "If she's my daughter, let's have a look!" (ff. 2:34a–b), p. 235.

Library of Congress Cataloging-in-Publication Data

Pihl, Marshall R.
    The Korean singer of tales / Marshall R. Pihl.
        p.   cm.—(Harvard-Yenching Institute monograph series ; 37)
    Includes bibliographical references and index.
    ISBN 0-674-50564-6
    1. P'ansori—History and criticism. 2. Folk music—Korean—History
and criticism. 3. Ballads, Korean—Korea—History and criticism.
4. Music and literature. I. Title. II. Series.
    ML1751.K7P5   1994
    782.42162'957—dc20   93-39953
                                                                  CIP
                                                                   MN

BOOK DESIGN: Adrianne Onderdonk Dudden
INDEX: Marshall R. Pihl

For Chang Chun-ha

ACKNOWLEDGMENTS

When I saw an operatic adaptation of the very popular "Song of Ch'un-hyang" in Seoul as a soldier in 1958, I was not aware of the p'ansori origins of the work. It was not until I returned to Korea for graduate study between 1960 and 1965 that I saw an authentic performance of p'ansori for the first time. After further study I followed the suggestion of the late Professor Kim Dong-uk, then of Yonsei University, that I concentrate on the "Song of Shim Ch'ŏng" for my doctoral research.

My formal study of the Korean language had begun under Professor Edward W. Wagner of Harvard University, whose continued support and guidance have been invaluable. I am also indebted to Professors Yi Sung-nyŏng, Lee Ki-moon, Chŏn Kwang-yong, and Chŏng Pyŏng-uk of Seoul National University for their direction of my graduate work there.

The research for the present study began under Professor Kim Dong-uk, with whom I read a Wanp'an edition of the "Song of Shim Ch'ŏng," analyzing some two thousand lines of verse word by word and producing nearly three thousand vocabulary cards of unusual examples over the course of a year's work. Subsequently, I re-read the same text with Professor Lee Ki-moon, paying special attention to linguistic questions.

Acknowledgments

In the later stages of preparation, I was greatly helped by Professor Lee Duhyŏn of Seoul National University and Mr. Kim Sung-ha of Harvard-Yenching Library. Mme. Kim So-hŭi has increased my understanding of p'ansori performance through the hours of interviews she so generously gave. I am grateful to Professors Albert B. Lord and Patrick D. Hanan of Harvard University for their guidance and encouragement when this work first emerged as a doctoral dissertation. Indeed, the title of this book reflects an intellectual debt to the late Professor Lord. As the manuscript took shape, Professors Charles W. Dunn, Edwin A. Cranston, Howard S. Hibbett, and Victor Mair of Harvard pointed out many possibilities for improvement; and Barbara Cooper invested long hours in computerizing the document. I am also beholden to such friends as Mark Belson, David McCann, Beverly Nelson, and Robert Provine. Part of the research for this undertaking was made possible by a grant from the Joint Committee on Korean Studies of the American Council of Learned Societies and the Social Science Research Council. The penultimate manuscript was researched and developed in Korea between May and August 1990 at the Academy of Korean Studies in Sŏngnam, where I was maintained by a fellowship from the International Cultural Society of Korea. The book, itself, emerged from an editorial process guided by the knowledgeable Katherine Keenum, diplomatic and persuasive Executive Editor of the Harvard Council on East Asian Studies.

Finally with sadness and gratitude, I remember Mr. Chang Chun-ha, Korean patriot, founder and publisher of *Sasanggye* magazine, and constant friend, who died too young on August 15, 1975. He, his wife, family, and colleagues have supported and encouraged me. They are the reason I study Korean literature.

CONTENTS

NOTE ON ROMANIZATIONS

The romanization systems used throughout this book are Ministry of Education for Korean, Wade-Giles for Chinese, and Kenkyusha standard for Japanese.

THE
KOREAN
SINGER
OF TALES

Introduction: Of Singers and Tales

The Korean singer of tales is called a *kwangdae*. His* oral narrative is known as *p'ansori,* a long form of vocal music in which he sings a work of narrative literature with appropriate dramatic gesture. P'ansori, a folk art and a popular art, evolved at first without the aid of scores or libretti. Although the *sori* of p'ansori is accepted as meaning "sound" or "song," there are various interpretations of *p'an.* Most commonly, *p'an* is taken as meaning "site," "arena," or "stage," with the term *p'ansori* interpreted as meaning "song sung in an arena." Some writers have used the expression "one-man opera" to explain the term. The oddity of the expression aside, it does succeed in conveying the four essential characteristics of p'ansori: it is a solo oral technique, it is dramatic, it is musical, and it is in verse.

Accompanied by only a drummer, who uses his hands and a stick to beat out a variety of rhythms, the kwangdae alternates between sung and

---

*The preponderant majority of kwangdae have historically been male, with only three females joining their ranks before the twentieth century. Therefore the male pronoun is used for convenience in this text.

spoken presentation. He performs within the area of a large mat, where he stands, kneels, sits, or moves as his story requires. His only props are his clothing, a fan, and, for some kwangdae, a handkerchief. At one moment, he is the narrator; at another, he becomes an actor playing the roles of his characters, with the voice and gestures appropriate to each.

Although he makes occasional asides to his drummer, who urges him on with cries of encouragement, the kwangdae relates primarily and directly to the members of his audience, who frequently shout out their approval after a particularly good turn. A full performance of one song may take as long as six hours, but it is traditionally presented in several installments over the course of a day. Some modern virtuosi have attempted nonstop performances, but older purists question this practice.

The musical function of the drummer is always distinguished from the histrionic role of the kwangdae, but the drummer's importance to the performance of p'ansori is suggested by the expression "one drummer is [worth] two singers."[1] When beginning his performance, a kwangdae customarily sings an opening, warm-up song to loosen his throat and gather the audience.[2] A song completely independent of the main tale may be sung for this opener; or the main work itself may have an opening section that is unconnected to the story but sung for this purpose.

Most traditional kwangdae performed alfresco, setting up shop in a farmer's marketplace or a fishing village. Some of the better singers, however, would be invited to perform at private homes or in government precincts. A leading female singer, Kim So-hŭi (b. 1917), describes a typical salon performance of p'ansori, as she has known it in this century:

> A proper place would be made in the courtyard of someone's house that would hold enough people. Otherwise, the performance would be given in a large receiving-room. The singer would be given some fruit juice on a small table and the drummer would take his place to one side. Then they would start and go for two or three hours. After that, they would all eat. That would give the singer a chance to rest. After clearing away all the food, they would start in again. Maybe at that point the drummer would be changed because his arms might be tired.[3]

Structure of the Story

Though coarse and unrefined in the early stages of its evolution, p'ansori developed its three aspects of music, drama, and literature in response to the demands of audiences. Some of the songs, while based upon simple and traditional folktales, incorporated realistic episodes and, thence, developed into believable works that reflected their social environment. Others lacked the narrative basis of a folktale altogether but put together diverse oral materials into the alternation of story and lyric that came to be recognizable as p'ansori. Whatever its origins, any given p'ansori was likely not only to interpolate folk and popular songs, but also to make abundant use of humorous sayings and idiomatic phrases. It might even borrow lines of Chinese poetry and classical allusions to decorate its sentences. Because the audience for p'ansori included members of the aristocracy, songs incorporated refined expressions suited to their tastes and even mimicked written-language narratives. In so doing, p'ansori developed its distinctive complexity, including even characteristics that resonated with aristocratic, written literature. In spite of all this, p'ansori did not lose its popular character. P'ansori was sung to any audience that would pay: fishermen or farmers in the markets, rich men at their banquets, or successful state examination candidates celebrating their good fortune. The kwangdae had to be ready to satisfy many demands: they reflected the viewpoint of the lower classes, but they also had to be responsive to aristocratic tastes.

In performance, the spoken passages are inserted by the kwangdae from time to time in order to link sung passages or rest his voice. The sung passages are characterized by their various rhythms, which change to reflect changes in feeling. The great variety of rhythms in p'ansori distinguish it from other kinds of vocal music. Another distinguishing characteristic is the wide range of pitch in which the kwangdae sings, moving freely from very high to very low. While the unique vocalization of p'ansori may sound complex to the uninitiated, it has great power and is capable of a wide variety of effects. It is difficult for untrained people to imitate the kwangdae's rhythm, range, and vocal quality because p'ansori is a refined and specialized vocal art, as distinguished from the folk songs that almost anyone can sing or poetry that can be sung with a modicum of training.

As can be expected of oral literature, p'ansori is essentially a product of serial composition by many singers over a long period of time. Thus, while the kwangdae receives an established tradition, he also innovates. The basic plot line of a given p'ansori work will be common to all performances, but the details may differ with the individual kwangdae and can also change from one of his performances to another. A plot may be drawn from a folktale; but, while the original content is simple, p'ansori turns it into a complex narrative. As the kwangdae strives to reflect everyday life and so mirror the realities of his listeners' lives, the sufferings and lamentations of his characters are frequently less in service of the plot than of an audience's need for catharsis. Although, in some p'ansori plots, distress and suffering lead eventually to a happy result, the process of suffering itself seems more important to the audience than the happy outcome—or, for that matter, than any laughter elicited by its critical view of the world. P'ansori distinguishes itself as popular literature by eliciting sympathy through suffering: it gives its audience a means to endure sorrow.

P'ansori is organized into episodes. Each episode has a distinct character and is sometimes associated with some famous kwangdae of the past who contributed it to the narrative tradition. Therefore, contradictions and inconsistencies can appear between episodes. While one may stress ideal moral codes and righteous sentiments, another may present a vivid image of unconforming life as it really is. Unconstrained by the need to maintain strict plausibility, p'ansori, with its episodic independence, can have a special, inventive liveliness and express, without the distortion of didactic narration, the contradictions inherent in real experience.

Some episodes consist of juxtaposed arias, couched in high-flown and erudite language, that express concepts especially dear to the traditional Confucian establishment. But others may take the form of a dramatic scene or a realistic dialogue where the kwangdae has a chance to use dramatic gesture and exploit his mimetic skills, reflecting a lifetime's experience of life in the lower class.

Social Aspects of P'ansori

As popular literature, p'ansori rejected the aristocratic assumption of a historical mandate for the social status quo and emphasized the contradictions and inequities of the real world in which the common people struggled to survive. But despite this outlook, it attracted an audience that included royalty as well as outcasts, a fact that not only suggests the extraordinarily wide social base of p'ansori, but also bears witness to the very adaptive nature of the form.

The occupation and social class of the traditional kwangdae, and those of his predecessors, were hereditary. Generally speaking, this hereditary characteristic was common to all occupations and classes in premodern Korea. Traditional Korean society tended to isolate one class from another in matters of residence, clothing, speech, and association; but the kwangdae and other entertainers belonged to one lowborn occupation in which one could break the rules and get away with it. We read about professional entertainers of lowborn origins performing before a range of audiences from kings and courtiers to the rabble of the streets and villages, about haughty performers dressed in finery and riding about in sedan chairs, and about kwangdae snubbing governors while on their way to visit with royalty.

Broadly conceived, the Korean social structure of the Chosŏn period (1392–1910), when p'ansori evolved and flourished, was based upon a contrast between "good people" and "lowborn." Within the good people were two major groupings: the ruling class of aristocratic officials and the bureaucratic specialists who supported them, on the one hand, and the ruled class of commoners (farmers, artisans, and merchants), on the other. At the very bottom of the structure was the lowborn class, the outcasts of society, which included kwangdae and other professional entertainers.[4] This class had existed in Korean society since prehistoric times. Its earliest categories, found in Shilla (57 B.C.–A.D. 935), were enslaved prisoners of war, criminals, and paupers, all of whom were made to live in specially designated, isolated communities. Although some were liberated during Koryŏ (918–1392), the system itself continued to be enforced rigorously with categories that included ferrymen, post-station attendants, acrobats, musicians, slaves, butchers, wicker-ware makers, actors, immigrant northern tribesmen, and other itinerants. The lowest of these lowborn, the slaves, were treated like land or other goods that could be bought, sold, pawned, given as gifts, and inherited.

During the Chosŏn period, considerable efforts were made by the government to liberate the lowborn but with little impact on the actual treatment accorded them by society. Indeed, the overall system of distinctions in social status was more strictly observed during Chosŏn then any other period. There being limited tolerance and mutual understanding between classes, those relegated to the lowborn category were ostracized by the rest of society. The "Eight Lowborn," an expression that was common in the Chosŏn period, designated private slaves, monks, butchers, shamans, kwangdae, pallbearers, *kisaeng* (female entertainers), and handicraftsmen.[5]

The word *kwangdae* existed as early as the Koryŏ period, when it appears to have designated a masked performer.[6] Later, as its meaning broadened, it came to refer to any variety entertainer; but by the late eighteenth century, it was applied narrowly and specifically to the singers of p'ansori. Early predecessors of the p'ansori kwangdae, bearers of medieval theatrical culture, were under government control and were frequently mobilized, without pay, for official state events. They had to eke out their day-to-day living by selling their talents as wanderers among the common people, where they were very much disdained.

Kwangdae were mostly from hereditary shaman households or were socially close to them. Lee Duhyŏn states that many famous kwangdae were still emerging from among the men of hereditary shaman households in the Chŏlla provinces of the southwest as late as the 1930s.[7] The highest aspiration for a male born into such circumstances was to become a kwangdae. Lacking that potential, he would become a musician and accompany a shaman. Failing that, he would turn to tumbling or rope-walking or become a blacksmith. As a last resort, he could serve as a helper at shaman ceremonies.[8]

Shaman Background

The roots of p'ansori are intertwined with those of the narrative shaman song.[9] Professional female shamans of Chŏlla Province, the heartland of p'ansori, learned their craft from their mothers-in-law;[10] and their husbands, who assisted them as accompanists, also became kwangdae. Greater diversity in kwangdae social origin and regional background was a latter-day phenomenon. While most of the early performers of p'ansori appear to have emerged from this lowborn culture of Chŏlla Province, the materials of their art came not only from the shaman culture but also from the traditions of the professional variety entertainers who preceded them and the general folk culture of their southwest region. From shaman narrative songs they gained rhythmic patterns of drumming and singing, techniques of vocalization, interweaving of sung and spoken passages, and the interpolation of songs from other traditions. From solo actors of farce and storytellers they inherited skills of characterization, improvisation, narrative development, and audience management. And the folk culture around them was an abundant source of such materials as myths, legends, stories, ballads, laments, and work songs.

As I shall show in the following pages, p'ansori emerged from these makings in the early eighteenth century and, by the late nineteenth century, was flourishing as a comprehensive embodiment of Korean popular culture. Its closest genetic affinity was to those forms and traditions in which the entire dramatic event was in the hands of an unassisted single performer, as distinguished from mask dance and puppet plays.

While p'ansori kwangdae of the latter half of the Chosŏn period inherited a disdained social status, some of those who flourished during the nineteenth-century heyday of the art earned considerable appreciation by their efforts to create a timely and interesting form which was both musical theater and narrative poetry. It is widely believed that the early p'ansori kwangdae, in order to adapt narrative shaman songs as secular and popular narrative poems, invested the music with greater rhythmic variation and introduced entertaining legendary materials which they supplemented with experience drawn from real life. It was because of their personal life experiences that these articulate products of the lowborn class could so sharply and perceptively satirize Korean social realities and also reveal the interior of the human experience as they knew it. By integrating their social insight with the rhythms and melodies of their unique folk and shaman music, they created a combination that not only rang true for their own people but also proved irresistible to those of other classes and regions.

Since kwangdae were improvisational performers who were dependent upon the whims of live audiences, they would tailor their performances to suit the tastes of their listeners, adding here and deleting there, emphasizing one theme at the expense of another, all in order to shape a whole that would gain the best response and, hence, financial reward. As the master singer Song Man-gap (1865–1939) is said to have remarked, "A singer is like a fabric seller. To the customer who asks for silk, he gives silk, and to the customer asking for cotton, he gives cotton."[11]

In this sense, popular audiences of the early nineteenth century were parties to the act of composition and, thus, had an indirect role in shaping the content and emphasis of p'ansori songs. Since the combined influences of the master-disciple relationship and guild affiliation contributed to a fixing of p'ansori texts later in the century and since surviving texts record the resulting tradition, we have available to us today, in p'ansori, an authentic reflection of nineteenth-century popular culture in Korea.

P'ansori's broad and receptive audience and its ability to adapt to changing needs have helped it survive the waves of social, political, and cultural change that have swept Korea since the late nineteenth century. Just after the turn of the twentieth century, it responded to the challenges of Chinese opera, new-wave drama, and Western theater by taking on its popular operatic form, called *ch'anggŭk,* in which kwangdae became theatrical stage performers, each taking on the role of an individual character. Although ch'anggŭk no longer called upon the kwangdae's special ability to conjure up many settings and characters with only voice and gesture, it did serve as a vehicle for the introduction of new works—something p'ansori had ceased to do after its repertoire became fixed in the later half of the nineteenth century, until its modern revival in the 1980s and 1990s.

From Mat to Proscenium

The event that brought p'ansori from a mat in the marketplace to the proscenium stage and from solo performance to multi-singer casting was the 1902 erection of Korea's first national theater, the Hŭidae, in preparation for a celebration of the reigning emperor's fortieth year on the throne. Although the celebration was never carried out as planned, the Hŭidae Theater was built, a company was assembled, and the first proscenium-stage, ch'anggŭk adaptation of p'ansori, was presented in the fall of 1903.

Although the Hŭidae Theater's structure had been inspired by grand facilities in Europe like London's Royal Albert Hall and the Royal Theater in Vienna, the adaptation of p'ansori to a stage format was influenced by Chinese Peking opera troupes then performing in Korea, according to leading performers in the Hŭidae Theater company. But, as it turned out, although many ch'anggŭk productions were mounted and can still be seen today, they developed into spectaculars in which theatrical effect displaced creative art. Traditional p'ansori, on the other hand, continued to be performed and, thanks to recent government subsidies, the surviving master singers can pass their art to a new generation of performers. But, while traditional, solo performances continue to be seen on stage and television, the most exciting innovations can be found in the adaptation of p'ansori techniques to the assertive literature and theater of political resistance, a fitting trend in view of the original protest nature of p'ansori during its nineteenth-century heyday among the common people.

So, why does solo performance seem to enjoy a better fit with the essential nature of p'ansori than does casted, proscenium opera? I believe an answer to this lies in the nature of the p'ansori narrator and his relationship with his characters and his audience.

There is a tension between narrator and character when the solo performer does both roles, for the narrator never quite eliminates himself and the character is never fully realized. That is, the audience never knows the character directly without the intervention of the narrator. The narrator does not "become" the character but, like a shaman, conveys his experience of the character, through himself, back to the audience. Hence, just as the shaman must be present to bring back the spirit so must the p'ansori performer be a constant party to the presentation of a character. Contrast this with the stage performer who wears the clothing and make-up of the character and, eliminating himself, asserts that he is, indeed, the character while we, suspending disbelief, accept his transformation.

Korea before the twentieth century had no experience in such fully realized characterization, unlike the cases of neighboring China and Japan. At court, there had been exorcistic tableaux with masked figures and farce plays with comedic characterization where the farce actor commented on the stereotype he ridiculed. And among the common people there had been puppeteers and masked dancers who also presented only stereotypes. But in all cases, the performer had always been present in a mediating role.

Evidence of the unwillingness of a Korean audience in 1900 to accept self-eliminating, fully realized characterization can be found in two anecdotes from the period. When the first realistic ch'angguk on a contemporary theme—about a wildly rapacious governor and a commoner who suffered and died because of him—was performed at the Huidae Theater in 1908, the audience reacted emotionally. People sympathetic to the victim rose from their seats and mobbed the actor playing the victim, praising him and hanging strings of cash around his neck; and on another occasion, newspapers reported that some seven spectators raised a ruckus during a climactic scene one night when they yelled at the same actor, claiming it wrong to perform such scenes of immorality and asking where such acts would lead. The second anecdote concerns a provincial ch'angguk troupe that could not perform the full version of a certain work because it called for three female characters and there was only one female singer in their company. This was in spite of the fact that a traditional male solo p'ansori performer of course "played" all three roles and male performers in mask dance drama were also playing all roles, including those of women. And at the same time, of course, men were still playing women in traditional Chinese and Japanese theater.

All of this suggests to me that characterization, as managed in p'ansori and mask dance, was something quite different from that of proscenium theater, where individual actors appeared in full character without any mediation. This also suggests to me that the mediating role of the narrator is essential to p'ansori and that the move from mat to proscenium cut the heart out of the art when it relegated the central figure of the narrator to a marginal place off to one side of the stage.

It may be better to say that ch'angguk is not so much a developmental stage of p'ansori as it is an imported theatrical format which drew upon p'ansori for its materials. And, at the same time, we should be looking for the survival of the art of p'ansori, not on the stage but, rather, on the "mat" again, where the narrator is still master of all he conjures up for us.

水晶宮中에
母女相逢

ONE

THE SINGER:
KWANGDAE

1

Where Did the Kwangdae Come From?

Until urbanization and modern mass communications altered the traditional balance, popular literary cultures existed alongside, but distinguished from, the higher cultures of the same peoples of East Asia. In China, for example, the formal, written literature of the gentry had long been distinguished from its oral (and orally derived), popular counterparts, not only by content and style but by language as well. Indeed, neither the spoken language nor the written vernacular was recognized as a proper literary medium by the Chinese literati until the beginning of the twentieth century. In spite of the distinctions that separated these literatures in China, there was a complex interaction between them, marked by a general upward flow of subject-matter from one to the other.[1]

In the Chosŏn period of Korea, there existed a set of conditions that tended to separate popular culture from the orthodox culture of the society. The higher culture of traditional Korea based its institutions on Chinese models and consciously shunned the popular culture as a source of artistic inspiration; there was no upward flow of literary materials and only piece-meal borrowing from the higher culture by the popular culture. Chinese Neo-Confucianism dominated the philosophy and aesthetics of the former, while Buddhism and indigenous shamanism invested the latter; the litera-ture of the former was written, while that of the latter was oral; the literary language of the former was mainly Chinese, while that of the latter was Korean. Along with Korea's hereditary class standings and professions, these conditions made for a dual cultural tradition in Korea, assuring the survival of the oral narrative, which throve in the context of the popular culture until the twentieth century, when it was absorbed by the written literary tradition of the society.

The kwangdae had no occupation (such as farming) other than the per-formance of oral narratives. His training was lengthy, specialized, and rig-orous. He was born into the lowest of social classes, grew up in poverty, banded together with others of his profession, and had an ambiguous social status and access that varied with his skill, popularity, and patronage. This professional singer of tales survived by dint of his wit and eloquence and, jealous of his art, regarded outsiders with suspicion and kept any written texts a secret. He developed his lengthy songs during performance and had to think quickly under these conditions, improvising rapidly and fluently to satisfy his audience.

Hwarang *Tradition and Shaman Culture*

The earliest identifiable predecessors of the kwangdae are usually sought amongst participants in the festivals of community and state. The history of state-sponsored performance in Korea dates back to the formative years of ancient society when the founding rulers were chief shamans in whom were combined both political and religious functions.[2] Before the introduction and subsequent success of Buddhism during the Shilla period, the religious life of the country was shamanistic and court entertainment reflected this native culture. Young members of the nobility sometimes played a religious role that included the performance of song and dance, as members of the aristocratic *hwarang* order. The order is said to have been established by King Chinhŭng (r. 534–576) in the last year of his reign for ethical, artistic, and military training.[3] Young men were admitted to it at ages thirteen to fifteen and later graduated to serve the country as civil and military leaders.

Although the *hwarang* order may not itself have been a shaman insti-

tution nor its members themselves shamans, their activities basically reflected a native shamanistic outlook.[4] The *hwarang* visited "celebrated"
(probably sacred) mountains and rivers, where they sang and danced, pray-
ing for national peace and progress.[5] This was consistent with the fact that
the Council of Elders, the highest organ of the Shilla state, would retire to
one of the four sacred mountains surrounding the capital when they had to
discuss and decide questions of particular importance to the nation.[6] The
choice of mountain sites for prayer and debate by the *hwarang* and the
elders was appropriate for the shamanistic context of early Shilla society
and may be related to the ancient mountain worship found also in Japan
and Mongolia.[7]

From its inception, the *hwarang* order continued to enjoy the personal
interest and patronage of the king, who frequently exercised his right to
name new members, selecting them from among the sons of the high nobility. At least one king, Kyŏngmun (r. 861–875), was himself a *hwarang* in
his youth, having joined the order at the age of eighteen.[8]

Chinhŭng, the king who first sanctioned the *hwarang* order, also instituted an annual court entertainment, the *p'algwanhoe,* at which members of
the *hwarang* order performed.[9] This celebration, held in the palace gardens,
was a formalization of the annual and semi-annual custom of heaven-wor-
ship, which had been observed by primitive Koreans and has survived today
in remote country villages in the form of periodic festivals such as the mask
play at Hahoe. According to Hong Pong-han's encyclopedic *Tongguk munhŏn
pigo* (Collected Korean documents; 1770), participants "amused themselves
with singing, dancing, and variety acts and, also, prayed for blessings."[10]

At their height, the *hwarang* had enjoyed high popular regard; but, toward
the end of the Shilla period, their status gradually declined. With the coming of the Koryŏ period, there was no longer a place for them in the official
order of things; they lost their political base and the path to power that
their order had afforded them. The decline of the *hwarang* was probably
related to the disintegration of the royal establishment, rise of the local
nobility, and concomitant philosophical transformation that characterized
the late-Shilla period. The *hwarang* exemplified the warrior ideal and native
beliefs that had built the state and assured its social order. But now a much
different philosophy was on the rise, influenced by Chinese thought and
espoused by non-royal nobility. Oral culture was giving way to the written
as lords of the word were yielding to those of the letter, for it was descendants of the lettered nobles of Shilla who would eventually assume political
leadership in the coming Koryŏ period.[11]

Modern Korean scholarship assumes that this degraded *hwarang* tradition merged with other shamanistic aspects of the popular culture during the Koryŏ period.[12] In the shadow of a Koryŏ state policy favoring Buddhism, the *hwarang* became displaced and dispersed; and their religious activity took on the form of popular shamanistic rituals. Their martial skills were turned to tumbling, acrobatics, and rope-walking; and their music became accompaniment for shaman ritual or the stuff of itinerant band performances. Furthermore, after the establishment in the middle tenth century of the Koryŏ examination system and the subsequent growth of a bureaucratic class with no less a status than the noble officialdom of Shilla, the scattered *hwarang* were demeaned as a group of wandering outcasts who were unregistered and difficult to control, reminiscent of Europe's Gypsies.

Although the social status of actors, singers, musicians, dancers, and other entertainers had thus declined to that of a degraded minority, there was still a demand for their services at court that was to increase over the years of the Koryŏ period. There were three major periodic events that took place in the Koryŏ court over the course of a year: the *p'algwanhoe* mentioned above, the *yŏndŭnghoe,* and *narye.* They were like state religious rites that were meant to assure national peace and prevent disaster through song and dance. The *p'algwanhoe,* dating back to the Shilla period, sought national peace through prayers addressed to mountain and river spirits; the *yŏndŭnghoe,* introduced during Koryŏ, sought the blessings of Buddha; and the *narye,* instituted in early Koryŏ and influenced by Chinese models, served as the annual exorcism of the court. Though of differing religious import, all three events were performed on the same sort of large, festooned stage and shared a common core of secular songs, dances, acrobatic feats, and variety acts.[13]

The founding king of Koryŏ, T'aejo (r. 918–935), revived the Shilla *p'algwanhoe* for his court, where it was held in the eleventh lunar month. This Koryŏ version of the Shilla *p'algwanhoe* preserved some parts of its predecessor, particularly a section called *sasŏn akpu* (music troupe of the four *hwarang*), which was dominated by the music, singing, and dancing of *hwarang*. Although its actual content is not clearly understood, Lee Duhyŏn stresses, "The expression *sasŏn akpu* was not related only to dancing in a narrow sense; but, rather, we should see the term as associated with the totality of the song, music, and dance—in the broad sense—that had been the responsibility of the *hwarang* order."[14]

Many professional actors and entertainers—apart from musicians—were attached to the Koryŏ court (160 people at one point) with exclusive re-

sponsibility for theatrical events. And, in addition to these court entertainers, there were also many entertainers and musicians throughout the
country, living in the midst of a populace that appeared to have sufficient
resources to support them as professionals.[15]

Although an attempt was made under Sŏngjong (r. 982–997) to eliminate the *p'algwanhoe* on grounds that it incorporated "inappropriate and
annoying, motley amusements," foreshadowing comparable attitudes of the
Chosŏn period, it was soon revived and went on to flourish well into the
twelfth century. As the *hwarang,* who had maintained the *p'algwanhoe* tradition, began to disappear in the twelfth century, aristocrats and rich people
took over its management, with the result that it gradually became secular-
ized and its once-dominant religious aspect was reduced to a side event
accompanying a show composed of worldly variety acts. The *p'algwanhoe*
declined during the thirteenth century and had disappeared from court life
by the reign of Wŏnjong (r. 1260–1274).[16]

I infer from two descriptive poems[17] by the late-Koryŏ scholar Yi Saek
(Mogŭn, 1328–1396) that variety entertainment at court by the fourteenth
century was called *sandae chapkŭk* (stage theatricals), as distinguished from
the exorcistic *narye* rituals. The late-Koryŏ expression *sandae,* meaning an
elevated platform, here replaced the earlier and more descriptive designation, *ch'aebung,* which had meant a stage draped with silk. The term *sandae*
became more commonly used during the Chosŏn period, when court entertainments were generally known as *sandaehŭi* (stage play).[18]

After 1392, the new Chosŏn government rejected Buddhism and adopted
Confucianism as the state ethic. Subsequently, Buddhist monks were relegated to a station similar to that of the *hwarang.* But the Buddhists still had
their temples in the mountains, the protection of tradition and popular belief, and an income of sacrificial rice and offerings with which they were
able to survive. The *hwarang,* however, were left with no such means and
had no choice but to tour and perform their songs and participate in shamanistic rituals. Some built shrines in various localities for shaman worship
and restricted their activities to a district surrounding the shrine. While the
women conducted rituals, the men assisted by providing a musical accompaniment. As a regular relationship developed with their believers, they
managed to get along on the money and grain received for their rituals,
prayers, and fortune-telling.[19] This shaman "parish" system, called the *tan-
gol* system, is common today in Chŏlla and Kyŏngsang Provinces. It is centered on a hereditary shaman who, carrying on priestly authority passed
through the generations, is not spiritually possessed but has been ordained

by human agency. This type of shaman functions within a systematic institutional structure and exercises jurisdiction over a fixed territory.[20]

The men had several specialties and were grouped into three classifications: instrumentalists, called *agin* or *kongin,* who played flute and drum; physical performers, called *chaein,* who did tumbling, rope-walking, and acrobatics; and singers, called *kwangdae.* All three were commonly lumped together as *chaein* or *kwangdae.* As a matter of natural evolution, the husband of a shaman, who had served as accompanist and assistant to his wife, eventually emerged as a professional actor or singer on his own. The set of skills he already possessed were easily transferred to a secular context.

A continuous stream of comments—frequently demeaning and abusive—from private and official sources throughout the Chosŏn period makes it clear that such lowborn entertainers as these successors to the *hwarang* were destined to remain relegated to a status determined by their social, cultural, and economic circumstances until those circumstances finally began to change with the coming of the twentieth century.

A modern study of *tan'gol* shamans allows some glimpses of these years of change and also documents the presence of male p'ansori singers in *tan-gol* shaman family lineages.[21] Three families were examined in considerable detail for the personal background of the primary shaman, family structure and lineage, ritual practices, and ritual texts. The lineages, of which two were interrelated, covered from four to six generations and the earliest birth date that can be inferred would have been about 1840 (from a daughter given as born in 1856). In all, fifteen women and nineteen men were clearly accounted for by name, age, and occupational specialty.

It is clear that the women had little choice but to be shamans, except for two young women who were identified as "popular singers," an occupation consistent with their backgrounds. The name of one of the popular singers was withheld from the report. The men, however, had a variety of specialties including *tan'gol* shaman, p'ansori singer (both nineteenth-century and contemporary), musician (zither, flute, drum), tumbler, shrine helper, businessman, and college dropout. The name of one of the p'ansori singers (a registered Intangible Cultural Treasure at the time) was withheld; the businessman's company name was not given; and the college dropout, who had previously done some shaman duties, had a "pessimistic view towards having been born into a *tan'gol* shaman family."[22]

The 1969 report describes a modern shaman culture that looks essentially the same as its early-Chosŏn antecedent, as reconstructed in modern Korean scholarship. In both cases, we find a socially outcast, hereditary profession that is organized on a territorial basis. While the women are virtually all practicing shamans, the men have a variety of specialities, chief among which is musician-accompanist. Useful in the context of this present study is the fact that the men are also frequently active as variety entertainers.

The Chosŏn Court and Its Popular Entertainers

Although Chosŏn officials had no interest in popular culture, they did have a use for popular entertainers. As was the case in earlier periods, the Chosŏn court sponsored periodic and occasional entertainments for which they employed such variety performers as masked dancers, musicians, singers, jugglers, rope-walkers, acrobats, tumblers, magicians, comedians, and puppeteers. The Chosŏn court and aristocracy served as an unintentional catalyst in the transformation of folk entertainments into extended and refined works of oral narrative, playing a role not unlike that of the feudal domains and religious establishments of medieval Japan in the development of Japanese narrative literature.[23] Unlike China and Japan, however, Korea had neither great urban centers with a monied mercantile class that would support professional theater nor sufficient sources of aristocratic protection and patronage in the countryside to nurture a class of itinerant entertainers.

Korea did develop a practical and necessary system of linkage involving the royal court, local officialdom, literati, and rural entertainers.[24] Through this mechanism, which developed during the seventeenth and eighteenth centuries, erstwhile outcast singers and actors came to perform in the capital, gain access to forbidden precincts of the palace, absorb elements of aristocratic literary culture, compete with their colleagues, and exchange materials with performers from other parts of the country. Thus, the professional singer of tales, the kwangdae, was able to gain exposure to the lettered world. Eventually, seminal performers of the p'ansori oral narrative emerged and populated the nineteenth and twentieth centuries with their artistic progeny.

While the Chosŏn court eliminated the Koryŏ p'algwanhoe and yŏndŭnghoe, they did continue the sandaehŭi variety show and the exorcistic narye, which became known as naryehŭi (exorcism and plays). The naryehŭi, held on the last day of the twelfth lunar month, still served to exorcize malevolent spirits; and the sandaehŭi, performed on its decorated stage, was held on such occasions as days of national celebration. Both the sandaehŭi and *naryehŭi* provided professional entertainers with continuing opportunities to perform in the capital city. The two events overlapped in content and personnel and, indeed, eventually became confused with each other.

The *naryehŭi* got its name from the fact that its program customarily consisted of an exorcism (*narye*) followed by various entertaining plays (*hŭi*), which actually involved all kinds of singing, dancing, acrobatics, and witty talk. These plays and their performers were the same as those employed in *sandaehŭi* variety shows. As a result of the fact that people paid more attention to performance than to function, the two events came to be grouped under the one term, *sandaehŭi*.[25] According to a notice in the *Munjong Shillok* for the sixth month of 1451, these *sandaehŭi* were divided into three aspects: acrobatic and spectacle shows, farces, and music.[26] The acrobatic and spectacle shows were made up of such stunts as rope-walking, juggling, and tumbling; the farces consisted of humorous talk; and the music included singing, dancing, and playing on instruments.[27]

Sandaehŭi—particularly the farces—provided opportunities for quick-witted, improvisational performers to develop their technical skills as they encountered sophisticated and demanding audiences, lettered culture, and professional competition. In the capital, they worked in an artistically comprehensive context that would eventually support the development of an improvisational oral narrative literature that combined prose and poetry and was vocally demanding, full of musical and rhythmic variation, rich in gesture and characterization, structurally complex, witty and poignant, and abounding in audience give-and-take. For more than three hundred years, the *sandaehŭi* and other opportunities to perform in the capital provided an enriching complement to the boisterous cauldron of the rural marketplace theater and so, by the opening of the eighteenth century, a fully formed, extended oral narrative song—called p'ansori—began to appear and attract the attention of the lettered populace, who could document its existence.

Sandaehŭi were given on stages erected within court precincts or on the wayside as part of royal banquets and progresses, state receptions, various periodic festivals, and other occasional official observances.[28] The most ambitious *sandaehŭi* were held to mark the visit of Chinese embassies: large-scale performances were given not only at provincial centers along the route from the Chinese border, but also in the capital. In his "Ch'ao-hsien fu" (Rhymeprose on Chosŏn), the Chinese envoy Tung Yueh described a performance he had seen in Seoul when he visited in 1488 to announce the ascension of the Ming emperor, Hsiao Tsung.[29] According to Tung Yueh, this variety show, rather like a circus, included such acts as fire-eating, dragon-dancing, children's dancing, tumbling, rope-walking, puppet shows, and grotesque mask-dancing. It was performed on a stage housed within a structure that he judged to be as high as the palace gates, which would have been about forty feet.

From the size and shape of the *sandaehŭi* stage, it appears that many of these productions were major undertakings, consuming great amounts of human and material resources.[30] More than just platforms, the stages were decorative objects in themselves. Though simple in the Koryŏ period, the stages of the Chosŏn period were painted, festooned, and decorated with portraits of historical and legendary figures. So heavy was the cost of building and decorating them that some kinds of expensive stages were eliminated at times and efforts were made to reuse others in following years.[31] The government office responsible for such events was called the *Sandae togam* or *Narye togam* (a *togam* was an office set up to supervise a special event). While the *togam* staff, on temporary reassignment from other offices, handled planning and preparations, actual stage management of the production was left to the lowborn signers, actors, acrobats, and other itinerant entertainers—all conscripted to perform without compensation.[32]

For most of these performers, life was a harsh affair, lived from day to day, hand to mouth. Remarks appear in the *Shillok* from time to time, noting that they did not farm but begged for food or that they even turned to thievery when they could not otherwise survive, since their livelihoods depended totally on performing.[33] A *Shillok* entry for 1481 notes that performers also banded together to give performances.[34] Their usual audience, as impoverished as they, was found in farming and fishing villages, around temples and shrines, and in the periodic marketplaces. They were of the common people and reflected the tastes and sensibilities of that audience.[35] Therefore, a chance to perform in the capital was a golden opportunity that often attracted performers in sufficient numbers to disconcert court officials, some of whom already had a very low opinion of them.

Controlling these performers, particular the farce players, proved to be a challenge. The passage from the *Munjong Shillok* for the sixth month of 1451, quoted above, that divides *sandaehŭi* into spectacle, farce, and music, also reflects official attitudes toward the content and performers of farce. While recommending that both the music and spectacles be continued "as from days of yore," the passage singles out the farces as being acceptable only if they are "kept to a limited number."[36] But, although the farces were not essential to the *sandaehŭi,* they were nevertheless included because they were the strong suit of the performers who were themselves essential to all aspects of *sandaehŭi*.[37]

Since these farces could not be eliminated, they became the subject of ongoing debate within the government. Those Confucian officials who argued against the retention of old practices and in favor of a whole new order based on Neo-Confucianism also took the *sandaehŭi* for their whipping boy because of their particular distaste for farce plays. The debate lasted as long as *sandaehŭi* itself.

While the entertainers were needed at court, they were still despised for their rustic vulgarity. Indeed, these rowdy country folk were the very antithesis of what many members of the Confucian establishment regarded as civilized. A minister of King Myŏngjong (r. 1545–1567) asked in 1561, "How can we call this a civilized state and yet have these plays of puppets and actors?" Arguing against making such plays a part of formal court events, particularly in the forbidden precincts, the same minister summed up, "These plays are, all of them, the vulgar and ragged affairs of the streets and villages."[38]

Court officials were especially displeased with the popular reaction to *sandaehŭi* performers, who would attract swarms of onlookers at their public performances in Seoul. The presence of women and students in the crowds, in particular, aroused their ire.[39] The Inspector General in 1431, Shin Kae, submitted a memorial which condemned the *sandaehŭi* for its bad influence on the morals of women and asked that they be kept away, saying, "It would be most unfortunate if we do not succeed in reforming these evil customs and rectifying the way of women."[40] King Sejong (r. 1418–1450), however, did not approve the memorial. The performers appear to have continued to be very popular among women; for another Inspector General reported to the throne in 1537, "Recently women gather in vacant houses to see the plays of actors. They say there are also such occurrences even within the palace."[41]

A prohibition against aristocratic women attending welcoming ceremonies for the 1606 Ming embassy was recorded in the *Shillok*: "On the day when customary ceremonies are held to welcome the Chinese embassy, aristocratic women of the capital take in the sight. Their mule-litters stretch in lines and their adornment and cosmetics cause confusion. The Third Royal Secretary was told that, on the day of welcome for the Chinese embassy, there would be a strict curfew imposed on the families of aristocrats with the head of household held responsible."[42]

In 1703, a prohibition was applied to students when King Sukchong (r.

1674–1720) approved a request from the headmaster of the National Academy that "students discovered watching the *sandaehŭi* be kept from sitting for state examinations for a period of three years." In making his request, the headmaster reported, "The capital is thrown into chaos at the time of a *sandaehŭi* performance; noisy arguments erupt and every place is in confusion. I have seen, in this midst, the evil of many students getting into fights and knocking people down!"[43]

Sandaehŭi performances ceased by the end of the eighteenth century.[44] The heavy cost of preparations may have helped bring about the end of large-scale government patronage; for the record is dotted with notices suggesting preparations on a smaller scale, saving materials for reuse on later occasions, and other measures to reduce expenses.[45] By the time that the noted octogenarian scholar of the New Learning School, Yi Ik (Sŏngho, 1681–1763), was writing his *Sŏngho sasŏl* (Sŏngho's jottings) in the middle of the eighteenth century, the *sandaehŭi* had become a major expense. In the opinion of Yi Ik, the court would be well rid of this waste of money that served only to "dissipate the mind." In *Sŏngho sasŏl* he makes the following comments: "First there was wastefulness and then it became excessive, flowing over to harm the people and even disrupt the world. Why do these things continue unabated? In the present age an office was specially established to build stages of the left and right each time a Chinese embassy came. The competitions were novel. Each time it grew bigger and the expense was great. Could this not be lessened each time and then finally be abolished?"[46]

The *sandaehŭi* farces, which were so popular with the public and so disturbing to some members of the establishment, consisted of witty talk intended to evoke laughter. A single player could do a monologue of questions and answers, or several players could take individual roles. There is an early reference to this kind of farce, albeit alfresco, given in the *Koryŏ sa* (History of Koryŏ; 1451) and assigned to the reign of King Kongmin (r. 1352–1374). It is contained in a biography of the stern Koryŏ bureaucrat, Yŏm Hŭng-bang (d. 1388). According to this account, Yŏm Hŭng-bang was returning from a visit to relatives when he came upon a place where the street was packed with spectators watching a player do a scene in which the slave of a very powerful household is tormenting a commoner in order to collect tenant farm rent. Yŏm is said to have watched with amusement.[47] Not only does this anecdote help link Chosŏn-period farce to its Koryŏ antecedents, but it also reminds us of the social function of farce and of its origins among the common people.

While the kings and nobles of Koryŏ openly enjoyed their court entertainments, even to the extent of participating themselves, their straight-laced Chosŏn counterparts customarily sat motionless, only watching and listening, no matter what was being performed. Nevertheless, there were times when even a Chosŏn monarch would have a farce player called in for unofficial diversion to relieve tedium. But a pretext was needed to justify letting the king listen to what was regarded as utter nonsense from a lowborn clown, hence the almost ubiquitous endnotes added to documentary accounts of farces performed in the royal presence to the effect that the king lent an ear to farces in order to hear things that would help him grasp the sentiment of the people and, thus, better rule the country.[48]

But the king was not alone in having a hidden agenda. Just as he sought amusement in the guise of grasping popular sentiment, so the farce player, for his part, sought to plead the people's case in the guise of performing nonsensical farce. All the while, the player knew well that he risked punishment as payment for his efforts.

The Yŏnsan'gun (r. 1495–1506) seems to have been easily irked by incautious farce players. When a player named Konggyŏl in the twelfth month of 1499 ridiculed the Confucian classic canon in several particulars, he was declared insolent, lashed, and expelled to work as a post-station attendant.[49] And, in the twelfth month of 1504, a player named Konggil was beaten and banished for presenting a farce in which he said that it is difficult to find an ideal king but that splendid ministers always abound. The wretched Konggil had the courage to remonstrate against the tyrannical Yŏnsan'gun when no one else dared to speak!

Two stories in *P'aegwan chapki* (A collector's miscellany) by Ŏ Suk-kwŏn (fl. 1525–1554) demonstrate that farce players on occasion could achieve redress for the people. The first story regards a heavy cloth tax the government had been levying on shamans in particular. When tax collectors appeared at the shaman's gate, shouting and carrying on, the entire household would hastily prepare food and wine to receive them and then beg for a postponement. Such encounters could stretch on for days. When a player took one of these incidents and, fashioning it into a farce, performed it in the courtyard of the palace, the king listened and had the discriminatory shaman cloth tax abolished. Since the player would have come from or been closely connected to a shaman family, he could perform on the basis of detailed knowledge. According to Ŏ Suk-kwŏn's account, the actors "preserved this play and still perform it to this day,"[50] suggesting that farce plays were not necessarily always newly improvised at the time of their performance and that they enjoyed some measure of lasting popularity among the common people.[51]

While this farce satirized an institutional practice that needed correction, other farces were directed at specific corrupt or covetous officials whose behavior was eventually rectified as a direct result of the farce players' efforts, such as the case of Ku Se-jang, magistrate of Chŏngp'yŏng in the reign of Chungjong (r. 1506–1544). Ŏ Suk-kwŏn tells how actors one New Year's day performed a play for the king in which this greedy magistrate haggled tyrannously with a saddle dealer and finally bought himself a saddle with government money. The king, hearing this, ordered the magistrate arrested, flogged, and punished for misappropriation of funds. "Indeed," concludes Ŏ Suk-kwŏn, "the actors could impeach a corrupt official!"[52]

Players on Their Own

Reports of individual farce players, performing at court or before the king, disappear from official records and private writings in the early seventeenth century.[53] Nevertheless, *sandaehŭi* continue to be performed at court and court records reflect that unnamed *sandaehŭi* performers continue to raise official ire. Here, however, a new emphasis appears: officials are now also criticizing entrepreneurial public performances outside the province of court *sandaehŭi*. I do not know what became of the role that farce players performed at court but, on the basis of their popular following and the hereditary nature of their calling, I assume that they continued their professional activity. Presumably they were attracted by opportunities to continue performing, for compensation, in other, undocumented contexts. Indeed, this moment, when farce plays and their players no longer evoke comment in the court record or other, private sources, coincides with early stages of the development of commerce and the growth of private capital among commoners, which made it increasingly possible for entertainers to make a living by selling their talents among the common people.

The seventeenth century in Korea set the scene for the prosperous eighteenth, when aristocratic intellectuals were to explore new ways of thought and popular culture would enjoy an awakening. Economic developments of the seventeenth century served to create new wealth in non-aristocratic hands. New agricultural technology enriched enterprising peasant farmers, and changing tax laws permitted the emergence of powerful wholesale merchants. While shops appeared in Seoul and periodic markets developed in the countryside (where entertainers could gather their audiences), rural brokers and itinerant peddlers grew in number. Middlemen began to offer support services to merchants, ranging from warehousing to banking.[54]

In such an environment, the newly rising commoners were increasingly able to purchase the services of professional entertainers and thereby provide them with both employment and a new kind of audience. Popular entertainment, thitherto, had been presented basically in two very contrasting environments: farming and fishing villages, on the one hand, and the royal court and mansions of the aristocracy, on the other. However, this third, urban audience did not record its culture as fully as did the court and aristocracy and, therefore, left an incomplete record of the popular entertainment they enjoyed.

In addition to performing within the palace, out-of-doors on a stage, or as party to a royal progress, entertainers, called "kwangdae" also served in the entourages of the aristocracy and guests of the court in the capital city, literally dancing attendance upon the central figure in the procession. As early as the eighteenth century, performers were attending successful state examination candidates on their triumphal tours of celebration. In his *Sŏngho sasŏl,* Yi Ik observes, "Nowadays the successful examination candidate must have a player to make music."[55] A generation later, Yu Tŭk-kong (1748–1807) gives a more detailed account of this custom in his *Kyŏngdo chapki* (Capital miscellany): "The successful examination candidate receives his diploma and goes in a procession with musicians, kwangdae, and acrobats in attendance. A kwangdae is a player who wears brocade robes and a yellow straw hat in which are stuck silk flowers and peacock feathers. He dances a vigorous dance and makes merry patter. The acrobat does rope-walking, tumbling, and performs various turns."[56]

This custom of performers' attending a new licentiate continued into the nineteenth century. In "Hanyang ka" (Song of the capital), a lengthy narrative poem in the *kasa* form, an anonymous poet with the pen name Hansan Kŏsa described the scene as he saw it in 1844. Dancers greeted the celebrants as they emerged from the palace and formed a grand retinue that paraded through the streets:

> Amidst the flowers and the willows,
> Music at a quick-beat followed;
> Dancers dancing, servants calling—
> Sound reverberating everywhere.[57]

The early modern scholar Ch'oe Nam-sŏn (1890–1957) has described these triumphal tours as he knew them at the turn of the twentieth century. A central event in the celebration of a new licentiate was the *yuga* procession, a three-day tour through the streets of the capital with stops to call upon examination officials, older licentiates, and relatives. This was followed by a visit to the licentiate's home village to honor his parents, sacrifice to his ancestors, and hold banquets. Ch'oe Nam-sŏn concludes, "In the *yuga* procession, singing actors lead the way, displaying their skills. At every banquet or sacrifice, such publicly performed music and entertainment is necessarily included."[58]

The poet Song Man-jae (1788–1851) refers to an interesting aspect of this practice of attending the licentiate in his Chinese poem, "Kwanuhŭi" (On seeing the plays of actors; 1843), in which he describes a variety entertainment by musicians, actors, singers, and tumblers. One of his allusive stanzas reads:

> With diploma given, they chant the *tŏktam*
> Of soaring rank and ambition won—
> From Secretariat Recorder to State Councilor:
> One leap to the sweet realm of an Acacia Dream.[59]

This refers to the practice of a kwangdae's returning with the new licentiate to his home and there conducting rites to ensure the young man's future success. Drawing upon the testimony of one famous drummer to kwangdae, Han Sŏng-jun (1875–1935), Yi Hye-gu gives the following account of this ritual, which is called a *tŏktam*:

> When the licentiate, accompanied by a kwangdae, reaches his country home, the kwangdae sets a table in the garden and places rice on top of it. On top of the rice he places the diploma and then intones rites. These consist of a summary of history since the Creation, of the Three Kingdoms, and of the Koryŏ and Yi dynasties. Then he chants, describing the furnishings of the house, speaking of the new licentiate, and asking that they be blessed with wealth and rank in the future.[60]

To this, Yi Hye-gu adds that *tŏktam* is another word for *kosa* (a ritual offering to spirits for good fortune). He goes on to remark that, in a radio broadcast made prior to the Second World War, one Pang Ŭng-gyo[61] said that the *tŏktam* was sung in the *chung mori* rhythm from beginning to end. In view of this, Yi Hye-gu concludes, "We can see a relationship between p'an-sori and shaman ritual."[62] Yi Hye-gu's conclusion is based upon the fact that the *chung mori* rhythm, which is fundamental to p'ansori, is also heard in this shaman ritual for the licentiate and his family.

This *tŏktam* is recorded by the ethnographers Akamatsu Chijō and Akiba Takashi in their study on Korean shamanism as part of a widespread shaman ceremony called *ch'ŏnshin kut* (rite for offering first produce to god), which was performed annually to celebrate the first of a new crop.[63] The *tŏktam* occurs in a section of the ceremony called the *Ch'angbu*, named for the *ch'angbu* song which the shaman sings at that point in the proceedings. *Ch'angbu* designates the husband of a shaman. The rendering that Akamatsu and Akiba give of this *ch'angbu* song and its incorporated *tŏktam* appears to be a narration of the same ceremony which the drummer Han Sŏng-jun described to Yi Hye-gu.[64]

According to the drummer Han, the state examinations in Seoul also provided the assembled kwangdae a parallel opportunity to hold their own formal, competitive examination. Singers would gather in the reception hall of some high government official and there compete for recognition on the basis of their talent. The winners would then be engaged by the new licentiates and given generous rewards of silk and other gifts, being enriched to the degree of their standing in the competitions.[65]

2
The Kwangdae's Nineteenth-Century Heyday

The evolution of p'ansori, like that of any art, is a process with no fixed beginning. Practical definitions must, in fact, work backward from attested nineteenth-century practices in order to define the form. Within that process, the first recognizable example is the so-called Manhwa text of the "Song of Ch'un-hyang," by Yu Chin-han (Manhwaje, 1711–1791), which was recorded in a document of 1754.[1] Its appearance at that time leads us to assume that the final stage of p'ansori's gestation belongs to the first half of the eighteenth century. Chŏng Pyŏng-hŏn chooses 1800 to mark the approximate end of the genre's formative period.[2] This year roughly coincides with the birth dates of early master singers. Some forty years later, when these singers were in their prime, Song Man-jae composed his historically valuable poem, "Kwanuhŭi," which describes p'ansori as part of a variety show.

Prior to the time Song Man-jae was writing, however, individual p'ansori kwangdae had already begun to take advantage of opportunities to perform separately from troupes of variety entertainers. Since p'ansori, unlike other forms of variety entertainment, was performed by a solo artist and could be a complete show unto itself, it was especially easy for p'ansori kwangdae to perform outside the troupes of which they had already become the star attractions. They could set up and entertain almost anywhere since all that it took was for the kwangdae to stand, the drummer to sit, the kwangdae to sing, and the drummer to handle the accompaniment while calling out encouragement.

There is a document that picks up these kwangdae at the end of the eighteenth century and chronicles many aspects of their personal and professional lives through the late nineteenth century: family, training, professional relationships, performances, special skills, personalities, romantic affairs, and patrons. This singular document is the 1940 book, *Chosŏn ch'anggŭk sa* (History of Korean singing drama), in which the scholar-aficionado Chŏng No-shik records the reminiscences of p'ansori kwangdae who had been born in the last half of the nineteenth century and whom he interviewed in the 1930s. Although the title of Chŏng's book uses the term *ch'anggŭk,* which designates the popular twentieth-century ensemble performance of p'ansori, the book is actually a history of the nineteenth-century solo performers of p'ansori.

Though not a professional kwangdae himself, Chŏng spent some three years traveling around the country to interview as many performers as possible. His history contains eighty-nine individual biographies and was facilitated by the kwangdae tradition of orally transmitting their professional genealogies. He quotes the kwangdae Chŏn To-sŏng (b. 1863) on this tradition: "When I was young I visited performances of the famous singers Pak Man-sun, Yi Nal-ch'i, and others, where I heard them recite the names of great performers of the past in order."[3] The master-disciple relationship, which served to transmit much of the wording and interpretation of the repertoire, also provided the kwangdae with a way of preserving a detailed oral history of their art and of their predecessors.

Five Professional Generations

Drawing upon this oral tradition, Chŏng was able to include in each biography both the place and date of the kwangdae's birth, as well as information about his professional relationships, such as the names of his teachers, seniors, colleagues, juniors, and students. The resulting large body of information is entirely free of internal inconsistencies such as contradictions which might describe two singers as colleagues in one biography but as senior and junior in another. The historical scheme that emerges from these facts provides our first inkling of the stages of development that p'ansori passed through during the nineteenth century.

The period between the late eighteenth century and the early twentieth century (when Chŏng conducted his study) may be divided into five professional generations of kwangdae, all linked in a matrix of master-disciple relationships: 1) late eighteenth century, 2) early nineteenth century, 3) middle nineteenth century, 4) late nineteenth century, and 5) early twentieth century. Within each of these five generations there were a number of colleague groups. Each group was made up of kwangdae who regarded each other as strictly contemporary. Any such colleague group, therefore, was distinguished from another such group of the same generation by their relative seniority. On the whole, one generation of kwangdae generally served as teachers to the next.

The first generation, which flourished in the late eighteenth century (and into the early nineteenth), is known for a few, nearly legendary, figures who were thought of as the progenitors of the nineteenth-century p'ansori tradition. All modern histories of p'ansori start with reference to the shadowy Ha Han-dam (also known as Ha Ŭn-dam) and Ch'oe Sŏn-dal, with whose names the oral genealogies typically begin.[4] Only one concrete and detailed personal history of a member of the founding generation survived in the oral record until Chŏng No-shik's day. This describes Kwŏn Sam-dŭk (1771–1841), a kwangdae of aristocratic origins and therefore called a *pigabi* (outsider) in the argot of the profession. While his family was closer to rural gentry than high aristocracy, they were, nevertheless, at one time about to execute him for having taken up such a dishonorable calling. But they settled for expelling him and having his name expunged from the clan records. This incident suggests that considerable changes must have taken place in the once-disdained art of p'ansori, generating an appeal that was compelling enough to entice such *pigabi* kwangdae as Kwŏn Sam-dŭk.

The second generation of kwangdae was larger, and their accomplishments are better known. Four of its master singers—Ko Su-gwan (b. ca. 1800), Song Hŭng-nok (b. ca. 1790), Yŏm Kye-dal (b. ca. 1800), and Mo Hŭng-gap (b. ca. 1800)—are celebrated in one line of a poem by the poet-official Shin Wi (1769–1847), "Kwan'gŭkshi chŏlgu" (Quatrains upon seeing a dramatic poem; 1826): "Ko, Song, Yŏm, and Mo—the talents of a generation!" The dating of this poem provides a valuable basis for estimating their birth dates.[5] In view of the fact that only Song Hŭng-nok came from the p'ansori heartland of Chŏlla Province and the three others were from Ch'ungch'ŏng and Kyŏnggi, we can confirm a spread of p'ansori into the central regions of the country in the early decades of the nineteenth century.[6]

When members of this second generation matured as singers and became masters of their art, they naturally attracted the following of younger and would-be kwangdae who sought them out as models and teachers. In this process, two schools of performance developed during the first half of the nineteenth century as disciples gathered around Song Hŭng-nok and Pak Yu-jŏn (b. 1834), in particular, and adopted their styles, which reflected the regional characteristics of the two master singers. The two schools, Song's *Tongp'yŏn-je* (Eastern school) and Pak's *Sŏp'yŏn-je* (Western school), were each named after the location of the leader's home, relative to the Sŏmjin River that runs south through Chŏlla Province.[7]

As opportunities to perform multiplied, the better kwangdae moved out of the marketplace and into the salons of the rich and powerful, who came to dote upon their favorite singers. The governor of Taegu once praised Song Hŭng-nok as the "King of Song" and King Hŏnjong (r. 1835–1849) rewarded Yŏm Kye-dal for his talents with an appointment to the rank of *tongji,* an honorary Fourth Minister. Chŏng No-shik's biographies reveal that kwangdae of the early nineteenth century were already flaunting the prestige that came with such notoriety as they rode about in sedan chairs, were treated to sumptuous meals, and stood out as popular personalities for whom *kisaeng* vied as lovers.

The third generation, a teaching generation, flourished in the middle third of the century. These teachers established classical interpretations and populated the remainder of the century with their disciples. During the dominance of the third generation, kwangdae contributed new episodes to old songs and also created entirely new works to bring their common repertoire to twelve songs. Since each singer would perform a song in his own individual manner, for which he became famous, new versions of established works were easily generated. The task of revision and refinement was not carried out by just the kwangdae alone. They had the help of educated men of letters. Chŏng No-shik reports, for example, that the kwangdae Pang Man-ch'un (fl. ca. 1830), who was of the same generation as Song Hŭng-nok and Yŏm Kye-dal, worked at length with a "man of letters who was a master of music and poetics" in Hwanghae Province (Pang's second home) to revise and embellish earlier versions of the "Song of the Red Cliff" and "Song of Shim Ch'ŏng." Their rough draft of the "Song of the Red Cliff" had been passed around and read by so many people that it was nearly in tatters.[8]

The fourth generation dominated the last third of the nineteenth century, producing students who maintained the classical tradition. They and their students also took part in the operatic adaptation of p'ansori, the establishment of flourishing theaters in the capital, and the formation of provincial touring companies. In the same period, two important patrons of kwangdae emerged, who contributed to the development of the p'ansori art and to the acceptability of these performers as entertainers to polite society. One of these was a rich petty official from the countryside, Shin Chae-hyo (1812–1884), and the other was the father of King Kojong (r. 1863–1907), the Regent Taewŏn'gun (1820–1898). As a devotee of p'ansori, the Taewŏn-gun came to play a considerable role, which was carried on by his son.

Before he became regent for his minor son in 1863, the Taewŏn'gun had spent considerable time with members of the commoner, petty-official class and enjoyed their entertainments, central among which was p'ansori.[9] With the patronage and frequent invitations of the regent, such kwangdae as Pak Man-sun (1830–1898) and Pak Yu-jŏn gained fame; and, while still members of the lowborn class, they were honored with official appointments and would travel frequently to the capital.

Shin Chae-hyo, as an outsider, made a significant contribution to the development of p'ansori in his patronage and training of kwangdae, consolidation and editing of extant textual materials, exposition of theory, and composition of p'ansori itself. From about 1867 until his death in 1884, Shin devoted himself thoroughly to p'ansori, both as scholar and patron. His activity exemplifies the interest of the commoner, petty-official class in the performance and development of p'ansori.[10]

The members of the fifth generation were born in the last decades of the nineteenth century and were to carry the p'ansori tradition into the twentieth century and recite to Chŏng No-shik the oral history of their art. These singers, then, are the link to the present day, for it is they whom Koreans in their seventies can still remember hearing on the radio and seeing on the stage in the 1930s and 1940s when they were children.

It is evident from Chŏng No-sik's study that the craft of the kwangdae was mostly hereditary during the nineteenth century. The wide variety of family relationships among the kwangdae in Chŏng's sampling suggests that he recorded only fragments of a widespread and ramified network of kinship ties. Many less famous members of kwangdae families are presumably not mentioned in his study.

A significant number of Chŏng's subjects are related to each other by blood or marriage (brother, brother-in-law, cousin, uncle, father, grandfather, and so forth). Those related constitute 27 percent of the total. Several more are either related to other, unnamed kwangdae, or began training at such an early age that such a relationship could be inferred (based on the fact that most of the 27 percent who were related also received their early training from such relatives as fathers and uncles). In addition to this evidence and the overall hereditary nature of occupation and social status during the Chosŏn period,[11] there is also the general tendency for vocations in the lower social classes to be hereditary on account of the lack of alternatives and the economic need to involve children productively in the family's work as early as possible. In the case of entertainers, the range of specialties within their craft allowed a place for all members of a family, regardless of age or native talent.[12] The Song family of kwangdae is a case in point. This very famous dynasty of singers dates from the great Song Hŭng-nok, who flourished at the beginning of the nineteenth century. Song Kwang-nok (1803–?), Song Hŭng-nok's brother, served his older brother as a drummer until he could train himself to perform as a kwangdae.[13] Then he and a brother-in-law passed on the family tradition to their sons and grandsons (the grandsons were both alive when Chŏng conducted his study).[14]

Entertainers were frequently married to female shamans, who were of the same low social status.[15] In the terminology of Korean shamanism, the musician-husband of a shaman was called a *ch'angbu* or *mubu*. He would serve as her accompanist on the drum and could also perform as a singer himself.[16] In the *ch'angbu* song, mentioned above, we encountered a shaman narrative that describes these singers as individual performers in their own right, working outside a shamanistic milieu, who journeyed to the capital where they met new licentiates and then accompanied them home to perform sacrificial rites.

National Association of Performers

Another function of the husband, particularly in Chŏlla Province (the heartland of p'ansori where shamans were mostly women), was to run the local shaman association which was centered in a business office called the *shin ch'ŏng, chaein ch'ŏng,* or *ch'angbu ch'ŏng.*[17] The business office maintained a *sŏnsaeng an* (record of teachers), which was a "statement of the basic principles of the shaman organization with a roster of the names of their predecessors."[18] This document was the focus of annual rites, funded by membership dues, that were celebrated as others might perform ancestor worship.

This office also appears to have linked the male performers with the government, for which they served as occasionally conscripted entertainers. Among documents of the Kyŏnggi Province *chaein ch'ŏng,* uncovered by the ethnographers Akamatsu and Akiba, is an introduction to the office records, dated 1836, which notes that affiliates of the *chaein ch'ŏng* had "performed plays to the approbation of others on stages built at the time of foreign embassies to the country."[19] We shall presently look at a memorial submitted to the government by eminent kwangdae of the same period which describes similar functions in similar terms.

Just before the Second World War, two unique and valuable documents came into the possession of the Vocal Music Research Society. The documents are known as the *Kapshin wanmun* (Kapshin disposition; 1824) and the *Chŏnghae soji* (Chŏnghae appeal; 1827).[20] Until then, scholars had been unaware of the existence, as early as the seventeenth century, of anything like a professional guild of entertainers.[21] The *Kapshin wanmun,* submitted to the Board of Taxation by seven eminent performers, proposed the reorganization of their national association, then called "Chaein of the Eight Provinces" (the term *chaein* here was a general designation for variety performers of all specialties and degrees of skill). According to the introductory portion of the text, a national association of experienced performers had been established "after the Manchu Invasion [1636]" as a result of a meeting held in Seoul to which responsible delegates were sent from throughout the country. Although the organization continued to function through the end of the nineteenth century, we learn that large-scale pageants in Seoul were discontinued in the late eighteenth century: "Stages of the left and right were not erected for performance after the year of *kapchin* [1784]."

In the *Kapshin wanmun,* the performers propose that the *chaein* of each province keep a branch office of the association in readiness to eliminate the need for special orders and also to avoid the disorderly convergence of performers in Seoul on the occasion of the arrival of a Chinese embassy. The text states that leadership of the organization was vested primarily in men from the three provinces of Kyŏnggi, Ch'ungch'ŏng, and Chŏlla, with lesser representation from Kyŏngsang and Kangwŏn. The three northern provinces were grouped as one in their administrative structure.

Yi Chong-man, who had served as a provincial assistant director in 1908, described the structure as he knew it to Akamatsu and Akiba in 1938:

> The *chaein ch'ŏng* is also called *kwangdae ch'ŏng* or *hwarang ch'ŏng*. There is one in each *kun* of the three provinces of Kyŏnggi, Ch'ungch'ŏng, and Chŏlla. In each province the director is called *taebang*. Under each director are two assistant directors, one for the left province (*chwado tosanju*) and one for the right province (*udo tosanju*). One province is divided into left and right as a matter of jurisdictional form. A *tosanju* assists the *taebang*, and it is his task to deliberate with him on important matters. Under each assistant director, there are four stewards (*chipkang*), four secretaries (*kongwŏn*), and two clerks (*sangmu*). The stewards and secretaries manage affairs and the clerks do general administration. In contrast to this, the head of the *chaein ch'ŏng* in each *kun* is called a *ch'ŏngsu* and, under him, are a secretary and a clerk.[22]

Kim Dong-uk has charted the organizational structure both as written in the *Kapshin wanmun* and as described by Yi Chong-man and found them to coincide.[23] In view of such long-term stability, it may well be that essentially the same structure had existed since the seventeenth century.

According to the *Kapshin wanmun*, each officer of the association was selected by consensus. And, once they were selected, other members of the association were expected to be obedient to them. In like manner, members were chosen by consensus to perform in Seoul. On the occasion of an embassy, in addition to giving a performance, they were always subordinate to the association, as on-call kwangdae, each waiting his turn to perform.

Corporate authority was symbolized by a seal, held by each local office, which was to be used on the official minutes of their deliberations. This seal was also essential for any petition made to the government. Its importance and usefulness are reflected in the 1827 *Chŏnghae soji*, presented by forty members of the Kongju *chaein* office to the local Office of Criminal Prosecution. In the document, they ask severe punishment of four musicians from Kongju who stole the office seal from its custodian, Song Il-mun of Ch'ŏngyang,[24] and used it to forward an unsanctioned document (which, unfortunately, has not been preserved).

Among the forty-seven names signed to the *Kapshin wanmun* and *Chŏnghae soji*, five also appear in Chŏng No-sik's biographical sketches of noted kwangdae, suggesting that some of the leading p'ansori singers of the time were members of the *chaein* association when it was functioning. But, since Chŏng presents his subjects as free agents and never mentions the association, it is doubtful that the *chaein* group had much control over appearances of eminent performers at the capital or elsewhere. The singers of whom Chŏng writes seem to have received their invitations directly from their patrons. The *chaein* association, of which they appear to have been a leading element, was more likely concerned with lower-ranking entertainers, whose uncontrolled movement to the capital was reported to have created confusion.

We have seen that some p'ansori kwangdae, while every bit as lowborn as any rope-walker, tumbler, or other wandering entertainer, were able to gain special recognition which would let them leap over the hierarchical order of the status-based society of Chosŏn. Although this was due in part to their ability, based on arduous training, to sing erudite lyrics with refined melodies, there were social and economic changes during the nineteenth century that contributed to the remarkable mobility of prominent kwangdae like those who appear in Chŏng No-shik's book. In addition to the growth of commerce and the concentration of wealth in the hands of successful commoner merchants, which created a bourgeoisie, it is important to take note of increasing instability in the class system. With money or grain, anyone could get rank or buy lineage and become a yangban or aristocrat. The cash-hungry Chosŏn government had a schedule of prices for a variety of titles.[25] Whereas the population of Taegu, for example, was only 8.3 percent yangban in 1690, that figure had risen to 34.7 percent by 1789, and to 65.5 percent in 1858.[26]

In such a climate, leading kwangdae enjoyed an entrée at court and in the homes of high officials and the rich and powerful. This privilege, enjoyed only at the pleasure of their patrons, may have been tenuous; but some prominent kwangdae were proud and haughty men whose remarkable talent gave them license to flaunt convention. Many were royal favorites and gave frequent command performances at court. Chŏng Ch'un-p'ung (fl. 1850), a great favorite of the Regent Taewŏn'gun, was a frequent visitor at the palace, "using the guest quarters like his personal bedroom."[27] Every ruler of the last half of the nineteenth century was entertained at court by kwangdae, and it was common for them to bestow title and rank on their favorites. One turn-of-the-century great, Song Man-gap, was successively named by King Sunjong as a *ch'ambong* (junior ninth grade position), a *kamch'al* (inspector), and a Royal Household Secret Inspector.

Patrons of the great kwangdae, in addition to kings and the Regent Taewŏn'gun, included ministers of state, provincial governors, military commanders, powerful politicians, and the landed rich. Some favored singers adopted lifestyles as elevated as those of their patrons, not only affecting a formidable hauteur but also dressing with suitable elegance.

The famous kwangdae of the middle nineteenth century, Pak Man-sun, was one such remarkable entertainer. Chŏng No-shik relates an incident in which Pak Man-sun's arrogance toward the governor of Ch'ungch'ŏng Province might have led to his death had not his phenomenal talent turned away the wrath of that official, who was intent upon an execution.

When the Regent Taewŏn'gun once called Pak to Seoul for a performance, his route to the capital took him through Ch'ungch'ŏng, where the governor, Cho Pyŏng-shik, summoned him to perform. Pak refused.

"The Taewŏn'gun has called me to the capital for a command performance and I shall not open up until then," he responded and continued on to the capital, where he stayed several months to perform for the regent.

When it came time for him to return home, Pak told the regent of his refusal and begged for his life, claiming that he would surely be killed by the hot-tempered governor. After hearing the story, the regent ordered a personal letter sent to Governor Cho.

"To summarize in a few words, Pak's behavior merits execution and you may deal with him as you see fit. However, it would be best to listen once to his matchless p'ansori and then kill him."

Governor Cho realized that the regent's implication was against killing the singer and, relenting, asked for one p'ansori performance. Pak, rescued from the brink of death, did his very best with the result that he earned the protection of Governor Cho, it is said.[28]

3

Singers in the Twentieth Century

During the last third of the nineteenth century, even while traditional p'ansori was still in its heyday as a solo male art form, a new stage in its development was already taking shape. This process was to culminate in the emergence of the new theatrical form of p'ansori called *ch'anggŭk* (singing drama), in which both male and female singers were assigned individual roles to play and appeared on stage together. The first ch'anggŭk, an adaptation of the "Song of Ch'un-hyang," was offered in 1903. This event was more than a new departure for a traditional form; it was an epoch-making transition in the performing arts that marked the beginning of modern theater in Korea.

Developments leading up to this turn of events had been taking place both in the countryside and in the capital. While the capital city of Seoul was experiencing social, cultural, and economic changes that would stimulate the necessary popular demand and, hence, paying audience for staged dramatic events, Chŏlla Province in the countryside was witnessing the addition of new aspects to p'ansori and a refinement of what was already effective.

While famous master singers were hobnobbing with nobles like the Regent Taewŏn'gun and powerful government officials, less accomplished or less fortunate kwangdae worked among the hordes of itinerant storytellers, jugglers, comedians, actors, acrobats, singing girls, and dancers who made their living in the countryside. In such circumstances, where there were too many kwangdae with too little territory to share, ordinary singers could not do very well for themselves. As a matter of economic necessity, they joined itinerant variety troupes that offered performances incorporating such acts as p'ansori, rope-walking, musical song-and-dance acts, witty talk, and farmer's music.[1] The term for these troupes, hyŏmnyulsa, which later became widely used to designate companies specializing in ch'anggŭk, is said to have been introduced in the 1860s from a Chinese expression for "opera," pronounced hyŏmnyul ch'anghŭi in Korean.[2] In this Chinese operatic form, more than one singing actor performed on stage at the same time, a potentially attractive notion to p'ansori kwangdae and one that would lead to a revolution in their art as ch'anggŭk evolved at the end of the century.

At about this time a historic change occurred in the profession of p'ansori singing, one without which the later emergence of ch'anggŭk would not have been possible. Until the 1860s, solo dramatic singing had been the exclusive province of men; but the staging of ch'anggŭk would depend upon the availability of female performers, as well as male.[3] Professional women having the greatest affinity with the p'ansori art would have been kisaeng, female shamans, itinerant female performers, or wandering prostitute-entertainers called sadangp'ae.[4] While a kisaeng had highly developed skills, an attempted transition to dramatic singing—well beneath her station—would have been disastrous for her career. The shaman had no need to switch, for she enjoyed better status than a male singer, and a guaranteed territory and audience into the bargain. Other itinerant female entertainers were already committed to different specialties and had skills that would not give them a competitive edge in dramatic singing. All of which is to say that a successful female dramatic singer would have had to start fresh at an early age and go through long and arduous training in order to compete with a successful male kwangdae who already had such a background.

Finally, in mid-century, the person who was to become the first female kwangdae that history has noted, Chin Ch'ae-sŏn (1847–1901), was born in Koch'ang County of North Chŏlla Province. Although the details are now unknown, she came to study under the noted patron and scholar of p'ansori, Shin Chae-hyo, whose home was also in Koch'ang County; and she appears to have made her Seoul debut at age twenty-one in July 1868, under Shin's sponsorship, at a banquet held in Kyŏnghoeru Pavilion to celebrate the reconstruction of Kyŏngbok Palace. "Her voice astonished the world, one woman in a sea of men,"[5] as she sang the love song from the "Song of Ch'un-hyang" and "Kosa ch'ang" (Prayer for blessing), which was composed for her by Shin. She immediately became a favorite of the Regent Taewŏn'gun.[6] For the remainder of the century, she was followed by only a few other female singers, including Hŏ Kŭm-p'a and Kang So-ch'un.[7]

Hŏ Kŭm-p'a, also born in Koch'ang County, was a contemporary of Kang So-ch'un and flourished at the turn of the twentieth century. She was trained early in her career by Kim Se-jong, the master singer and theorist who had studied under Shin Chae-hyo. Hŏ Kŭm-p'a and Kang So-ch'un were to perform together in Seoul, participating in experiments that served as stepping-stones from p'ansori to ch'anggŭk.

A *hyŏmnyulsa* is said to have been operating just before 1900 in the East Gate area of Seoul. Later, in the same location, a theater called Kwangmudae was built and had the popular name of Kwangmudae hyŏmnyulsa. There they emphasized p'ansori but also offered folk songs, *kisaeng* songs and dances, rope-walking, witty talk with slight-of-hand, and variety acts. Leading male singers like Kim Ch'ang-hwan (1854–1927) and Song Man-gap, together with Hŏ Kŭm-p'a and Kang So-ch'un, tried a form of presentation there called "dialogue singing" (*taehwa ch'ang*) involving characters from p'ansori works.

For example, given a scene from the "Song of Ch'un-hyang" involving the hero Toryŏng and the heroine Ch'un-hyang, a male singer and a female singer would step on stage together and play the two roles, exchanging songs in dialogue style between them.[8] The task of creating believable characters for these dialogues was facilitated by the fact that kwangdae had already developed the ability to sing in the character of each role they played. As early as the 1860s, p'ansori scholars, theorists, and master performers had been stressing the use of dramatic gesture in order to convey character and emotion believably; thus, kwangdae were already equipped with mimetic skills that were appropriate to the portrayal of individual characters. This dialogue singing, a precursor of ch'anggŭk, was very novel to audiences at the time and continued to be practiced until the p'ansori works "Song of Ch'un-hyang" and "Song of Shim Ch'ŏng" were turned into ch'anggŭk in 1903 and 1904, respectively.

Somber Seoul Becomes a Theater Town

Meanwhile, the capital city itself had been experiencing its own dramatic changes. Seoul in the 1860s had a population of just a little over two hundred thousand. The people who lived within the walls and gates of Seoul were grouped into five residential districts that reflected their social status: royals and high officials in the north, lesser aristocrats in the south, civil officials in the west, military officials in the southeast, and, in the center, the petty bureaucrats who were known by their district as the "middle people." When foreigners began living in Seoul by 1882, they settled in the western end of the central district, together with the middle people. While Americans and Europeans moved into the Chŏng-dong area behind Tŏksu Palace, the Japanese chose Chin kogae (now called Myŏng-dong), and the Chinese community located itself near the southwestern banks of Ch'ŏnggye Stream (now paved over and called Ch'ŏnggye-ch'ŏn Avenue).[9] There appears to have been some friction caused by this influx, as suggested by an entry for February 25, 1887, in the Chronological Index of Horace N. Allen's *Korea: Fact and Fancy*: "Seoul shops closed because of a local demonstration in favor of compelling foreigners to remove to Ryongsan."[10] The Seoul of 1886 that diplomat and author Percival Lowell described in *Chosŏn: The Land of the Morning Calm* was a quiet and somber city that sent its merchants away at night, closed its gates, and barred men from the dark and silent streets between eight and midnight, when their cloistered women had their only opportunity to move about freely.[11]

But within ten years much had changed. The Reforms of 1894, undertaken at the behest of the Japanese, restructured the government and called for sweeping social changes. In the same year, peasant armies launched the massive Tonghak Rebellion, which led to the outbreak in Korea of the Sino-Japanese War. Queen Min was assassinated by a Japanese agent late in 1895, and the king had taken refuge in the Russian Legation early in the next year. Korea had been thrust into an international maelstrom. Isabella Bird Bishop, world traveler and writer, who made four trips to Korea between 1894 and 1897, published her observations in *Korea and Her Neighbours* (1898). Bishop's penultimate chapter, "Seoul in 1897," devotes considerable space to her impressions of change since her previous visit. She describes a Seoul that had become "literally not recognizable" as a result of improved drainage, new paving, and widened streets and lanes. "Shops with glass fronts had been erected in numbers, an order forbidding the throwing of refuse into the streets was enforced . . . and Seoul, from having been the foulest is now on its way to being the cleanest city of the Far East!" In addition, she remarks upon her inability to find a remaining "representative slum" to photograph as a basis for comparison in illustrating the physical changes that had taken place. "Along the fine broad streets thus restored, tiled roofs have largely replaced thatch, in many cases the lower parts of the walls have been rebuilt of stone instead of wattle, and attempts at decoration and neatness are apparent in many of the house and shop fronts. . . . Some miles of broad streets are now available as promenades, and are largely taken advantage of; business looked much brisker than formerly, the shops made more display, and there was an air of greater prosperity . . . ."[12]

Although Bishop reports the presence of a Japanese theater, she states that there were no Korean theaters in Seoul as of 1894.[13] The modern journalist Yi Kyu-tae, in a retrospective article for the *Chosun ilbo* in the 1960s, writes of stereoscopic exhibitions, magic shows, and circuses put on during the late 1890s by enterprising Japanese in tents that they pitched on the banks of the Ch'ŏnggye Stream near their residential area of Chin kogae. But, Yi continues, the Japanese consul had to discourage performers from visiting Korea for a while after a Korean mob broke up the magic show being given by a man named Miyagi. They ruined both his tent and equipment, "shouting that he was a robber who was stealing Korean money with magic."[14]

The 1894 Chinese community in Seoul, according to Bishop, was nearly as large as the Japanese.[15] It is widely known that Chinese opera was being performed for the Chinese community in the 1890s in a theater called the Ch'anghŭigwan, but there is no record of when the theater was built. Noted singers visited from Beijing to perform·such works as the "Romance of the Three Kingdoms" and were well received. The p'ansori scholar Pak Hwang quotes Yi Tong-baek (1866–1947), a noted kwangdae of his age, on details of the Ch'anghŭigwan, which was located within the Chinese community in the second block of today's Ch'ŏnggye-ch'ŏn Avenue on the southwest side, across from the present Samil Building:

> In the amusement quarter of that district, the Chinese had an opera house where Chinese singing actors performed operas every day. . . . In addition to Chinese, many Koreans also attended. Unlike today, one did not buy a ticket to get in. Instead, anyone could go inside and take a seat. Then, after the first act ended, a Chinese employee would go through the audience collecting fees. . . . Korean singers who happened to be in Seoul at the

time would visit out of interest and curiosity . . . and the master singer Kang Yong-hwan [1865–1938] would attend whenever he had a chance, nearly living there. Kang Yong-hwan developed the p'ansori "Song of Ch'un-hyang" into a ch'angguk on the model of this kind of Chinese opera.[16]

Starting in 1899, there was a boom in Korean theater openings in response to the increased demand for entertainment in a growing and prospering capital city. "Nowadays, in the capital, theaters are everywhere; and men and women of no discernable occupation flock to them!" reported the *Hwangsong shinmun* on May 14, 1904.[17] Master singer Yi Tong-baek recalled the situation for the *Chosun ilbo* on March 30, 1939:

> Those days, though I really don't know why, they had merrymaking even at court. They thought so well of amusements that they had a lot of rope-walking and mask dance performed in front of the king. And, since this sort of inclination was prevalent also among the people, places like what we call music halls today suddenly popped up—like the Kwangmudae, Wŏngaksa, Yŏnhŭngsa, and Changansa. And so, those folks who had a little talent to show off—telling jokes, ropewalking, or whatever—came swarming up to Seoul, all bent on getting their share. What's more, even the great master singers of the age, like Kim Ch'ang-hwan and Song Man-gap, were making big names for themselves back then.[18]

In the decade from 1899 to 1908, eight theaters opened in Seoul. Similar to the Japanese and Chinese theaters, these Korean theaters were built in locations close to their source of both financial capital and paying customers, Korean merchants and petty officials.[19] One exceptional case was a theater originally called the Hŭidae (Theatrical stage), built at government expense and located just west of the modern Kwanghwamun intersection, on the site of the present Saemunan Church.[20] Most descriptions of this event in Korean theatrical history begin with reference to the most detailed account, a brief 1947 essay by the early modern scholar Ch'oe Nam-sŏn (1890–1957), who was born and raised a few blocks from the theater and was a teenager there during its heyday. His recollections can be confirmed in 1902 newspaper accounts.[21]

> In the fall of 1902, it was determined to hold a ceremony in Seoul to celebrate the fortieth anniversary of King Kojong's ascension, for which . . . all kinds of modern facilities were hastily prepared. . . . As one of these, the government cut away one part of the Office of Rites and Titles and constructed a small theater . . . which was a round, brick structure

modeled on the Colosseum in Rome. . . . Though built on a small scale, this was Korea's first theater; and it was equipped with a stage, terraced audience seating on three sides, draw curtain, and preparation room. It was, in fact, a unique national theater that they intended to be comparable to London's Royal Albert Hall or the Royal Theater in Vienna.

In order to deal with the administrative matters there entailed, an organ called the Hyŏmnyulsa was established under the jurisdiction of the Department of the Royal Household. They started out by having *kisaeng* and entertainers conduct rehearsals for the celebration; but then, unfortunately, that fall, observances were postponed until the next year because of a cholera epidemic. Therefore, the Hyŏmnyulsa Office, functioning as a general entertainment organ, put on performances by *kisaeng,* actors, dancers, and others while waiting for the next year. But, after a second postponement due to the prince's smallpox, the anniversary celebration was finally given only a nominal observance because of concern for the agricultural situation and a crisis in relations between Russia and Japan.

Whereas the theater was left unused in the wake of all this, the Hyŏmnyulsa Office quietly turned it into a commercial enterprise. Public chagrin was stirred by the popular shows and by the fact that this office had turned into a management agency for *kisaeng* and actors. The Hyŏmnyulsa Office was abolished by royal command in April 1906 in response to a memorial submitted by a vice administrator in the Office of Rites and Titles. But, at the same time, the demand for entertainment increased by the day; and, since there was then no other structure in Seoul sufficient for use as a theater, there were plenty of producers to use the building.[22]

Thus, the Hyŏmnyulsa Office operated the Hŭidae Theater for three years and five months, starting with its first production in early December 1902, "Diversions for Greeting the Spring," until the office was closed down in late April 1906. The Hŭidae Theater facility itself continued to be used by various groups until it was destroyed by fire in the spring of 1914. The most famous production company to have used it was the Wŏngaksa Company (1908–1909), as a result of which the Hŭidae became known to history as the Wŏngaksa Theater.

Putting P'ansori on the Stage

In addition to being Korea's first national theater and one of its first theatrical structures, the Hŭidae Theater also earned its place in the history of Korean dramatic arts for two transitional productions that were staged there. The first, offered in the fall of 1903, was the ground-breaking ch'anggŭk adaptation of the p'ansori "Song of Ch'un-hyang." The second, which opened on November 13, 1908, was "Silver World," a ch'anggŭk adaptation of oral materials that also appeared immediately thereafter in the form of a popular, "new" novel.[23] A third, and unintended, outcome of the Hŭidae Theater period was the formation of provincial touring companies that brought ch'anggŭk to the countryside. These were organized by such greats as Kim Ch'ang-hwan and Song Man-gap, after ch'anggŭk became the object of interference by the Japanese through their Korean colleagues, who saw such things as the antithesis of the cultural modernity they advocated for Korea.[24]

The original Hŭidae Theater troupe, under management of the Hyŏmnyulsa Office, had been recruited and hired by Kim Ch'ang-hwan and Song Man-gap at the direct command of King Kojong. They had assembled a company in 1902 of 170 men and women from all over the country. These performers were put on salary and immediately went into rehearsal to prepare for the king's fortieth anniversary celebration. But when the celebration was postponed and then finally given only perfunctory observance in 1903, they decided to go ahead with a ch'anggŭk version of the p'ansori "Song of Ch'un-hyang" in the fall of that year. One person was assigned to sing the descriptive passages[25] while male and female singers appeared on the stage and sang as characters in the story, each dressed and carrying properties appropriate to the character. They performed in front of a white curtain, without scenery and equipment, and illuminated only by bare light bulbs in the ceiling.[26]

Thus began a short but exciting era that many performers of the time considered the most satisfying in the history of their art. For the first time, entertainers were actually put on regular (and generous) government salaries, were surrounded with many opportunities to perform, enjoyed the adulation of a public hungry for entertainment, and so played to packed theaters day after day. The recollections of drummer Han Sŏng-jun and singer Yi Tong-baek, published in the March 1941 issue of *Ch'unch'u,* suggest the spirit of these times and, even, the attitude of Kings Kojong and Sunjong toward the performers.

> *Yi:* When would you say was the finest time for us all? For both singers and drummers?
>
> *Han:* Oh, that would have to be the days of the Wŏngaksa, without question!
>
> *Yi:* Yes, I think so, too. People used to look down on us in the early days. But when King Kojong received us as a patron, it made all that sing-

ing and dancing worth while! Yes, we even played for King Sunjong in the Great Hall. That was fun.

Han: I still remember, even today. Han In-ho was doing his toad somersault, when he slipped and landed in Sunjong's lap! I was afraid he was in for some terrible punishment but the king just laughed happily—remember? I think Sunjong favored you the most of all. When you were singing at the Wŏngaksa, Sunjong would listen to you through a telephone pressed against his ear!

Yi: Yes, he did. But, when we did the ch'anggŭk "Song of Ch'un-hyang" back then, it was on a scale much bigger than today. And more people could understand us, don't you think? That's why those of us on stage got excited, too.[27]

With the ch'anggŭk undertaking at the Hŭidae Theater at an end and the players dispersed, Kim Ch'ang-hwan and several other leading singers mustered some fifty colleagues from the Chŏlla area and organized a company in 1907 to tour the three provinces of the south. According to one member of the troupe who spoke with Pak Hwang in later years,[28] they attracted oceans of people wherever they went. Their procession from one locale to the next was a spectacle in itself, reminiscent of a circus parade. Kim Ch'ang-hwan led the way, riding in a four-bearer palanquin, followed by leading singers on donkeys. Other performers rode in formal costumes aboard festooned, horse-drawn wagons with the remaining actors following on foot. Musicians playing cymbals, gongs, drums, oboes, and other instruments were deployed ahead of the procession. At the stops, many miles apart, they would settle in to perform for some three to five days.

While Kim Ch'ang-hwan was touring the provinces in 1907, Song Man-gap put in a year with colleagues in the newly rebuilt Kwangmudae Theater at East Gate, continuing to perform p'ansori and ch'anggŭk, but on a diminished scale. With his disciples multiplying, however, he decided in 1908 to organize his own hyŏmnyulsa around them and other colleagues and set out to tour the provinces. Now, with these two companies touring the country, many rural people—who had until then known only lesser fare—were given a unique chance to see these famous singers in person and to sample the theatrical form of ch'anggŭk for the first time.

Song Man-gap's troupe moved from place to place in spectacular processions that were every bit as impressive as those of Kim Ch'ang-hwan. Song Man-gap and Yi Tong-baek led the way, riding in open sedan chairs, wearing formal crowns and luxurious robes, and sporting other regalia. They were followed by their one-and-only female kwangdae, Kang So-ch'un, in her flower-bedecked palanquin, and by other leading players mounted on donkeys. After this came the horse carts, actors on foot, and wagons loaded with the complete apparatus of a temporary theater and stage. Rumors would precede the procession, bringing out tumultuous throngs to greet them wherever they went.[29] According to Pak Hwang's description, men and women of all ages packed the tent theaters to give these star performers a wildly enthusiastic reception. And, after a performance, the singers would join in merrymaking with their fans and local officials. Never before had there been such a wave of first-rate talent ranging over the Korean countryside at the same time.[30]

But, for all the glory and popularity of the moment, the long-term prospects of the ch'angguk form were not good. The last regional tour before a hiatus of twenty years was mounted in 1912, offering the "Song of Ch'un-hyang" and "Song of Shim Ch'ŏng" to the three southern provinces. After a 1915 production of the "Song of Hŭng-bu" in Seoul, all ch'angguk disappeared from sight until 1935–1936, when favorites from the traditional p'ansori repertoire were mounted as ch'angguk, but beefed up with additional dialogue to satisfy contemporary tastes in entertainment. After that, although ch'angguk continued to be a productive form, only two of the thirty-six titles offered over the next two decades were based on the five-song, traditional p'ansori repertoire. In 1936–1938, however, several works were resurrected from the novels in which their oral progenitors had been preserved during the nineteenth century.[31] But the remainder were predominantly ch'angguk based upon historical incidents or materials. It is also noteworthy that the ch'angguk form was not building up its own repertoire, for only one title was produced twice in the twenty years cited.[32]

Heyday of Singing Drama

The period 1935–1939, when the Chosŏn Vocal Music Research Society was active, saw a productive reflowering of ch'angguk. During this time, seven of the original twelve p'ansori songs (including three revivals of lost works) were adapted and produced by Chŏng Chŏng-nyŏl (1875–1938), the most ever credited to any one person. His death in 1938, however, cut short his attempt to mount all twelve works and subsequent singers limited their repertoire to only the "five songs."

With the loss of both Chŏng Chŏng-nyŏl and Song Man-gap in 1939, ch'angguk began to undergo changes that were to result in a distinctly different form. By then, there was nobody left who was familiar with the twelve classical works. Only a few had mastered all five songs; and, since their disciples usually began their studies with the songs of Ch'un-hyang, Shim Ch'ŏng and Hŭng-bu, the three ch'anggŭk versions of these three were the most easily preserved.

The process by which classical p'ansori emerged on the twentieth century stage as ch'anggŭk and by which ch'anggŭk itself developed its own distinctive form and content can be summarized as follows. Before 1903 was the heyday of classical "one singer, one drummer" p'ansori in which the traditional, solo kwangdae performed both as narrator and as the individual characters of his story. Next, from 1903 to 1935, came the period of p'ansori-based, ensemble ch'anggŭk, in which a "lead singer" took over the function of narrator while male and female singers played the characters but no new material was added to the libretto. Finally, after 1935, rewritten, dialogue-based ch'anggŭk was introduced and newly created, historical works emerged. In terms of music, original p'ansori arias were replaced after 1935 by shorter songs sung in imitation of the old arias, an accommodation to the popular tastes of the times.

These developmental stages can be illustrated by comparing the same scene from the "Song of Ch'un-hyang" as performed in each of the three periods. The excerpts in Table 1 are taken from the beginning of the "Separation Scene." I have edited them to make the overall length more manageable and the differences between examples easier to grasp. (Omissions are indicated by ellipses, and the singing rhythms—*chung chung mori* and *chung mori*—are noted in parentheses.)

In this scene, the hero, Toryŏng, has come to the house of his lover, Ch'un-hyang, to tell her that his father, the governor, has been reassigned to the capital and that he must follow, with the result that they will be separated. Toryŏng is greeted at the beginning by Hyang-dan, Ch'un-hyang's maid. The first of the three examples follows the classical tradition of Kim Se-jong (fl. late nineteenth century) and is a transcription of a performance by Sŏng U-hyang (b. 1935).[33] This is in the pre-1903, classical, solo p'ansori form, in which the one singer plays all four roles—Hyang-dan, Ch'un-hyang, Toryŏng, the narrator—and must adjust his voice, gesture, and interpretation each time he changes persona. The second example is taken from the text of a pre-1935 ch'anggŭk production as reported by Pak Hwang.[34] It demonstrates how the characters have been distinguished from each other and assigned to individual singers. In addition, a "lead singer" has been created to sing the narrative portions that had not been assigned to any one

TABLE 1. P'ansori and Ch'angguk Compared

column 3- paste-up position

TRADITIONAL P'ANSORI (Before 1903)	EARLY CH'ANGGŬK (1903–1935)	LATER CH'ANGGŬK (After 1935)
Solo Kwangdae (chung chung mori) "Ah! You've come, Toryŏng, sir!	*Hyang-dan* (chung chung mori) Ah! You've come, Toryŏng, sir! My mistress is waiting for you.	*Hyang-dan* (speaking) Your Toryŏng is on his way! Miss! Miss! Your Toryŏng is coming!
Usually when you come We know you're here by Your footsteps near the wall Or a quiet cough at the gate. But, today, who is it that You wish to startle, Coming here So very, very quietly?" . . .	Usually when you come We know you're here by Your footsteps near the wall Or a quiet cough at the gate. But, today, who is it that You wish to startle, Coming here So very, very quietly? . . . **Lead Singer**	**Ch'un-hyang** Toryŏng, you're here! You've come at last, Toryŏng! How is it you're so late today? Did you have a visitor at your study? . . . Toryŏng! Why are you crying?
Toryŏng, without an answer, Opens the door and enters the room. At that moment, Ch'un-hyang Is embroidering a purse To give to Toryŏng. She greets Toryŏng happily And rises, smiling, to her feet. She takes his fine hand, saying:	Toryŏng, without an answer, Goes inside the room. At that moment, Ch'un-hyang Sets her basket by the candle. She was embroidering a purse To give to Toryŏng when She greets Toryŏng happily And clears her basket away. . . . She rises to her feet And takes his fine hand, saying: **Ch'un-hyang**	**Toryŏng** No, no. Cry? Why should I cry? I wasn't crying. **Ch'un-hyang** What, did some letter come from your family seat? Did, perhaps, a death notice come, announcing the death of some kin? **Toryŏng** If one hundred members of my family died, could I be this crushed? **Ch'un-hyang** If that's not it, then, what has happened? Oh, please speak to me!
"Your face is o'erspread by concern: What is this about? There wasn't any note from you— Did Pangja become ill? Did a friend arrive from somewhere That you're already as vexed as this! Were you scolded by the governor Or get teased for seeing me? Have you had too much wine And now your mind's befuddled?"	Did some matter come up Today in your study room? There wasn't any note from you— Did Pangja become ill? Did a friend arrive from somewhere? You are already so vexed as this! Usually when you see me, You seem to be pleased. But today are you so troubled for Having heard bad talk of me? . . .	**Toryŏng** Oh, Ch'un-hyang! What's the best way of dealing with this thing? **Ch'un-hyang** You've got to tell me what this is all about if I am going to understand, don't you? **Toryŏng** The governor has been promoted to Sixth Royal Secretary and so is going up to Seoul, he says. **Ch'un-hyang** Oh, what a fortunate thing for

**TRADITIONAL P'ANSORI
(Before 1903)**

She goes around behind him
  and
Slips her hands into his arm-
  pits.
Though she pokes him sharply
There is no response at all.
  (chung mori)
Ch'un-hyang feels embar-
  rassed,
Pulls away from him, and sits.

"I've not known you,
Really haven't known you.
I just don't understand
What's in Toryŏng's heart!
You, Toryŏng,
Are an aristocrat
And I, Ch'un-hyang,
Am just a lowborn girl.
You think it right to cast me
  off
After dallying just a while!
And so now you've come
To break away from me!''

**EARLY CH'ANGGŬK
(1903–1935)**

Have you had too much wine
And now your mind's befud-
  dled? . . .
Lead Singer
She slips her hands into his
  armpits
And pokes sharply at him
But, still, there is no response
From him at all.

  (chung mori)
Ch'un-hyang feels embar-
  rassed and
And pulls her hands away;
She sits back away from him
And speaks to him with feel-
  ing.
Ch'un-hyang
I've not known you,
Really haven't known you.
I just don't understand
What's in Toryŏng's heart!
You, Toryŏng, are the son
Of an aristocratic house
And I, Ch'un-hyang,
Am just a lowborn girl.
You couldn't still a passing
  fancy
And so dallied for a while.
But, then, chastised by par-
  ents,
And hearing others' attitudes,
Do you think it right to break
  away
And so come here to say
  goodbye?

**LATER CH'ANGGŬK
(After 1935)**

  your family, then! It is sure?
Toryŏng
It's sure. He's going to Seoul
  tomorrow, he says.
Ch'un-hyang
So, I'll get to go to Seoul!
  (singing)
It's been a life-long wish,
And now I'm going to Seoul!
Look here, Toryŏng!
Are you so happy that you
  cry?
The good people of Namwŏn
Lose a great governor.
They lament, indeed,
But for your family, good
  news!
The proper thing for you, Tor-
  yŏng,
Would be to dance for joy.
What, then, is this crying?
Ah! Now I understand!
While Toryŏng goes to Seoul
He cries for fear that I won't
  go!
Women are to follow men,
  they say.
One or ten thousand li, wher-
  ever,
I shall follow my Toryŏng!

character. In spite of these changes, the libretto is still entirely sung and follows the text of the traditional version very closely. In the third example, from a post-1935 ch'anggŭk production also reported by Pak Hwang,[35] we find fundamental changes. Here the lead singer's function has been reduced and the passage is dominated by spoken dialogue, newly written in a realistic style that is comparable to the lines of modern drama. And, at the same time, the singing has been reduced to short song buried deep in the dialogue.

At the same time that ch'angguk was flourishing with new materials and productions between the late 1930s and late 1950s, the profession was losing the great p'ansori kwangdae who had shepherded their time-honored tradition into the twentieth century. Every year but one in the decade of the 1930s saw the death of one or more master singers who had been born the late nineteenth century.[36] Some twenty-five more died in the twenty years of the 1950s and 1960s[37] and, of course, the rest were lost in the following years. Realizing that the art of p'ansori could be preserved, though the loss of the artists was inevitable, the government in the 1960s recognized certain living master singers as "intangible cultural treasures" and instituted a program to promote public appreciation of these artists, contribute to their support, and encourage them to pass on their p'ansori skills to a new generation of students.

While the classical, solo p'ansori remains alive and well today, so does ch'angguk. With the notable exception of the successful 1950 Western-style "grand opera" adaptation by Hyŏn Che-myŏng (Rody Hyun) of the "Song of Ch'un-hyang," the native ch'angguk style has dominated p'ansori-related stage productions.[38] Theatricality has been the salient characteristic of ch'angguk since the late 1930s, asserting itself as physical facilities have grown larger and more complex over the years. Although p'ansori and ch'angguk were little performed in the 1960s and early 1970s, the tempo of production increased during the late 1970s in response to government subvention and blossomed in the 1980s. Ch'angguk productions of the 1980s and 1990s incorporate elaborate scenic effects, full-stage ballets, and massive production numbers of a scale that was unheard-of half a century before. Since the opening of the new national theater on the slopes of Namsan in the late 1980s, there have been monthly, "full-work" p'ansori recitals by noted solo artists and annual ch'angguk productions of lavish proportions, complete with simultaneously projected titles in both standard Korean and English translation.[39]

女必從夫말이옷타
갓치가는생덕어미

TWO

THE TALE:
P'ANSORI

4

How Did P'ansori Evolve?

While we may speculate that the art of the story singer in Korea and the other countries of East Asia can be traced back to the utterances of priests and historians of a pre-literate age, we are not given abundant evidence of orally performed literature until the arrival in East Asia of proselytizing Indian Buddhism, the major outside cultural impact East Asia had known prior to the coming of the Europeans. Introduced in the first century A.D., Buddhism spread rapidly throughout China in the next few centuries and, thence, into Korea in the fourth century and Japan in the sixth. Between the mid-fourth century and the end of the eighth, Buddhism was the dominant religion of the Asian continent, embracing half its population as believers. During the heyday of the new religion in each country of East Asia, Buddhist monasteries became centers of cultural, economic, and political influence—not unlike the Christian monasteries of medieval Europe.[1] From these powerful establishments, proselytizing monks carried their belief to the peasantry, many times in the form of popularizations of scripture and adaptations of Indian tales that illustrated the meaning of their religion.[2]

During the T'ang dynasty, an active period for Chinese Buddhism, the

Japanese pilgrim, Ennin, traveled to China. In his travel diary, he describes Buddhist "lecture" series in the middle of the ninth century that ran for as long as a month at a time, serving both the clerics of the monasteries and laymen in the local cities.[3] Ennin found such monastic establishments not only in all the Chinese cities and towns he visited, but also in the numerous and flourishing Korean communities along the southern littoral of China's Shantung peninsula (on the coast facing Korea).[4] The largest he encountered was the Mount Ch'ih Cloister of twenty-nine Korean monks, serving one of the most populous of these Korean communities, a settlement large enough to supply an audience of 250 people for lectures.[5]

The fact that these lectures were conducted in the Korean language suggests similar activities at the same time for Koreans back home, where Buddhist monasteries had become rich and powerful with the support of the court and aristocracy during the Shilla period. Although there are no contemporary records of Buddhist storytelling in Shilla, the many edifying tales preserved in the *Samguk sagi* (History of the Three Kingdoms; 1145) and the *Samguk yusa* (Memorabilia of the Three Kingdoms; ca. 1285), in particular, suggest a flourishing narrative tradition.

Religious establishments in Japan, both Buddhist monasteries and Shintō shrines, emerged as major cultural centers with the decline of central authority during the four-hundred-year medieval epoch that followed the end of the Heian period in 1185. During the comparatively tranquil middle years of that epoch, a time known as the Muromachi period (1336–1573), a popular literary tradition emerged and was carried along the highways and into the villages by a variety of jongleurs: both secular professionals in search of a livelihood and proselytizing priests and nuns in search of converts. As Barbara Ruch says, these medieval entertainers "did more than probably any other groups to build what can be called Japan's first body of a truly national literature and to spread it throughout the country."[6] In a manner reminiscent of the Chinese experience, powerful monasteries and shrines facilitated the rise of these jongleurs by giving them home, audience, protection, and patronage.

Most noteworthy among these jongleurs was the secular *biwa-hōshi* (lute-priest), a blind and itinerant singer, self-accompanied on the lute, who created narrative cycles about powerful feudal houses at war that evolved into such saga-like chronicles as the *Heike monogatari* (Tale of the Heike). The textual development of the *Heike monogatari* has been traced from origins in orally composed tales, through transcriptions of oral performances, then written versions intended to be read silently and, finally, to later revisions made for the purpose of oral presentation as recitations—a process that produced more than one hundred variant manuscripts over several centuries.[7]

While the orally performed literature of temples and shrines made a contribution to later popular fiction and drama in both China and Japan, such a connection between Buddhism and popular literature has not been established for Korea after the Shilla period. In spite of the fact that the economic and political fortunes of the Buddhist church gained ground as Korea moved into the Koryŏ period, the intellectual and artistic vigor of Shilla Buddhism gave way to "blind formalism and false magnificence."[8] Several factors help to explain the non-involvement of Korean Buddhism with popular literature at the very time when Chinese monk-storytellers were already introducing their tales in the marketplaces and Japanese jongleurs were just beginning to spread their literature from temple and shrine out among the people.

Buddhism was effectively the state religion of Koryŏ and, as such, was deeply involved in the politics and life of the court. As a powerful and prosperous church of the aristocracy, Koryŏ Buddhism was uninterested in proselytization, vernacular literature, or popular culture. As early as 953, monks could sit for special state examinations and receive clerical rank appropriate to their performance. The two highest of these ranks were *wangsa* (royal master) and *kuksa* (national master); and the incumbents, being the king's own priest or embodiment of the state religion, were greatly respected.[9]

Many princes and sons of the aristocracy became monks, which is believed to have contributed to relationships that led to the enrichment of monastic establishments.[10] Since the state granted land to priests and also exempted them from conscripted service, their ranks became so swelled that the government by 1059 permitted a young man to become a monk only if there were already three or more sons in his family.[11] The secular power of the Buddhist church was demonstrated when monks took up arms to defend their establishments. By the early eleventh century, these priest-soldiers had already multiplied to the extent that they even supplemented government troops, as in the fighting against the Jurchen in 1033–1044.[12]

The Buddhist church was becoming powerful enough to challenge the secular leadership for control of the state; and, in 1135, the influential but erratic, geomancer monk Myoch'ŏng raised an army and proclaimed his own state with its capital at P'yŏngyang, his birthplace. But within a year, government troops from Kaesŏng, then the actual capital, had put him down.[13]

In such a milieu, the attitude of the Koryŏ Buddhist establishment, hardly conducive to the growth of popular culture, actually helped to harden the distinctions of Korea's dual cultural tradition and forestall such creative exchanges between the popular and formal cultures as occurred in both China and Japan.

Shaman Culture as P'ansori Seedbed

Although shaman culture, a basic vehicle of the Korean narrative tradition, was officially suppressed in the Chosŏn period, the actual practice of its rites continued unabated not only among the common people but even in the very bosom of the royal family. In the later Chosŏn period, to satisfy changing popular tastes and a growing demand for secular entertainment, shamanistic performances became popularized and the narrative shaman song itself grew increasingly vulgar as it tended to incorporate comic expressions. Such a shift in public sentiment was a product of rising popular consciousness and can also be associated with emergence of a monied bourgeoisie that found realistic arts to be more entertaining than religious or magical ones. The increased humor and satire in the narrative shaman song was paralleled by similar developments in mask dance, and also in *shijo* and *kasa* poetry.[14] In the hundred-odd shaman songs that have been collected in the field by modern researchers,[15] it is evident that these narratives, originally meant to entertain an invoked spirit, had accrued substantial entertaining and secular aspects that could hold the attention of the peasant audience. The extant narrative songs are of considerable variety and intersperse spoken passages, improvisational dialogues, and comic patter.

While the narrative folk song is sung and transmitted by untrained common people and is the more simple in content and plain in narrative structure, p'ansori and the shaman song are performed and transmitted by professional singers and, therefore, have similarly complicated structures and varied content. The shaman song, however, is distinguished from the other two by virtue of its function in religious rites. It does, at the same time, also bear the earmarks of myth, the earliest form of narrative, from which all other forms later emerged.[16]

Whereas the narrative shaman song sets forth the hero's life in panoramic terms, the narrative folk song focuses on a single incident that arises in the life of an ordinary person, such as a daughter-in-law. Such narratives naturally begin with a hardship, proceed to an attempt to resolve the difficulty, and usually end in failure (though occasionally a second attempt at resolution ends in success). Narrative folk songs can be divided generally into two large groups, depending upon whether the attempt at resolution is normal or extraordinary. In cases where the attempt at resolution is normal, the singer is closely identified with the main character and the story develops with a tendency towards the tragic. In cases where the attempt at resolution is extraordinary, however, the singer maintains a critical distance from the main character and the story displays comic development. In contrast to songs of lament, the comic narrative folk song attributes the central event of the song to someone other than the singer, who is therefore free to treat the event as an object of humor.[17]

It is widely accepted that p'ansori emerged from the narrative shaman song in the area of Chŏlla Province.[18] The narrative shaman song and p'ansori share certain distinguishing features: they are based on the same typical Chŏlla-area rhythmic structures and also employ alternating spoken and sung delivery. Nevertheless, p'ansori differs sharply from the narrative shaman song because it is an independent form of entertainment performed outside the context of the shaman rites and because it deals with realistic issues of human life, attracting the attention of its audience by using common people, rather than gods and heroes, as protagonists.[19] In addition, p'ansori is distinguished as a consciously creative art with its own developing vocal technique and theory of performance.

But until the seminal study by Seo Dae-seok in 1979, "A Comparative Study of P'ansori and the Narrative Shaman Song," there was only circumstantial evidence to support the belief that p'ansori arose in the southwestern region, that its most immediate folk background was the culture of the hereditary shaman, and that the formative context of p'ansori was the narrative shaman song. Seo earlier postulated in "Questions in the Formation of P'ansori"[20] that the region of origin of p'ansori had to be limited to the southwest in view of the fact that most of the singers of p'ansori were natives of the southwest and that the music of p'ansori is the same as the folk music of that region.

In the 1979 study, Seo demonstrates that the performance form of the narrative shaman song is nearly identical to that of modern p'ansori and goes on to compare the oral forms of p'ansori with those of the narrative shaman song, concluding that p'ansori had gone through a transformation from a recitational chant to a dramatic song.[21] According to Seo's formulation, when the narrative shaman song lost its mythic nature and began to assume a more epic, literary quality, the shaman could become an epic poet, singing more for the benefit of the congregation than of the spirits. Such a transformation led to a distinction between two kinds of shaman songs: the prior monotonic religious chant addressed to a spirit and the later melodious theatrical song addressed to an audience. Hence, the chanting shaman typically sits facing the deity with her back to the audience, while the dramatic singer stands facing her audience with her back to the deity and the accompanist to one side. The audience-consciousness of hereditary shamans, who do the dramatic singing, is consistent with their parish-oriented religious practice.

Seo Dae-seok rejects storytelling and the folktale as parent forms of p'ansori on grounds that such an assumption disregards p'ansori's obvious affinity with the narrative shaman song and overlooks the unique vocalization techniques of p'ansori and the shaman song that are lacking in other folk arts. Even though we can identify folktale materials that match the content of certain p'ansori songs, this means only that we have found a source of materials, not the origin of the genre itself. Seo Dae-seok does not specify the stage at which, nor the process by which, p'ansori took shape from within shaman dramatic singing. He does, however, posit, with some evidence, a formative stage when p'ansori was self-accompanied on the drum, had weak gesture, and enjoyed no supportive interaction with an accompanist.[22] But, in view of the fact that kwangdae continued to emerge from shaman households and remained a part of the shaman-based culture, we may easily speculate that the two performance forms developed in tandem.

In its earliest stages, p'ansori probably reflected the culture of its low-born performers for the most part, a position implicit in Kim Dong-uk's proposal that early p'ansori of the Chŏlla region may have been like a variety of oral narrative found in the northwestern P'yŏngan area and represented by the narrative "Paebaengi kut" (Rite for Paebaengi), in which a bogus shaman burlesques the shaman invocation of a dead person's soul and, imitating the speech and melodies of a shaman, deceives the parents of the dead maiden Paebaengi.[23] Unlike p'ansori, "Paebaengi kut" is simple in content, its expression is sparse, and its rhythmic changes are unclear; but it is, like p'ansori, an oral narrative poem that is satirical and describes everyday life realistically. The performer of "Paebaengi kut" beat on a drum while he sang alone, the rhythmic changes were ill-defined, and the language was coarse. But, while the northwestern narrative did not develop beyond this stage, southwestern p'ansori divided functions between singer and drummer, clearly distinguished the rhythms, refined its language while expanding materials, and finally spread throughout the country.[24]

As mentioned earlier, the evidence of Yu Chin-han's text of the "Song of Ch'un-hyang" suggests that p'ansori took its present shape in the eighteenth century; but, as Song Man-jae's "Kwanuhŭi" indicates, even in the middle of the nineteenth, it was still being performed together with variety acts.[25] The p'ansori corpus described in "Kwanuhŭi" consisted of twelve songs with the "Song of Ch'un-hyang" apparently already more refined than the others. The term Song Man-jae uses for a "song" is *madang,* a word that had once indicated the place ("yard") where a performance took place and later came to designate the work itself. Since a p'ansori *madang* is apt to be performed differently depending upon the kwangdae and the occasion, the word *madang* should be taken as designating a group of p'ansori works sharing the same story line. Song Man-jae's reference to "the twelve *madang*" might well have meant something more like "the many p'ansori," rather than exactly twelve works. While it is possible that the number twelve was used figuratively to parallel the traditional number of sections in a shaman ritual, we should note that it was later echoed in the poem "Kwanghallu akpu" (A *yueh-fu* song of Kwanghan Pavilion; 1852) by Yun Tal-sŏn (b. 1822), who referred explicitly to the "twelve vernacular songs."[26]

From Twelve Madang *to Five Songs*

The repertoire of *madang* shrank to six late in the nineteenth century, and today only five are still extant and performed. Table 2 lists fifteen by name, as drawn from sources including Song Man-jae's "Kwanuhŭi,"[27] Chŏng No-shik's *Chosŏn ch'anggŭk sa,*[28] Shin Chae-hyo's *P'ansori sasŏl chip,*[29] and Yi Sŏn-yu's (b. 1872) *Oga chŏnjip.*[30] While Song Man-jae gives an eyewitness description of 1843, Chŏng No-shik bases his listing on the oral tradition of master singers whom he interviewed in the 1930s. Shin Chae-hyo's collection of six songs reflect both his taste and what was popular when he was sorting and editing between 1867 and 1884.[31] The collection by Yi Sŏn-yu consists of transcriptions of the five-song repertoire that he performed in the 1930s and are still being sung. The table also notes which of the oral repertoire were performed on stage in ch'anggŭk style and which appeared in novel form.

Song Man-jae and Chŏng No-shik agree upon their first ten entries but they round out their tallies of "twelve *madang*" differently: where Song has the "Ballad of Walcha" and "Ballad of the False Immortal," Chŏng gives the "Ballad of Musugi" and "Tale of the Maiden Sug-yŏng," respectively. The

TABLE 2. Occurrences of the Nineteenth-Century Oral Repertoire

ORAL REPERTOIRE	SONG	CHŎNG	SHIN	YI	STAGE	NOVEL	COMMENT
Song of Ch'un-hyang (Ch'un-hyang ka)	√	√	√	√	√	√	—
Song of Shim Ch'ŏng (Shim Ch'ŏng ka)	√	√	√	√	√	√	—
Song of Hŭng-bu (Hŭng-bu ka, Pak t'aryŏng)	√	√	√	√	√	√	—
Song of the Water Palace (Sugung ka, T'obyŏl ka, T'okki t'aryŏng, Pyŏlchubu t'aryŏng)	√	√	√	√	√	√	—
Song of the Red Cliff (Chŏkpyŏk ka, Hwayong-do)	√	√	√	√	—	√	Novel based upo Chinese original
Song of Pyŏn Kang-soe (Pyŏn Kang-soe ka, Karujigi t'aryŏng)	√	√	√	—	√	—	—
Ballad of Chief Aide Pae (Pae-bijang t'aryŏng)	√	√	—	—	√	√	P'ansori libretto no longer extant
Tale of Ong Ko-jip (Ong Ko-jip)	√	√	—	—	√	√	P'ansori libretto no longer extant
Ballad of the Cock Pheasant (Changkki t'aryŏng)	√	√	—	—	—	√	P'ansori libretto no longer extant
Ballad of Maehwa of Kangnŭng (Kangnŭng Maehwa t'aryŏng)	√	√	—	—	—	—	—
Ballad of Walcha (Walcha t'aryŏng)	√	—	—	—	—	—	—
Ballad of the False Immortal (Katcha shinsŏn t'aryŏng)	√	—	—	—	—	—	—
Ballad of Musugi (Musugi t'aryŏng)	—	√	—	—	—	—	—
Tale of the Maiden Sug-yŏng (Sug-yŏng nangja chŏn)	—	√	—	—	√	√	P'ansori libretto no longer extant
Ballad of Ch'oe Pyŏng-do (Ch'oe Pyŏng-do t'aryŏng)	—	—	—	—	√	√	Novel is Yi In-jik's "Silver World"

last title listed in the table, "Ballad of Ch'oe Pyŏng-do," was not introduced until the twentieth century.

Today we know the content of eleven of the songs in the table but only the titles of the remaining four. Five p'ansori works are to this day performed in their traditional solo form and on the stage as ch'anggŭk operas; they have been recorded in many versions and are published as novels.

They are the "Song of Ch'un-hyang," "Song of Shim Ch'ŏng," "Song of Hŭng-bu," "Song of the Water Palace," and "Song of the Red Cliff." Like them, the "Song of Pyŏn Kang-soe" was transcribed by Shin Chae-hyo, but it is no longer widely sung and has never been published as a novel. Four other works from the traditional lists survive only in their novelistic form: "Ballad of Chief Aide Pae," "Ballad of the Cock Pheasant," "Tale of Ong Ko-jip," and "Tale of the Maiden Sug-yŏng." The remaining four works, for which we have no texts, appear only as titles in the lists of Song Man-jae and Chŏng No-shik: the "Ballad of Maehwa of Kangnŭng," "Ballad of Walcha," "Ballad of the False Immortal," and "Ballad of Musugi."

A work closely related to p'ansori, the "Ballad of Ch'oe Pyŏng-do," was performed as a ch'anggŭk only once in 1908; it concerns one Ch'oe Pyŏng-do who is persecuted and then flogged to death by the governor of Kang-wŏn Province. Materials related to this actual event had been transmitted orally by kwangdae. The noted singer Kang Yong-hwan fashioned them into a ch'anggŭk[32] called the "Ballad of Ch'oe Pyŏng-do" but gave it the title "Silver World" when it was performed. Through hard work, the historical Ch'oe Pyŏng-do had managed to amass a fortune but fell into the clutches of the wildly avaricious Kangwŏn governor, who had him thrown into jail. Ch'oe Pyŏng-do refused to yield to threats and resisted until he finally suffered his widely noted death. The incident, conveyed in p'ansori's uniquely expressive style that can evoke intense feelings of emotion, had such an impact on the audience that many people rose from their seats and shouted out to the singers on stage, according to an interview with master singer Yi Tong-baek which appeared in the magazine *Ch'unch'u* for March 1941.[33]

The script for "Silver World" no longer exists, and we can only guess at its content and style through Yi In-jik's novel of the same name. Although it was once thought that Yi's novel was the basis for the drama, recent scholarship has demonstrated that the play was rehearsed and performed while Yi was away in Japan. The novel was not published until after the ch'anggŭk had opened.[34]

Of the six songs represented in Shin Chae-hyo's collection, only the "Song of Pyŏn Kang-soe" exists solely as a p'ansori libretto; the other five are extant in many variants, including both libretti and novels. The plebeian origin and transmission of this tale is reflected in its lewd and amoral content and in its hopeless, dead-end story line, which helps account for its failure to circulate as a novel among a literate audience. The two major characters in the work are the woman Ong-nyŏ and the man Pyŏn Kang-soe. After telling how the two wander in search of a living, happen to meet, and then marry, it goes on to bawdy heights as it describes scenes in which the slattern and libertine go in search of pleasure.[35]

Although no single reason can account entirely for the shrinkage of the p'ansori repertoire from twelve to six and then to five *madang,* it was largely due to efforts of aficionados like Shin Chae-hyo at winning acceptability for p'ansori among the upper classes. His choices were consistent with the bias of influential kwangdae when p'ansori was on the rise in the late nineteenth century. The great singers of that age, patronized by an audience of high lineage and favored by those able to provide them with a venue, avoided libretti that suited lower-class tastes and concentrated on catering to the tastes of their growing upper-class audience.

The five favored songs had, for instance, ostensible themes—like filial piety, loyalty, comradeship—that were helpful in garnering acceptance for p'ansori among the elite. Being commodious, they could, moreover, easily accept the interpolation of decorous passages pleasing to aristocratic tastes. Nevertheless, the fundamental character of the works did not change; and in contrast to the superficial, external themes, their internal, central themes still addressed social reality by exposing contradictions that could not be explained with ordinary logic. Since p'ansori's inherent empathy for the lower class was not lost during the course of its cultural elevation, the resulting thematic contrast gave the kwangdae an opportunity to develop an individual interpretation that would bring unity to such a duality. This contributed to the tendency of the five songs to develop as clusters of differing versions.[36]

Although I assume, on the basis of formulaic analysis, that early kwangdae were skilled in techniques of oral composition, as defined by the Parry-Lord formulaic theory,[37] it is clear that they were already working with written source materials and using singers' texts during the first half of the nineteenth century. I earlier related that the kwangdae, Pang Man-ch'un, worked at length with a knowledgeable man of letters to revise and embellish earlier versions of the "Song of the Red Cliff" and "Song of Shim Ch'ŏng." The existence of a singer's text that came of this effort is confirmed by an anecdote in Pak Hŏn-bong's 1966 p'ansori anthology, in which he tells how he was able to attribute certain passages directly to Pang Man-ch'un himself. He explains that "Pang's original singer's text is now in the library of the late Hyŏn Chŏl, who had obtained it from Pang Ŭng-gyu, the singer's grandnephew. And, as a colleague in Korean music for many years, it was easy for the author to inspect this original text."[38]

In similar fashion, Pak Hŏn-bong is able to quote the early-nineteenth-century master, Pak Yu-jŏn, because "one of Pak's disciples, the great Chŏng Chae-gŭn, who was the uncle of Chŏng Ŭng-min, is the father of Chŏng Kwŏn-jin, presently an instructor at the School of National Musical Arts. Accordingly, Pak Yu-jŏn's singer's text, being a faithful transcription, is preserved by Chŏng Kwŏn-jin; and, with this text that has been passed on through several generations, we can appreciate how well Pak Yu-jŏn sang certain passages." Pak reports that, generally speaking, as for master singers of the distant past, he had access to the original singers' texts and to the singers' texts as transcribed by living singers of note who had studied under them.

Hence, it appears that the p'ansori libretti passed down to the present day are not necessarily all transcriptions of what had been purely oral until the moment of their recording. For it is clear that written scripts played an important role in learning and developing p'ansori libretti. When seen as reading material, they were read as fiction and, as they circulated, would have been picked up by entrepreneurial printers, who issued woodblock editions for profit. Such printed editions are known as "p'ansori novels," which are so similar to known libretti that there is little basis to distinguish them as a separate genre.[39]

With the exception of the adaptation of the "Ballad of Ch'oe Pyŏng-do" as the ch'anggŭk "Silver World" in 1908, literary composition related to p'ansori was limited to conservative revisions to produce colorful performances in the ch'anggŭk style. Although master singers naturally had the ability to produce more highly developed works that could have played a meaningful role in the literature of the early twentieth century, no one did so. Perhaps the now comfortable and popular kwangdae had lost the fire and insight that had so inspired their earlier work. Meanwhile, though p'ansori novels were being widely read, they were regarded only as amusements that did not deal with reality. Yi Hae-jo (1869–1927) provided a new model for p'ansori novels when he adapted four works from the oral tradition but did not contribute any fresh interpretation of his own. These were no more than a commercial effort that took advantage of an established popularity.

Shin Chae-hyo and Yi Hae-jo, separated by an interval of some fifty years, between them twice reworked the libretti of p'ansori. Shin Chae-hyo's revisions were made in the period 1867 to 1884 and Yi Hae-jo's revisions were accomplished in the year of 1912. If we were to say that Shin Chae-hyo promoted p'ansori when it was still in social disfavor, then Yi Hae-jo produced best-sellers by exploiting the great success of p'ansori, which had by then become the most favored of the traditional arts. P'ansori gained in status as it rode the rising tide of popular culture but, in the process, suffered a weakening of the critical weaponry that had been effectively wielded by kwangdae back when they were still being held in contempt.

5
The Nature of the Text

Core and Realization

Generally speaking, a p'ansori song does not have an original plot. For the traditional audience, who took interest, primarily, in how the pieces went together and how they were performed, all the elements of the performance were, in one way or another, already known (or knowable). The plots had been borrowed from the pervasive library of folk literature and fleshed out in the telling by the addition of other materials from the common culture.

The "Song of the Red Cliff" is based upon one chapter in the monumental Chinese novel, *Romance of the Three Kingdoms,* which had long been widely known in Korea; and the "Song of the Water Palace" is built around a folktale called the "Story of the Tortoise and the Hare," which was first recorded in the *Samguk sagi.* In the case of the "Song of Hŭng-bu," the basic story of mending the swallow's leg, which follows a widely distributed folktale pattern, was revised to emphasize issues that result from the contrasting natures of the brothers Hŭng-bu and Nol-bu. Whereas the "Ballad of Chief Aide Pae" and "Tale of Ong Ko-jip," on the one hand, use single anecdotes taken over from folktales, it would be fair to describe the "Song of Pyŏn Kang-soe," on the other, as fabricated from a combination of such anecdotes. While the "Song of Ch'un-hyang" could be an adaptation of the story pattern, "official snatches maiden from the people," it could also be seen as having come from shaman rites that consoled the spirits of those who had died in the course of such suffering.[1] And, as we shall soon see, the pattern underlying the "Song of Shim Ch'ŏng" has cognates widely distributed in Buddhist, Confucian, and shaman contexts and is noted in both *Samguk sagi* and *Samguk yusa.*

A full p'ansori song, as performed today, consists of many passages, both sung and spoken, which serve either to move the plot forward or to expand upon some theme, event, or characterization. The spoken passages, *aniri,* tend to introduce new action or bridge songs. By contrast, the sung passages, *ch'ang,* tend to flesh out the story and develop its emotional climate. In the version of the Shim Ch'ŏng story translated in Chapter Eight below, the text consists of eighty-four passages: twenty-five *aniri* and fifty-nine *ch'ang.* Even if the *ch'ang* were removed, the plot would remain intact, albeit without any emotional content; but elimination of the *aniri* would leave only a potpourri of songs that follow no apparent line of narrative development.

Kim Dong-uk identifies many of the *ch'ang* of p'ansori as "interpolated songs" (*sabip kayo*) that had been borrowed from elsewhere in the oral culture; and Seo Dae-seok treats them as formulaic structures that the singer can introduce at will, comparable to the "theme," as defined in the Parry-Lord theory of oral composition.[2] My analysis of the "Song of Shim Ch'ŏng" confirms Seo Dae-seok's conception of a process of p'ansori composition leading to the libretti that were later fixed by tradition. According to Seo, "A p'ansori libretto would be generated by taking some interesting story from popular tradition as an outline and then interpolating elements of popular song. The basic learning principle involved was, first, getting familiar with the singing of the songs and, next, grasping the situation and narrative context into which the songs were to be interpolated."[3]

In the case of the "Song of Shim Ch'ŏng," obviously interpolated songs come from other literary genres such as *kasa* and *shijo* poetry (e.g., storm scene at the Indang Sea); *tan'ga* songs (e.g., bird ballad, flower ballad); folk songs (e.g., lullabies, dirge, milling song, laments, and prayers); and Chinese poetry (e.g., Eight Sights on the Hsiao and Hsiang). All told, more than half of the *ch'ang* in the "Song of Shim Ch'ŏng" have been identified as interpolations.[4]

Thus we have what Cho Dong-il terms the "two aspects" of *p'ansori*: core and accretion.[5] The core story is a tidy schematic idea that is easily remembered and passed on; but its realizations, which result from the accretion of various materials, can take very different literary forms, including legend, folktale, narrative shaman song, narrative folk song, and p'ansori. There are three ways in which a p'ansori song and a folktale can differ, even while they are realizations of the same core story.

First, the p'ansori realization is always many times larger than that of the folktale to which it is related. Even the longest folktale could not match the quantity of material necessary for a p'ansori, which takes many hours to perform. Second, the structure of the p'ansori is typically complicated and unsystematic in contrast to the simple, regular, and clear character of the folktale. Third, the p'ansori realization contains contradictions and inconsistencies, both in fact and in characterization. Since the folktale is always remembered in terms of its core story, its realization is subordinated to the core, serving only to supplement and elucidate it. Hence, the contradictions and inconsistencies of one folktale teller would not necessarily be passed on to the next.

The distinction between core and realization helps to account for the contrasts in characterization and in concepts of time and reality that can exist within one p'ansori work. It explains, for example, the appearance within one work of two sorts of characters: the flat, symbolic stereotypes transmitted by the core, as opposed to the more believable, richly detailed secondary characters that are introduced in the p'ansori realization. It also explains why p'ansori is typically so vague and remote on matters of time and setting, yet invested with a wealth of realistic detail from everyday Korean life.

Let us take the setting of the "Song of Shim Ch'ŏng" as an example. Depending on the version, the time and place are given in the opening passage as the Sung or Ming dynasty in China or "in the days of yore." A typical opening goes, "In the last years of the reign of the Emperor Shen Tsung of the Sung dynasty there lived a man in Tohwa Ward of Hwangju." One version uses the Sung dynasty only to establish the time and then goes on to set the action in a country called "Yuri-guk," literally "Emerald-land," akin to a fairyland. The interior reality of the "Song of Shim Ch'ŏng," however, is always thoroughly Korean.

The core of the "Song of Shim Ch'ŏng," which can be found elsewhere in Korean myth, legend, and folklore, in Buddhist, Confucian, and shamanistic contexts,[6] contains four essential actions: 1) An incapacitated parent needs help; 2) a dutiful child sacrifices and suffers; 3) a benevolent power intervenes; 4) the child is rewarded and the parent helped. "The Filial Daughter Chiŭn," for instance, is a Confucian tale about a faithful daughter who sells herself as a slave to support her aged mother and so earns a reward for her sacrifice. It appears in the twelfth-century *Samguk sagi* and again, in more sparse style with less character detail, in the late-thirteenth-century *Samguk yusa*.[7] The foundation legend of Kwanŭm Temple in South Chŏlla Province was recorded by the ethnographer Ch'oe Sang-su in 1934.[8] This Buddhist tale, which explains the origin of the temple's statue of the bodhisattva Kuanyin, is very close to the "Song of Shim Ch'ŏng." A third example, "Princess Paridegi" occurs as the central chant in a ten-part ceremony performed by shamans in many parts of Korea to assure the safe journey of the spirit of a dead person to the next world. It is used in North Kyŏngsang Province to invoke and console the spirit of one who has died by drowning and was recorded there in 1965 by Kim T'ae-gon.[9]

The plot outlines in Table 3 demonstrate that the four core actions may be realized with different characters, in different settings, and within different time frames. Hence, one and the same plot has been realized as a story in four ways, ranging from the historian's reality of "The Filial Daughter Chiŭn," through the faithful Buddhist world of the Kwanŭm Temple legend and the fabulous, shamanistic realm of Princess Paridegi, to the comprehensive musical drama of Shim Ch'ŏng, which combines the real, the ideal, and the fantastic into a single work that resonates with the popular culture of the Chosŏn period. All four realizations are accomplished without any change in the core, but they succeed in evoking four very different worlds, reflecting the purposes of their tellers.

The story of "The Filial Daughter Chiŭn," faithful to the historical outlook of its source, is reported as an actual event, involving the people and places of the Shilla period: "The filial daughter Chiŭn was the child of one Yŏn'gwŏn, a commoner who lived in the Han'gibu district. . . . Hyojong was the son of the high noble, In'gyŏng, who had been prime minister of Shilla. The young man was called Hwadal as a boy."

The plight of Chiŭn and her mother would be commonplace in a society where widows could not easily remarry, and Chiŭn's decision to sell herself would be a realistic course of action in such a world. They live in a normal setting, in a house so near the thoroughfare that their sad laments can move even "passersby on the road." It is no supernatural power that

TABLE 3. Core Actions in the "Song of Shim Ch'ŏng" and Three Other Realizations

SONG OF SHIM CH'ŎNG	FILIAL DAUGHTER CHIÜN	KWANŬM TEMPLE LEGEND	PRINCESS PARIDEGI
1.			
An impoverished, blind widower named Shim Hak-kyu pledges 300 sacks of white rice to the Buddha in order to regain his sight.	A weak and aged widow is cared for by her dutiful daughter named Chiŭn. Their situation becomes untenable when they fall into poverty.	An impoverished, blind widower named Wŏn Yang pledges 50 sacks of rice to the Buddha to regain his sight but has no means to pay.	The great king is afflicted with a fatal illness that can be cured only by medicinal water found in another world.
2.			
His filial daughter, Shim Ch'ŏng, sells herself to ocean merchants as a sacrificial offering at the Indang Sea in return for 300 sacks of rice to be delivered to a temple.	Chiŭn sells herself as a slave to a rich man's house for 10 sacks of rice in order to support and continue caring for her mother.	His filial daughter, Hongjang, sells herself to sailors for 50 sacks of rice and is taken away.	His ninth (or seventh) daughter, Paridegi, goes in search of the water in spite of earlier cruelty of her father. She crosses into the other world and suffers many trials.
3.			
The Jade Emperor intervenes at the moment Shim Ch'ŏng makes her sacrificial leap into the sea and has her returned in a lotus, which the merchants later find and present to the emperor.	The king and many nobles are moved and take pity on them.	It turns out that the sailors had been sent by the widowed Chinese emperor to find a new empress, as instructed in a dream.	With the aid of supernatural powers, she procures the medicine and is returned to this world.
4.			
The emperor makes her his empress. She gives a banquet for all blind men, which her father attends, where he regains his sight upon hearing her call him, "Father!"	Chiŭn is set free. They are given food, clothing, a house, income, and security.	The emperor makes Hongjang his empress, and Wŏn Yang regains his sight.	After the medicinal water resurrects her now dead father, she and her progeny become gods.

intervenes, just the kind young noble Hyojong who "was out enjoying his leisure when he saw this sight." And what comes of his good offices? They are given what is needed: freedom for Chiŭn to do her filial duty as expected of her and also the necessities of their daily life. The record adds a believable reflection of the real world: "Furthermore, for fear that thieves would be attracted by all the millet, [the king] ordered the local authorities to assign soldiers to guard duty."

Finally, when the king arranges a marriage for Hyojong, as a reward for his generous efforts, it is not with a Cinderella-Chiŭn: "In view of the maturity he displayed at this early age, the king gave Hyojong as a bride the daughter of his older brother, King Hŏn'gang."

The Kwanŭm Temple legend is also presented with some of the believable formalities of historical reportage: "Wŏn Yang lived in a place called Taehŭng in Yesan County of South Ch'ungch'ŏng Province during the reign of Emperor Huei of the country of Chin." And, within the story, events seem to occupy real time, counted in days as in "The Filial Daughter Chiŭn." But then their concepts of reality begin to diverge: sailors are sent by a foreign emperor to whom God has spoken in a dream, identifying Hongjang as his empress-to-be, and a poor Korean girl becomes the empress of China.

The story of Paridegi presents still another world—one quite removed from everyday reality, a place where time is otherwise reckoned. The heroine goes to the next world in search of a medicine for her dying father and returns nine years later to find him only then being carried to his grave. In the world of Paridegi, mortals not only have dealings with supernatural beings but also become gods themselves.

In contrast to the "Song of Shim Ch'ŏng," these three realizations contain no more characters, narration, or dialogue than is needed to manifest the core. The p'ansori realization, on the other hand, introduces a variety of situations, involving additional characters, that contribute only indirectly to the unfolding of the plot. While the character of Shim Ch'ŏng is not well developed, her blind father gathers substance as he is played off against a variety of interesting secondary characters: his wife, the monk, neighbors, a local slattern, taunting youths, impudent peasant girls, passing officials on the road, the blind woman he marries in the end, and so forth. Shim Ch'ŏng, while given more dimension and functionality that her counterparts in the other realizations, remains more a paragon of filial piety than a real person; she is a mythic figure moving like a catalyst through her own story. Shim Ch'ŏng stands apart from the warm and earthy Korean world around her, carrying out a heroic function and assuming the didactic responsibilities of her character.

Structural Organization

Over the course of its lengthy evolution, p'ansori acquired a set of distinctive structural characteristics that were functionally related to the conditions of performance during its formative era. This unique structure of p'ansori can be considered on a number of levels: prosodic, formulaic, episodic, and dramatic.

Prosodic Structure. Traditional Korean poetry is a performed, not a written, literature; and in performance it has an instrumental as well as a vocal component. Although for analytical purposes its metrical foot can be calculated and is normally three or four syllables, the length of the foot is not actually fixed in terms of syllables. Instead, the fixed aspect of traditional Korean poetry is in the number of feet per line and in the rhythmic structure of the musical accompaniment.[10]

Two such feet constitute the smallest freestanding prosodic unit, that is, a unit followed by a caesura. This unit serves as a hemistich in p'ansori verse. It typically is balanced by another such hemistich, together with which it forms a full line. Two lines frequently form a paratactic pair. Such pairing is more common in p'ansori at faster rhythms than slower ones. Put another way, the hemistich, rather than the line, is the basic combining unit in p'ansori and a singer may use one in isolation or string three of them together on occasion, particularly at slower rhythms. In my translation of the "Song of Shim Ch'ŏng," I have decided to adopt the style of the p'ansori singer and treat all hemistichs as independent units—each starting flush left on its own line with a capital letter.

Since the metrical phrasing of p'ansori coincides with the syntactic phrasing of the language, enjambment is always avoided at the end of a full line, and typically at the end of a hemistich: each of the four feet which constitute a line also corresponds to a distinct syntactic unit within the sentence. Although we can find many instances of irregular syllabic counts in the lines of p'ansori texts, they are sufficiently consistent to satisfy the Parry-Lord condition that they follow a fixed pattern of length, meter, word boundary, syllabic count, and syntax.

The prosody of p'ansori is comparable to that of *kasa* verse, which is a form of discursive poetry that flourished during the Chosŏn period. While the underlying prosodic archetype that governs *kasa* is the same one that informs p'ansori, p'ansori is distinguished from *kasa* by its relative irregularity both in syllabic patterns and in pairing of hemistichs and lines.

The *kasa* form consists of a sequence of any number of lines, each made up of paired hemistichs. Lines frequently parallel each other. The most frequent full-line syllabic patterns I have found in a sample totaling 269 lines from four major *kasa* works are: 3-4 + 4-4 (26 percent), 3-4 + 3-4 (23 percent), 2-4 + 3-4 (10 percent), 2-3 + 4-4 (8 percent), and 4-4 + 4-4 (7 percent). The most common hemistich shapes are 3-4 and 4-4; atypical patterns include 6-5, 2-5, and 4-6. The *kasa* form avoids enjambment and the end of a line always coincides with a major syntactic break. Since every Korean sentence or clause must end with a verb form, it is appropriate that 81 percent of the hemistichs of our sampling of major *kasa* texts end in a verb form. A remaining 19 percent of the hemistichs end in a noun which, with its foregoing modifiers, serves as the subject, object, or indirect object of the verb coming at the end of the next hemistich. The caesura following a hemistich which ends in a noun generally coincides with the major syntactic break *within* a Korean sentence. That major break is the one that occurs between the two main sections of a Korean sentence: the nominal section (subject, object, indirect object) and the verbal section (predicate). In other words, the *kasa* verse form is a series of sentences that always terminate at the end of a hemistich, usually the second of the pair of hemistichs that forms a line. In sum, every prosodic unit of the verse form used in *kasa* or p'ansori—be it a foot, a hemistich, or a line—coincides with an essential syntactic constituent of the Korean sentence.[11]

Most of those who write about p'ansori today do so with little reference to its prosody or to the musical context of its performance. For this reason, the transcriptions that accompany their discussions nearly always have the appearance of prose, although the various passages are usually marked as "spoken" or "sung" and each song is marked with its appropriate rhythm. Even printing the poetry to look like poetry would not, however, be enough to capture fully the prosody of p'ansori; for in performance, the beating out of the various rhythmic patterns (*chung mori, nŭjin chung mori, chajin mori,* etc.) is integral to the effect. It is the irregular distribution of syllables against a regular drumming pattern that creates the characteristic prosodic complexity in p'ansori.

This complexity is difficult to capture on paper; but Figure 1 provides

FIGURE 1. Four P'ansori Hemistichs Set in Rhythmic Structure

This figure shows how the syllables of p'ansori verse are distributed irregularly against the fixed rhythmic setting of a barrel-drum *(puk)* accompaniment. Skin is stretched across both ends of the barrel-drum and the drummer strikes the left skin with his left hand and the right skin with a thick stick held in his right hand. With the stick, he also strikes the top and the rim of the drum's body.

1. Shim   Ch'ông   i ____   i   nal   pu   t'ôm
2.   pa —p   pi   rô   na sô ——l   che ____
3. wô————————   san e   hae pi————ch'i go
4. ap   ma   ûl————————   yôn   gi   na   myôn

Key to Drumming Notation

1 Strike left drum skin with palm of left hand
2 Strike right skin with stick in right hand
3 Strike top of drum body with stick in right hand
4 Strike rim of drum body with stick in right hand

Source: Extrapolated from Kim Ki-su, Han'guk ŭmak, pp. 272–273.

at least a notational analysis of the following four hemistichs from the beginning of the Begging Episode from the "Song of Shim Ch'ŏng":

Shim Ch'ŏng, from this day forward   Shim Ch'ŏng.i i nal pu-
                                                                   t'ŏm
When she goes out to beg the rice—   pap pirŏ na-sŏ.l che
As the sun shines on distant mountains   wŏn san.e hae pich'i.go
And smoke appears in the village yonder—   ap maŭl yŏn'gi na.myŏn.

These particular verses are sung against a drum playing the *nŭjin chung mori* rhythm of twelve beats in three-quarter time characteristic of Korean folk music. Therefore, whereas those who stress syllable counting as a means to account for prosody would describe these four hemistichs as "3-4, 3-3, 3-4, and 3-4," such an account does not convey the actual rhythmic effect of the singing in conjunction with the underlying rhythmic cycle. As the figure indicates, not only are there more drumbeats to the hemistich (twelve) than syllables (here, seven, six, seven, and seven), but an individual syllable may be drawn out over more than one stroke, or two syllables may be matched to a single stroke.

The frequent juxtaposition of an even number of syllables against an odd number of beats (e.g., four against three) leads to syncopation, clusters, and rests, which yield the characteristic complexity of p'ansori. Generally speaking, the slower the rhythm, the greater this complexity; and the more rapid the rhythm, the more monotonous the effect tends to be. This is because, in the slower rhythmic patterns like *nŭjin chung mori,* the singer can insert more than one syllable for each beat (in Figure 1, see *Shim Ch'ŏng* in row 1, *na-sŏ* in row 2, and *san.e, hae.pi,* and *ch'i.go* in row 3). In the relatively slow *chung mori* rhythm, as many as six syllables are commonly sung against a group of three beats. However, in the case of faster rhythms like *chajin mori,* even three syllables against three beats is difficult and the norm is more like two, with a result that is less complex.[12] The musical setting of p'ansori is further discussed in Chapter Six below.

Formulaic Structure.   The concept of the oral formula as the basic building block used by story singers was developed by Milman Parry in the 1930s and furthered in later years by Albert B. Lord.[13] According to the Parry-Lord theory, as a general precondition to qualifying as oral and formulaic, a given text must be sung verse and must fall into discrete lines that follow a fixed pattern of length, meter, word boundary, melody, syllable count, syntax, and acoustics. Such a text commonly uses parataxis but avoids enjambment.

The formula that is central to texts of this sort consists of "a group of words which is regularly employed under the same metrical conditions to express a given essential idea."[14] This formula may be a stable group of words associated with one of the more common ideas of the poetry, such as frequently repeated actions, revisited locales, recurrent times, and reappearing characters. In addition to the formula, there is a formulaic system, a group of phrases similar enough in their wording and the idea they express to be considered variants of a single formula.

The same formula will appear more than once in a given singer's repertoire, following the same basic pattern of rhythm and syntax. Some formulas may be shared by all singers belonging to a tradition, although no two singers would have identical repertoires of formulas. While seeming repetitious, the formula is useful and necessary to the singer, who must meet complex prosodic demands in the course of rapid oral composition. These often-repeated groups of words are known to students of the Homeric epic as "epic clichés"; and in classical Japanese poetry, the same phenomenon is called the *makura kotoba,* or "pillow-word."

There is no dividing line between formula and non-formula: everything in orally composed literature is potentially formulaic. After a group of words has been "regularly employed under the same metrical conditions to express a given essential idea," it may be recognized as a formula. Any group of words in any performance is a potential formula that may or may not attain some degree of frequency and, thence, recognition as a formula. Lord, having analyzed a sampling of twelve thousand lines from the songs of one singer, concluded, "The formulas in oral narrative style are not limited to a comparatively few 'epic tags,' but are in reality all pervasive. There is nothing in the poem that is not formulaic."[15]

Much of Korean p'ansori is, ultimately, a product of the same art of formulaic oral composition that Lord describes as the genius of the modern Yugoslav epic. In spite of the great cultural differences between the two traditions, the same formulaic technique has been useful to both for technical reasons that transcend local linguistic and cultural peculiarities. In both cases, the singer has needed the formula as a device to facilitate rapid oral composition before an audience and, at the same time, to adapt his work to the changing demands of his literature.

The Begging Episode from the Wanp'an text of the "Song of Shim Ch'ŏng" (ff. 1:12b–1:13a) can illustrate the role of the formula in p'ansori. I sought formulaic matches for each of its thirty-seven hemistichs throughout three versions of the entire, roughly four-thousand-hemistich work and also four versions of the equally long "Song of Hŭng-bu." I found that twenty-seven hemistichs (73 percent) appear to be formulas or formulaic systems: Formulas account for nine hemistichs (24 percent) and the formulaic systems for eighteen (49 percent).

Take, for example, the third and fourth hemistichs in the excerpt below: "wŏn san.e hae pich'i.go / ap maŭl yŏngi na.myŏn" (As sun shines on the distant mountains / And smoke appears in the village yonder—). As in the third hemistich, time of day is often expressed by reference to the sun or moon appearing and shining on objects below, such as we find in the opening of Ho Sŏk-kyun's *shijo* poem (Chŏng no. 675), "tongch'ang.e tal pich'i.go" (moon shines on the eastern window), or in the Wanp'an text of the "Song of Shim Ch'ŏng" (f. 1:24a), "ŏnŭdŏt tongbang.i palg.a-o.ni" (unnoticed, the east grows bright). As in the fourth hemistich, mealtimes— breakfast or dinner—are frequently suggested by references to the smoke rising from kitchen fires when the rice is being cooked, such as we find in the "Song of Shim Ch'ŏng" (f. 2:2a), "kyŏgan kangch'on yangsam ka.e / pap chin.nŭn yongi na.go" (at several houses of a river village on the far bank / smoke rises from the cooking rice). This fourth hemistich, then, incorporates a formulaic system for indicating the morning. Whereas the inflection *myŏn* means "when," *go* means "and." All thirty-seven hemistichs are analyzed in this fashion in my monograph, "Korea in the Bardic Tradition: P'ansori as an Oral Art."

In the following typographical rendering of this analysis, formulas are marked in boldface and formulaic systems in italic. Unmarked words do not appear as formulas elsewhere in the corpus selected for study. (The English translation has here been made as literal as possible while remaining intelligible, and the traditional orthography of the Wanp'an text has been corrected to the modern standard.)

Shim Ch'ŏng, from this day forward,	**Shim Ch'ŏng.i i nal put'ŏm**
When she goes out to beg the rice—	**pap pir.ŏ na-sŏ.l che**
As the sun shines on distant mountains	*wŏn san.e hae* **pich'i.go**
And smoke appears in the village yonder—	*ap maŭl* **yŏngi na.myŏn**
She binds old hemp trousers at the cuffs	*hŏn pe chungŭi taenim ch'i.go*
And, over a hemp skirt with just a waistband intact,	*mal* **man nam.ŭn** *pe ch'ima.e*
A jacket with no front,	*apsŏp* **ŏm.nŭn** *chŏp chŏgori*
She binds this way and that way.	*irŏng-jŏrŏng ŏlmae.go*
She pulls on a blue cotton cap,	ch'ŏngmok hwiyang null.ŏ-ssŭ.go
Bares her stockingless feet	**pŏsŏn ŏpsh.i par.ŭl pŏt.ko**
And pulls on sandals without heels.	*twich'ik* **ŏm.nŭn** *shin.ŭl kkŭl.go*
She tucks an old gourd under her arm	**hŏn pagaji yŏp'.e kki.go**
And carries a pot by some twine bound on it.	*tanji nokkŭn mae.ŏ* **son.e tŭl.go**
On the snowy days of deepest winter	**ŏmdong sŏrhan** *moji.n nal.e*
She is oblivious to the cold.	ch'u.un chur.ŭl morŭ.go
She steps inside gates of this house and that	*i chip chŏ chip munam-munap tŭr.ŏ-ga.sŏ*
With her pitifully begging words:	*aegung-hi pi.nŭn mar.i*

"That my mother has forsaken the
  world
And that my father, dim of eye,
Cannot see, who would not know?
Ten spoons make one meal, it is said.
If you eat one spoon less and give it,

My father, whose eyes are dim,
Would avoid being hungry."

The people who see and hear her
Are moved at heart;
Bowls of rice with pickles and sauce
They do not stint in giving her.
Sometimes they say, "Stay and eat!"
But Shim Ch'ŏng then replies:

"My old father in his cold room
Will surely be waiting.
Would I eat by myself?
I shall go right back quickly
And eat together with father."
For the rice she begs in this way,
Two or three houses are enough.

moch'in.ŭn sesang pŏri.shigo

uri puch'in nun ŏdu.ŏ
ap mot po.shin chul nwi morŭ.shilikka
shipshi ilban i.oni
pap han sul tŏl chapsu.shigo
  chu.shi.myŏn
nun ŏdu.un na.ŭi puch'in
shijang.ŭl myŏn-ha.gesso

po.go-tun.nun saram.dŭr.i
maŭm.i *kamgyŏk-hay.ŏ*
kŭrŭt pap kimch'i chang
akki.ji ank'o chu.myŏ
hog.ŭn mŏk.ko ka.ra ha.myŏn
Shim Ch'ŏng.i ha.nŭn mar.i

ch'u.un pang.e nulg.ŭn puch'in
ŭngdang kidari.l kŏs i.ni
na honja mŏk.saorikka
ŏsŏ pappi *tor.a-ga.sŏ*
abu hamkke mŏk.kennanida
irŏ-jŏrŏ ŏt.nŭn pab.i
tu se chip ŏd.ŭni chok-ha.njira

In the above passage, in order to help differentiate graphically between
what is fixed in a formula and what can be altered to fit a context (inflectional endings) or to generate a new formula (elements of a compound), a
period has been used to connect an inflection to a stem, and a hyphen
connects compound verbs and nouns. This punctuation draws attention to
an important feature of all oral formulaic poetry: a formula must be suited
to the syntax into which it fits.

In Korean, it takes a grammatical inflection appropriate to its role in a
given sentence, be it attributive, nominal, adverbial, or verbal. Hence, the
same formula may appear in several inflectional guises. Take, for instance,
the oft-repeated formulaic attribute of Shim Ch'ŏng's blind father that he
"cannot see ahead." The stem of this expression, *ap mot po-,* is altered by
changing the inflection to suit a variety of syntactic situations:

ap mot po.nŭn   (attributive)
ap mot po.gi   (nominal)

ap mot po.dŭshi   (adverbial)
ap mot po.go   (conjunctive verb)
ap mot po.nda   (final verb)

Consequently, the shape of a formula in a given sentence is governed to some extent by where the singer found himself in the construction of the sentence when he decided to use the formula. That is to say, the position of the formula within a hemistich or line is a factor that determines syntactic function and, hence, the inflectional form. For example, to return to the formula "cannot see ahead," the attributive *ap mot po.nŭn* would be avoided as the second or fourth foot of a line, while the final *ap mot po.nda* would probably be restricted to the fourth foot.

Episodic Structure.   Like all traditional oral narrative, a p'ansori song is made up of basic structural units that Lord calls "themes."[16] While creating lines of verse by the formulaic method, the traditional kwangdae was also mindful of the themes his verse constituted and the episodes into which those themes were grouped. Moreover, he was also aware of the final shape of the whole song that a sequence of episodes would ultimately produce.

Although Lord's Yugoslav singer had in his mind a "stable skeleton of the narrative," a "basic idea or combination of ideas that is fairly stable," or a "generic song,"[17] this basic formulation bore no name or independent identity in the folkloristic tradition of the culture, as do the songs of the present p'ansori repertoire.[18] In contrast to the amateur nature of Yugoslav oral composition, the Korean professional tradition was characterized by training through master-disciple relationships, by membership in professional organizations, by conscious competition among colleagues, and by the maintenance of professional genealogies. These all fostered an awareness of how others had performed a given song and, hence, reinforced certain traditions of performance and interpretation. As a result, some sequences of p'ansori episodes eventually came to be established as authoritative and were given names, producing the songs of the modern repertoire. Nevertheless, the various schools of interpretation still continued to maintain their distinctive traditions during the nineteenth century. Furthermore, individual singers remained free to add and drop themes and episodes, and also to alter the words as they saw fit. On the other hand, the inevitable hardening of tradition has produced many twentieth-century singers who reproduce the songs of their masters word for word and episode by episode.

While there may be considerable complexity within an episode, the internal ordering of the overall song is basically linear and chronological. Though time may pass at radically differing rates, depending upon the episode, the direction is always forward; though events may parallel each other in two episodes, overlapping to some extent, flashbacks do not occur. The one exception among major p'ansori works is a short episode in the "Song of Shim Ch'ŏng," interrupting the Crystal Palace Episode, which takes us back slightly to a point before Shim Ch'ŏng's sacrificial plunge into the Indang Sea: Lady Chang of Murŭng Village notices changes in the color of a scroll Shim Ch'ŏng had given her, signifying Shim Ch'ŏng's plunge and rescue. This episode occurs as a flashback only in the Wanp'an text (f. 2:10a); the only other text containing this episode places it immediately after the plunge (Chang Chi-yŏng text, pp. 198–200).

Whether established as an independent entity by convention or by the authority of some famous kwangdae of the past who made it his show-piece,[19] a given episode often acquired elements of style and content that contrasted sharply with other episodes within the same song. Such a contrast could be furthered by some later kwangdae who might momentarily disregard the song as a whole and concentrate his energy on a given episode in an effort to please his audience. As a result, while one episode might end up consisting mainly of realistic dialogue built of native Korean vocabulary and allusions, its neighbor in the same work could be an impressionistic pastiche of turgid Chinese verse. Such differences in style and content may be illustrated by two episodes from the "Song of Shim Ch'ŏng": the one in which the heroine visits the Crystal Palace beneath the waters of the Indang Sea and the one in which Blindman Shim is rescued by the alms-gathering monk and makes his impetuous pledge of three hundred sacks of rice.[20]

The Crystal Palace Episode is an impressionistic set piece in high-flown rhetorical style. But it is fraught with corruptions, lacunae, and opaque archaisms that suggest a history of uncritical transmission by many kwangdae after it had attained its unique shape. It is clearly meant to be an evocative *tour de force* that strives for an overall effect without particular concern for the logic of its minor details. The syntax of its language is many times only the simple concatenation of nouns, with predication forgotten in the rush of fantastic visions.

In the crucial Pledge Episode, by contrast, the kwangdae convincingly places Blindman Shim in a dilemma that his audience can accept as sufficient cause for the ensuing action. He deals in terms of his listeners' contemporary reality and uses a diction appropriate to that reality. No effect is without its cause and no action is without its motivation. Blindman Shim's anxiety over Shim Ch'ŏng's lateness, and hence his reason for going out in search of her, is convincing. His hunger and loneliness, the inclemency of the weather, and the lateness of the hour—these are all well established before he ventures out and falls into the drainage ditch. He is believably helpless when his cries are heard by the monk who, in turn, has reason for being the only one out on the path at that hour.

The Pledge Episode is artfully constructed. The bedraggled blind man is not only bewitched by talk of regaining his sight, but is prevented by stupid pride from any rational thought until, left alone, he finally does realize the enormity of what he has done. The overall purpose of the episode is realized in the closing monologue as Blindman Shim recounts his situation and considers the crucial dilemma in which he finds himself.

These stylistic contrasts between the two episodes have their parallels in the area of characterization. In the Crystal Palace Episode, there is none to speak of. Shim Ch'ŏng, who is given very little character detail throughout the whole work, appears here in her typical guise: self-sacrificing and demure. The other figures are but players in an elaborate spectacle. In the Pledge Episode, on the other hand, we find realistically detailed characters who interact in ways that move the plot forward. We learn new things about Blindman Shim and discover in him recognizable, human complexities. He seems lonely, proud, ironic, and angrily frustrated by his unjust lot in life. Furthermore, there is the suggestion that his feelings toward his daughter are entangled with his own self-esteem. The monk, however realistic, seems more functional, introduced as a necessity to promote the crucial pledge. This impression is strengthened when the kwangdae treats him as the butt of humor and, at his expense, makes an entertaining turn out of the undressing scene.

Further contrasts may be found in differing concepts of time and reality. As the kwangdae strives to conjure up the extravagant setting of the Crystal Palace, time hangs suspended and the reality that emerges is visionary. This timeless moment at the Crystal Palace is embedded in the temporal framework of Shim Ch'ŏng's real lifetime, as if it were a dream. And, like a dream, features of the known world appear in fantastic form—the court and all its trappings, social institutions, even historical men of yore. The account is invested with descriptions of people, titles, and articles known to the audience but not a part of their daily lives. This contrasts with the Pledge Episode, where time elapses at its normal rate and recognizable, realistic detail abounds.

The dramatic and aesthetic semi-independence of the p'ansori episode allows for another distinctive feature of the genre: the possibility of factual inconsistencies and even contradictions between episodes. The kwangdae, as an entertainer more concerned with immediate performance than with the literary work as an entity, would draw upon his capacity for improvisation to suit the tastes of his listeners, with the result that he might alter an episode in the course of its performance in a way inconsistent with other episodes of the narrative. He would skip some detail here and add some detail there, interpolate snatches of Chinese verse or Korean folk songs, indulge in impressionistic flights of cataloging (flowers, skills, clothing, place names, medicines, and so forth), and even change the sequence of the episodes themselves—practices to which surviving texts and modern performances bear witness.

Extant texts perpetuate inconsistencies and contradictions. In the beginning of the Wanp'an text, for instance, we are told that Blindman Shim had gone blind "before he was twenty." But his daughter, in a prayer several episodes later, reports to the gods that he had become blind "within thirty years." Although Blindman Shim is described as "facing eighty" upon the birth of his son near the end of the text, he is still described as the same age in the final episode, when his son's age is given as twenty. Shim Ch'ŏng's age, also, is inconsistently reckoned: she is sacrificed at fifteen but "three years later" is referred to as sixteen. In another example, a calligraphic scroll written in black ink in one episode is treated as if painted in color in another.

Other inconsistencies involve changes in characterization and the introduction of new characters for passing reasons that serve only the immediate episode and bear no relation to the greater story. And while time and place, vaguely established at best, are managed consistently within an episode, the work as a whole lacks any overall sense of such things.

Dramatic Structure.   P'ansori is narration, but dramatic narration. Although in performance it is, of course, dominated by the presence of a single singer and the attention of the audience is constantly on him, p'ansori is not limited to narrative exposition nor to the narrator's persona. Through the kwangdae's virtuosity, individual characters exist and speak in their own right.

Both the spoken and the sung passages can contribute to characterization and drama. The proportions of song and speech in p'ansori depend upon the style of the individual performer. From the orthodox, traditional point of view, the spoken passages do not demonstrate the singer's primary skills, but serve only to spell him in the arduous task of singing. Nevertheless, modern singers do exploit the technical contrast between sung and spoken passages to control dramatic pace and emphasis.

The spoken *aniri* passages are often loosely structured and serve as bridges between songs, scenes, and juxtaposed events. They are also a means of delivering dialogues in which the characters exchange numerous short lines. The sung *ch'ang* passages are built around single themes involving little action or dialogue and stand out as well-formed structures with their own internal integrity. When used as the vehicle for a monologue, a *ch'ang* is sung in the first person of the character involved. As a descriptive passage, it becomes an objective, third-person account of people, actions, places, goods, and so forth. On the whole, a given *aniri* passage is more apt to be related to the following *ch'ang* than to the one that comes before. That is, it sets the scene for a *ch'ang*, rather than resulting from one.

Let us look at the interplay of *ch'ang* and *aniri* in the context of a full work, Yi Sŏn-yu's performance of the "Song of Ch'un-hyang," which was published in 1933.[21] Yi's version contains fifty-five *aniri* passages and sixty-eight *ch'ang*. But, in sheer volume of words transcribed, the total space given to *ch'ang* is double that for *aniri*—613 printed lines as opposed to 305. Furthermore, since sung passages take longer to deliver, this dominance of the *ch'ang* becomes overwhelming in performance.

The introductory or bridging functions of *aniri* and the independent, unitary character of *ch'ang* are reflected in the grammatical forms with which each typically ends. Of the *ch'ang* in Yi Sŏn-yu's performance, a full 87 percent end with a sentence-final inflection. Only 47 percent of the *aniri* do; and even though these are grammatically conclusive, most of them (twenty-two out of twenty-six) have content which introduces the following *ch'ang*. That is to say, while most of the *ch'ang* in Yi's performance are independent entities, the *aniri* require the following *ch'ang* in order to stand.

The *aniri* which end in grammatically non-final inflections close with such expressions as "speaking, he says . . .," "upon doing . . .," "looking around and seeing . . .," "taking his leave . . .," "while doing . . .," and so forth. The *aniri* with grammatically conclusive endings (but which function as introductions) are mostly imperative, eliciting the action of the following *ch'ang* or foreshadowing an action or description which is to be given fuller treatment in it.

As mentioned, dialogue appears in both *aniri* and *ch'ang* passages. While speeches in *aniri* passages come in comparatively short, give-and-take bursts, those in *ch'ang* passages are more apt to be extended statements. Although the *ch'ang* is basically a vehicle for the lines of one character, two may sometimes (but not commonly) share the same *ch'ang*. More typically, when two characters are exchanging long statements, each is given his own *ch'ang,* sung in a rhythm appropriate to his temperament and the content of his speech. The two *ch'ang* are linked by a bridging line (spoken in the persona of the narrator) that marks the change of character.

The kwangdae almost never needs to juggle more than two dramatic roles at a time. First one major character and then a second is followed through a series of episodes. Two such characters dominate a p'ansori plot, the climax and resolution coinciding with the ultimate convergence of their two dramatic paths. Since the kwangdae usually deals with only one of them at a time, playing each off against a series of secondary characters, it is a simple matter for him to keep the dramatic speakers distinct in the minds of his listeners. A typical scene will involve a major and a minor character (and the narrator), and then, when each has been well established, the two major characters together. Three-way exchanges rarely occur in p'ansori.[22]

6

Music, Theory, and Transmission

Many general cultural studies in Korea today uncritically treat p'ansori as if it were a written literature. Worse, some people go so far as to perpetuate the mistaken belief that the entire tradition was derived from written sources that were somehow lost. In point of fact, p'ansori—like several other dominant literary forms of traditional Korea—has always been a performed literature, one presented in a musical setting. Despite many years of effort to the contrary, p'ansori resists classification in terms of only one of its four aspects, for it is an oral narrative, it is dramatic, it is musical, and much of it is in verse. An academic conference, held at Seoul National University in 1966 to discuss a definition of the genre, asked the question, "What is P'ansori?" After advocacies for poetry, prose, and drama were forwarded, one participant argued memorably for the notion that "p'ansori is p'ansori."

With this in mind, it would be appropriate to introduce here some aspects of p'ansori's music, performance, training, and transmission that argue against easy assignment of the form to one of the commonly cited, modern European bibliophilic genres. We shall look into the music setting of p'ansori, performance theory, and learning methods.

Music of P'ansori

The musical building blocks of p'ansori are rhythm, mode, and vocalization.[1] The kwangdae varies and mixes these elements in order to create effects that are appropriate to the content of the libretto and, thus, aid in the task of "revealing the inner meaning"[2] of the drama. Traditional kwangdae were judged by history more for these musical attributes than for their dramatic gestures or ability to learn and manipulate the words.

Although something will be said below to describe rhythmic cycles and modal structures, vocalization is another matter. Despite the fact that fifty-three different techniques of vocalization are named and defined in scholarly Korean texts, they can be taught only by demonstration and learned by imitation because of their complex structure of microtonal subtleties that can barely be explained in Korean, let alone in English, which lacks the technical vocabulary.

Rhythmic Cycles.   There are five basic rhythmic cycles (called *changdan*), each built on a particular sequence of beats and each distinguished by its own meter, tempo, rhythmic pattern, and affective attributes. Since any song is longer than a single rhythmic sequence, the drummer repeats the cycle as many times as necessary, adding variations and ornamentation as befits the emotive content and the singer's melodic inventions. At the beginning of a song, in reverse of the practice in Western music, the drummer lets the singer begin alone and then adds rhythmic accompaniment a few beats later, at the climax of the first rhythmic sequence (the loudest accent beat). Later in the song, the drummer also offers shouts of encouragement (*ch'uimsae*) at this same climactic beat of the reiterating phrase. The basic rhythmic patterns are given in Table 4, listed in order from slow to fast. Each of the first three is subdivided into three sub-types which differ from the fundamental cycle only in tempo, being slow, moderate, and fast. *Chajin mori,* however, is subdivided into only slow and fast. *Hwi mori* is used only in its basic rapid form. There are several more cycle patterns that are less frequently used.

Modal Structures.   The word *cho,* which appears in the names of such

Music, Theory, and Transmission

TABLE 4. Primary Rhythmic Cycles of P'ansori

CYCLE PATTERN	METER	METRO-NOME[a]	CYCLE BEATS	ACCENT BEATS	EFFECT
chinyang cho	18/8	45	6[b]	1, 5, 6	poignant
chung mori	12/4	85	12	1, 9	composed
chung chung mori	12/8	95	12	1, 9	elegant
chajin mori	12/8	100	4	1	lively
hwi mori	4/4	200	4	1	urgent

Notes: [a]These are averages, based upon a 1968 performance by Chŏng Kwŏn-jin as transcribed in Kim Ki-su, *Han'guk ŭmak*, pp. 237–369. The metronome number for *hwi mori* was extrapolated from the similar *ŏt mori*. [b]Usually repeated in sets of four cycles.

p'ansori singing modes as *p'yŏng cho, u cho,* and *kyemyŏn cho,* incorporates the sense of the Western musical concepts of mode and scale, in addition to the aesthetic effect of key. Each *cho,* moreover, is attributed certain impressionistic qualities which rise from the singer's vocal techniques and stage presence. The *cho,* therefore, is an arrangement of selected musical notes, usually five, which are used to create melodies. The selection and arrangement of these notes is said to impart characteristics to the melodies that are based on them and, therefore, suggest affective distinctions among *cho,* as expressed in such impressionistic terms as "brave," "harmonious," or "poignant." It is important to realize that these singing styles are not unique to p'ansori, but have long been widely distributed in Korean traditional music, both vocal and instrumental.

The *p'yŏng cho* is traditionally described as having a very tranquil and harmonious melodic line, characterized by balance and stability. To describe the feeling imparted by this mode, Chŏng Pyŏng-uk draws upon an introduction to *Haedong kayo* (Korean songs; 1763), a collection of *shijo* poetry and an important source of critical commentary.[3] In *Haedong kayo,* the feeling of the *p'yŏng cho* is compared to the sensation of "driving a carriage, with reins loosely held, through a garden alive with many kinds of flowers" or to the clear, fresh sensation of "seeing the moon risen high into the midnight sky or feeling a gentle breeze that strokes the placid surface of the water." The *p'yŏng cho* is thought to be appropriate for cheerful and peaceful scenes, like the description of the emperor's garden in the "Song of Shim Ch'ŏng."[4] While the effect of the *p'yŏng cho* is summed up as "balanced, peaceful, and profound," this is basically a relative matter to be best grasped through comparison of the *p'yŏng cho* to the *u cho* and *kyemyŏn cho.*

"If we were to characterize the *p'yŏng cho* as the backbone of p'ansori's musical nature," says Chŏng Pyŏng-uk, "then the *u cho* and *kyemyŏn cho* are expressions of p'ansori's potentialities, as arms and legs are extensions of the body's faculties."[5] The *u cho,* while very similar to the *p'yŏng cho* in its musical characteristics, is thought to have a cool and austere melodic line and is usually described as being brave and stately in character. It is used in such passages as that describing the heroine's voyage to her death in the "Song of Shim Ch'ŏng."[6] The *kyemyŏn cho* melodic line, on the other hand, is said to evoke soft and sad feelings in the listener and, therefore, is commonly used to express melancholy and lament and also to describe the behavior of women. An example from the "Song of Shim Ch'ŏng" is the last will and testament delivered by the heroine's mother.[7] This *cho,* which grew out of the folk songs of the Chŏlla region, is the predominant *cho* of p'ansori.[8]

Just as an artist mixes colors on a palette, so the p'ansori kwangdae selects and combines rhythms, *cho,* and vocalizations to convey the characterizations, emotional context, mood, tone, and level of artifice appropriate to the dramatic content of a given scene. That is, as suggested by the traditional dictum to "sing for the inner meaning," p'ansori has greater expressive capacity than shaman songs or *kasa* poetry. These other forms, though narrative in content, do not so evidently adjust their musical elements to suit the demands of their dramatic content.[9]

Many elements of classical p'ansori can be traced to the master singers of the first half of the nineteenth century. Chŏng No-shik devotes the lion's share of his book to setting down the accomplishments of such singers, whose unique contributions to the p'ansori tradition are detailed in oral history—their rhythms, vocalizations, melodies, and narrative interpretations. Most of these great artists came from the Chŏlla area and, therefore, with such broad and deep representation from this one region, p'ansori styles peculiar to certain Chŏlla localities became distinguished and then developed as distinct schools of performing style. The major schools that resulted from this localization are known as the Tongp'yŏn-je (Eastern school), Chunggo-je (Central school), Sŏp'yŏn-je (Western school), and Kangsanje (River and mountain school).

Since the Eastern School, for the most part, is based on *u cho,* it is noted for the brave and stately quality of its melodies. Widely performed by kwangdae from such towns on the east side of the Sŏmjin River as Kurye, Unbong, and Sunch'ang, its formation is traced back to the great Song Hŭngnok. The Western School, developed by kwangdae who hailed from Naju, Kwangju, Posŏng and other towns on the west of the Sŏmjin, dates back to the master Pak Yu-jŏn and is marked by the complex and haunting quality of the *kyemyŏn cho,* which it uses a great deal. The *chunggo-je,* which is associated with the Kyŏnggi and Ch'ungch'ŏng areas, is a subset of the Eastern School and is noted for a serene singing style that is reminiscent of the intoning of classical texts. Founding of this school is attributed to the noted Yŏm Kye-dal.[10]

Finally, the River and Mountain School, which was developed by Pak Yu-jŏn in later years as an extension of his Western School, is noted for its dense rhythmic subtlety and the innovative interaction of its words and drumming patterns.[11] This school of interpretation, which the Regent Taewŏn'gun particularly enjoyed, provided the wording of the Wanp'an text of the "Song of Shim Ch'ŏng" and is reflected today in the voice of the noted p'ansori singer Kim So-hŭi, who still performs occasionally.

Critical History and Performance Theory

The earliest references to p'ansori as it is known today come from writings left by aristocrats, who, as the literate elite, were the only members of Chosŏn-period culture with the means to make their observations part of the permanent record. What we know is therefore shaped by the biases and interests of upper-class members of the audience, rather than the practical experience of the performers or the tastes of the general populace. Nevertheless, not only did the writers describe actual performances they had seen, but, in contrast to the kwangdae, they had sufficient distance from the art to make critical comments. And we are indebted to them for recognizing p'ansori as a genre worthy of comment. These invaluable materials, nearly all in Chinese, began to appear in the middle of the eighteenth century and contain poetic retellings of songs, praise for accomplished kwangdae, descriptions of the audience and other entertainment, critical comments, and theoretical remarks. What follows are brief discussions of several of the key texts upon which a critical history of p'ansori must rest.

"Lyrics of the 'Song of Ch'un-hyang' in Two Hundred Stanzas." In tracing the critical history of p'ansori, we begin with Yu Chin-han's translation of lyrics from the "Song of Ch'un-hyang" into Chinese verse, which has already been mentioned in Chapter Two as indicating that the genre had been established in recognizable form by the middle of the eighteenth century. In 1754, Yu visited relatives in Chŏlla Province, where he witnessed a performance of the "Song of Ch'un-hyang." After he returned home to Ch'ungch'ŏng Province, he set down in Chinese translation his "Kasa Ch'un-hyang ka ibaek ku" (Lyrics of the "Song of Ch'un-hyang" in two hundred stanzas),[12] which was included in his collected papers and passed down through the family. Upon its discovery in the middle of the twentieth century,[13] in the keeping of his sixth-generation descendant, Yu Che-han, it became the earliest known version of the song and the first record of a p'ansori performance.[14] It also contains the earliest extant critical comment on p'ansori; for although the rest of it is devoted wholly to retelling the tale, the last four lines offer an word of appreciation:

> Of a remarkable tale that can be fully expressed only in song,
> This poet has set forth lyrics from the singer's ballad.
> These marvelous traces are worth printing in catalpa type:[15]
> Fine affairs to be handed down for the next one thousand years.[16]

Aside from these four lines, there is virtually no commentary accompanying the text and so the major critical significance of the event is that a man of letters of Yu Chin-han's pedigree[17] would value the song highly enough to retell it in a long poem of 2,800 characters and, furthermore, that the text would be included in his collected writings and preserved by his family for many generations. In this connection, it is worth noting that one Yang Chu-ik noted in *Mugŭk haengnok,* a travel diary of two years later (1756), that he, too, had composed such a work, in this case called *Ch'unmongyŏn* (The affinity of Spring [Ch'un-hyang] and Dream [Mong-nyong]).[18] Therefore, we may infer that p'ansori had already attained sufficient refinement by the middle of the eighteenth century to move beyond the confines of its plebeian origins and attract the interest of the scholarly elite of the society. This early acceptance set the groundwork for the later emergence of aristocratic kwangdae singers like Kwŏn Sam-dŭk.

"Quatrains upon Seeing a Dramatic Poem." As a fourteen-year-old boy, the poet-official Shin Wi (1769–1847) enjoyed the favor of King Chŏngjo, who would have him as a guest at the palace. Shin passed the government service examinations in 1799 and ultimately rose to the rank of Second Minister of Personnel. In literary history, he is noted for a critical anthology of Korean poetry since Shilla and for translations of *shijo* poetry into Chinese verse. In the spring of 1826, Shin Wi set down his feelings about p'ansori in the ten-stanza Chinese poem, "Kwan'gŭkshi chŏlgu" (Quatrains upon seeing a dramatic poem; 1826),[19] which contains the first recorded references to individual kwangdae and are particularly valued by historians for estimating the life dates of several important early master singers. Shin Wi opens his work by describing a festive scene:

> A spring crowd at the actor's arena, a mountain of embroidery:
> Countless voices drumming as they wander to and fro;
> Tired of sewing, bored with embroidery, idle fancy ladies.
> Then someone from atop the wall summons them with a single word.

Shin Wi continues in opaquely erudite wording to describe the nature of the music and the kwangdae's vocal technique. When suggesting the complexity of the p'ansori melodic line, he borrows terms for musical notes from classical Chinese music: "*Shang* rises, *kung* sinks; *chih* and *yü* fall low." Subsequent lines speak of the dramatic changes that are characteristic of rhythmic variations in p'ansori singing. In the third quatrain, the poet sings praises of the singers of his age:

> Ko, Song, Yŏm, and Mo—the talents of a generation! [20]
> Their liberated singing draws me, frees me from poetry's prison!

"On Seeing the Plays of Actors." It is apparent that Song Man-jae enjoyed p'ansori and was quite familiar with the content of the songs that were being sung in the 1840s. His "Kwanuhŭi" consists of an 800-character prose introduction, fifty-quatrain verse body, and a shorter prose colophon. In the colophon, Song explains that, since his household was too poor to mount a proper banquet to celebrate his son's success in the state examinations, he wrote this poem instead, describing in considerable detail the entertainment that would have been part of the banquet. The work is unique for its description of the overall context in which p'ansori was performed.

Before introducing each of the twelve p'ansori songs which were then current, Song Man-jae describes the variety acts that normally preceded the singing of a p'ansori song. Yi Hye-gu has observed that these acrobatics, tumbling, and other physical displays were of the same sort that the Chinese ambassador Tung Yueh had recounted in his "Rhymeprose on Chosŏn," written on the occasion of his visit in 1488. [21] In addition to the variety acts, there was the singing of songs in *kasa* and *kagok* styles. After these various turns, the p'ansori (called *ponsaga*, "main-event song") would begin and the audience would become attentive. From this audience reaction we can infer the relative popularity of p'ansori. In "Kwanuhŭi" we also encounter the earliest evidence of the p'ansori corpus having grown to twelve songs.

"A Song of Kwanghan Pavilion."   Another retelling of the "Song of Ch'un-hyang" in Chinese poetry is the 108-stanza composition by Yun Tal-sŏn, which is titled "Kwanghallu akpu" (A *yueh-fu* song of Kwanghan Pavilion; 1852). His piece is also known as "Honam akpu" (A *yueh-fu* song of Honam) and has introductions by Yi Kye-o, Yun Kyŏng-sun, and the author himself.[22] Although Yun Tal-sŏn's poem does not surpass the quality of Yu Chin-han's impressive work,[23] it is valuable for its description of the performance of p'ansori as seen in the middle of the nineteenth century. In contrast to both folk and formal music of the same era, which frequently involved accompaniment by more than one instrument, Yun Kyŏng-sun's introduction testifies to the one-singer, one-drummer arrangement of p'ansori: "In the plays by singing actors of our country, one man stands and one man sits. The standing one sings and the sitting one has a drum, with which he keeps time."[24] In addition to his reference to "plays by singing actors," Yun Kyŏng-sun also suggests the theatricality of p'ansori by describing it as a "farce play," which implies that the performances he saw in the middle of the nineteenth century contained more physical acting and movement than the plain recitation of narrative poetry. In the same passage, Yun Kyŏng-sun confirms that the p'ansori repertoire amounted to twelve works in 1852.

"Song of the Kwangdae."   Although not a kwangdae, himself, Shin Chae-hyo played a meaningful role in the late-nineteenth-century evolution of p'ansori. Of particular significance is his "Kwangdae ka" (Song of the kwangdae; ca. 1875),[25] which contains the earliest conscious criticism of either arts or literature in the Korean language. Shin Chae-hyo, a commoner, was born into a family of petty officials. His father came from Yangju in Kyŏnggi Province and had amassed a fortune serving in Seoul as a liaison for Koch'ang County of Chŏlla Province and later became a local official in Koch'ang where Shin himself was born and grew up. Shin managed and expanded the family fortunes to the extent that he was able to mount private relief efforts on the behalf of peasants ruined by a crop failure in 1876. At the same time, he was also able to advance himself politically by making a donation to the Taewŏn'gun's rebuilding of the Kyŏngbok Palace and like activities. As a result, and in recognition of his relief work, he received honorary military rank and became known as "Commander Shin." A man on the rise, he seems to have adopted involvement with p'ansori as the means of acquiring an intellectual identity proper to his position. An art form that was itself rising in social estimation was not a bad choice for a commoner who had taken on yangban status: he could make a name for himself among the elite without appearing socially presumptuous.

While it appears that Shin Chae-hyo himself did not sing p'ansori, he did use his considerable financial resources to gather p'ansori kwangdae around him, as their patron. He directed p'ansori performances, worked on p'ansori theory, and revised p'ansori libretti. In view of the fact that the Regent Taewŏn'gun had him manage the commemorative performance at a banquet celebrating the reconstruction of Kyŏngbok Palace, it would appear that Shin Chae-hyo was as talented as he was ambitious.

While it would have been difficult for him to express himself creatively when revising traditional libretti, he expressed unequivocally what he thought and advocated in original short works that he wrote to be performed. While his warm-up songs, meant to be sung by a kwangdae before launching into the main p'ansori song, make much use of erudite Chinese phrases mixed together with references to classical events, his "Song of the Kwangdae," opens with the assertion that the highly vaunted phrases of Chinese writing all come to naught in the face of p'ansori. He goes on to recall the most famous works of great Chinese poets and then asks, "How can we listen to their melancholy stories?" Next he turns to his chosen subject, the praise of Korean kwangdae.

> The world inside an inn, our pleasure;
> And the kwangdae's deed, how fine!
> But the kwangdae's deed
> Is difficult, so very difficult.
> For that which is called a kwangdae:
>
> First is fashioning a presence,
> Second is fashioning the narrative;
> And next is vocal attainment,
> And next is dramatic gesture.

Here Shin identifies and ranks what he believes to be the four major attributes of the accomplished kwangdae: first, presence; second, narrative; next, voice; and next, gesture. A leading contemporary scholar of p'ansori, Kang Han-yŏng, considers these requisites the "four great laws of the kwangdae . . . . a tetrad of principles, the golden rules of p'ansori theory."[26]

Presence. Regarding the requisite he ranks first, Shin Chae-hyo observes that, while the p'ansori kwangdae must have presence, this grows out of inborn nature and cannot be changed. He is saying that a commanding and effective stage presence is more a matter of native talent than of training. But with the other three requisites, he insists that a kwangdae can accomplish remarkable things by devoted practice. It is notable that Shin chooses to identify presence as the *first* of his four requisite attributes, seeming to give it the greatest weight. To give the kwangdae's presence such prominence is to regard the kwangdae, first and foremost, as an actor, thus stressing the theatrical nature of his art.

Narrative. In view of the fact that p'ansori incorporates elements of verse, narrative, and drama, it is possible to consider the words of the libretto separately from the performance that brings them to life. Shin Chae-hyo, in particular, devoted himself to the refinement of p'ansori wording; but, ironically, the later "p'ansori novels" were based, not upon Shin's labor, but upon the living traditions of the singers as represented in their family prompt-books. Nevertheless, Shin stressed the importance of elegance in expression and asserts in his "Song of the Kwangdae" that the narrative must be fashioned of words that are "as pure as gold and fair as jade."

> Clearly said and full of color,
> Adding flowers to embroidery:
> Like a beauty wearing seven treasures
> Coming from inside a screen;
> Like the full moon on its eve
> Emerging from behind the clouds.

Vocal Attainment. In the matter of "vocal attainment," Shin asserts that the singer must "strive to distinguish the five tones, employ the six pitches, and then manipulate and draw forth sound from deep within the viscera." Elsewhere in his poem, Shin Chae-hyo describes the impression given by a singer of great attainment, exploiting the potentials of his voice in its several ranges: "Gushing like a waterfall, long and short are counterpoised against high and low in voices of unlimited variation." Kang Han-yŏng expands on Shin by stressing that color and tone must be based on realism and that words and music must be matched to each other, not only in their outer forms but also in emotional content. Vocal attainment, he adds, demands that the modal *cho* (*p'yŏng cho, u cho, kyemyŏn cho,* etc.) and schools (*tongp'yŏn-je, sŏp'yŏn-je,* etc.) match the images of the libretto, concluding, "There can be no 'vocal attainment' without an understanding of the words.' "[27]

Dramatic Gesture.   Since the kwangdae portrays all the people who appear in his story, he must distinguish them for his audience by giving them individual characteristics that are reflected not only in the words and vocal quality but in dramatic gesture as well. The notion that gesture is fundamental to p'ansori testifies to its inherent theatricality, an essential element of its theory. Regarding such gesture, Shin Chae-hyo says that the kwangdae must capture his audience with skills that surpass the abilities of ordinary people.

> That which is called dramatic gesture is
> Rich in grace and full of style.
> Myriad manners and images, all in a twinkling:
> Countless changes from an immortal to a demon.
> The old and young, men and women of the audience,
> Who watch this show of elegance and heroics!
> This grace and this style
> That makes them laugh and cry—
> How could it not be difficult?

"Myriad manners and images all in a twinkling" speaks of the simultaneous integration of various forms of expression in a single moment. To the extent that p'ansori must describe a wide range of action and emotion, it is provided with a wide variety of rhythmic patterns and melodic lines. In like fashion, so must the kwangdae become a master of dramatic suggestion that runs from immortal to demon in order to enthrall his audience. The fan, held by the kwangdae and used in a great variety of gestures, is an essential tool: a stick when folded or a letter when spread, it can be transformed into anything that the moment demands.

"Just one man holding just one fan. A minimal cast with minimal properties but capable of maximum expression: this is the essence, the charm of p'ansori," says Cho Dong-il.[28] But, as essential as it is, this essence cannot be conveyed by audio recordings or ch'anggŭk adaptations. Since p'ansori does not use theatrical scenery of any kind, the kwangdae can change his setting at will with the use of dramatic gesture. But when staged as ch'anggŭk with scenery, restraints are placed upon the changing of locale.

After explaining techniques associated with rhythmic variations, using various metaphors, Shin Chae-hyo rounds off his "Song of the Kwangdae" with praise for the talents of great master singers of the past in such terms as the following, which he lavishes on Song Hŭng-nok.

Master Song, Song Hŭng-nok,
Unleashes excellence beyond compare!
He is brilliant spring in full luxuriance,
The King of Song, a veritable Li Po!

"Scores of the Music Office" and a Letter to Shin Chae-hyo. We learn something of the late-nineteenth-century aristocratic attitude toward p'ansori in two documents from the brush of Chŏng Hyŏn-sŏk (b. 1811).[29] Chŏng was a successful scholar-official who enjoyed the favor of the throne and served as magistrate of Chinyang and, later, as governor of Hwanghae Province in the course of his public career. While magistrate of Chinyang, he set up a facility in his yamen for teaching music, dance, singing, and other performing arts to government *kisaeng*; and he also composed a textbook for them, called *Kyobang chebo* (Scores of the music office; 1872).[30] This work contains a section titled "Songs of the Actors," in which Chŏng Hyŏn-sŏk summarizes the content and purpose of six p'ansori. As a traditional aristocrat, Chŏng sees in p'ansori only the superficial references to Confucian mores, such as the Three Bonds and Five Moral Rules,[31] and overlooks themes more reflective of the commoner's world view. Each of Chŏng's six lines refers to a separate narrative:

Ch'un-hyang is faithful to Yi Toryŏng; this promotes faithfulness.
Shim Ch'ŏng sacrifices herself for her blind father; this promotes filial piety.
The Gourd Ballad concerns a gentle brother and an ill-natured brother; this promotes brotherly love.
In the Ballad of Maehwa, a man loses himself to a courtesan; this reproves lewdness.
In the Rabbit Ballad, a rabbit deceives the Dragon King and escapes with his life; this reproves foolishness.
The Ballad of Huayung-tao celebrates a wise general and reproves a great villain.[32]

These themes were superficial pretexts. They were not what held popular audiences and moved them at heart. Such Confucian notions actually may have added up to an excuse for aristocrats to enjoy the vulgarity of p'ansori. What they probably enjoyed most was not the didactic message itself but, rather, the criticism of that very message that lay at the heart of p'ansori.[33]

Chŏng Hyŏn-sŏk, who enjoyed p'ansori but had never met Shin Chae-hyo, one day in 1873 met a kwangdae named Yi Kyŏng-t'ae, who performed for him. Chŏng praised the kwangdae for his clear articulation and intelligent interpretation. When their conversation turned to Shin Chae-hyo, Chŏng composed a letter to Shin and entrusted it to Yi for delivery.

In the letter, Chŏng quotes Yi as saying the following about activity at Shin's home in Koch'ang:

> Shin Chae-hyo invites kwangdae to stay at his house where he trains them in letters, correcting their pronunciation and interpretation. He rewords passages that are excessively vulgar and guides their practice sessions. Thereby, his house is filled every day with those who come from near and far to get instruction. And he houses and feeds them all. He lives to have actors and music around him always but everyone thinks him strange. Upon hearing this, I say "Here is a scholar of true purpose!"[34]

At the end of the letter, Chŏng adds, "Yi Kyŏng-t'ae articulates with clarity and his words make sense. Even without a hearing, he would be a good disciple for you, I am convinced. By all means, it would be well if he received more instruction to bring forth his talent."[35] In the same letter, Chŏng also speaks of certain "abuses" committed by kwangdae in the performance of p'ansori.

> To correct such abuses, one must first take control of the libretto to get rid of those things that are vulgar or illogical and, embellishing with words, describe the situation so as to make an integrated literary whole and provide a language that is elegant and proper. Furthermore, select from among singers those whose presence is attractive and whose voices are strong and sonorous. Train them in some thousands of characters and, after having awakened them clearly to tones and sounds, teach them with libretti so that they can recite them as their own words. Next, teach them using the singing modes: the basic mode, which must be grand, deep, and harmonious; the commanding mode, which must be clear, brave, and powerful; and the wailing mode, which must be of sad and piteous lament. The reverberations of the voice should make the rafters ring and the clouds stand still. When the singer takes his place and tries to sing, his articulation must be so clear and the narrative so consistent that he can assume that none of his listeners fails to understand. In addition, he must carry himself erect and proper; and, whether he sits, stands, raises his fan, or gestures with his hand, all of these must be done with moderation. Only then may he for the first time be called a "great singer."

Chŏng Hyŏn-sŏk's letter is in agreement both with the points made in Shin Chae-hyo's "Song of the Kwangdae" and with later statements (which are quoted below) made by the master singer Kim Se-jong, who had trained under Shin. There is no evidence to support a causal relationship between Chŏng's letter and the theories of Shin and Kim, but it is worth observing that the letter was preserved by Shin Chae-hyo's family and was reported to be in the safekeeping of his great-grandson, Shin Ki-ŏp of Koch'ang, in 1970.[36]

Aesthetic Awareness among Kwangdae.   In Chŏng No-shik's collection of biographical sketches of kwangdae, there is revealed an awareness on the part of kwangdae that their craft was one worthy of artistic criticism. Such matters as voice quality, projection, mimetic ability, stage presence, and knowledge of literary materials figure into the many comments that Chŏng elicits from his informants. One also gains the impression that audiences of the late nineteenth century could be as perceptive and critically demanding as the performers themselves. When the two great singers, Pak Man-sun and Yi Nal-ch'i (1820–1892), shared the same stage, "their audience, drunk with the pleasure of their skills, would never let them bow out." But when they were followed to the stage by any other performer, "the listeners would begin to leave by twos and threes until the arena was quite desolate," so well was the difference appreciated.[37]

Unlike aristocrats quoted above, kwangdae did not talk about p'ansori as an art form—as an object to be appreciated, described, and commented upon. They were practical men whose focus was on the immediate fact of the performance itself, and their oral history, therefore, is rich in stories about the artistic accomplishments of great singers of the past. Though they never talked about p'ansori as an abstraction, they did develop a rich vocabulary of specialized terms to describe and evaluate the elements of its performance. That is, while they were acutely aware of the aesthetics of actual delivery they were relatively unconcerned about p'ansori's attributes as a genre. The latter was the province of the scholar, the man of letters who commanded the critical vocabulary of literature and could write down his impressions.

The words of praise for great singers of the past that kwangdae passed down in their oral tradition and Chŏng No-shik captures in his book emphasized vocal quality and technique above anything else. Vocal strength, power, and endurance were secondary considerations, for the audience asked to be emotionally moved rather than technically overwhelmed. Chŏng's anecdotes relate that Mo Hŭng-gap's resonant voice could be heard "as far away as ten li," that Pang Man-ch'un had the ability to make his audience feel "surrounded by water and fire" when he sang the conflagration scene from the "Song of the Red Cliff," and that not only could Yi Nal-ch'i make the bells of neighboring villages vibrate in response to his voice, but the ampleness of his voice would bring forth an inundation of shouts of praise and encouragement from his audience. Such remarks, however, are far out-weighed by accounts of beauty, subtlety, and emotional effect achieved by other singers. Although Chŏn To-sŏng lacked sufficient projection to engulf a mass of listeners, "only the best of drummers could keep up with his melodic complexity and varied technique." Kwŏn Sam-dŭk's voice was "so innately beautiful that people would swoon upon hearing it." When Song Hŭng-nok sang in his saddest voice, "the entire audience was soon swim-ming in its own tears" and those who witnessed a performance by Pak Man-sun were "moved beyond their ability to describe it."[38]

But vocal quality and technique were only part of what made the real "master singers" great. They were also skilled in the use of gesture and phrasing. The great Shin Hak-cho (fl. 1850) is reported by Chŏng to have performed "with all the richness of a storyteller, surprising his audience with abrupt changes in rhythm and mode at climactic moments." And, of Kim Ch'ang-hwan, we are told, "His gesture was even more facile than his singing. Not a single movement was without its own beauty, so skilled was he in matching gesture to the song and the story."

In the process of being trained by example, the disciple learned the kwangdae's extensive technical vocabulary from his master. Appended to a recent anthology of biographical sketches of living kwangdae is a technical glossary of ninety-five entries divided into five categories: general, rhythms, singing modes, schools, and vocal characteristics.[39] The fifty-three vocal characteristics, in particular, give evidence of the close attention p'ansori singers have paid to the subtle details of vocalization. In addition to the expected "hoarse," "nasal," "muted," and "tremulous," we also encounter such qualities as "bent in the throat," "like a cracked cymbal," "ghostly," "pulled back then let loose."

A Master Singer Comments on P'ansori Theory. Even such a skilled and haughty artist as Pak Man-sun had to acknowledge comments by the educated and respected critic of p'ansori technique and theory, Kim Se-jong, who was also a leading kwangdae. Says Chŏng No-shik, "In the days when no one dared to open his mouth in front of Pak Man-sun and, if he did, found his criticism dismissed out of hand, only Kim Se-jong could freely criticize Pak and meet with agreement when he was right."[40] Kim Se-jong, who flourished in the late nineteenth century, had studied a number of years under Shin Chae-hyo and was famous for his critical views, which have been passed on in the oral tradition. He was regarded as a "nobleman" among singers. Kim saw p'ansori as a branch of theater and urged kwangdae to develop their stage presence, gesture, and movement with as much care as their vocal technique, emphasizing the need to match words and feelings with appropriate body movement:

> In p'ansori, the singing is a prime element and one must also apply regulation to the placement of words and structures, intonational changes in singing, and pitch and rhythm. But one must not be negligent about the descriptive movement. That is to say, to the extent that p'ansori is sung drama, one must not lose sight of its dramatic significance.
>
> Suppose that one is to cry. At that moment he should actually cover his face with a handkerchief and fall forward to cry, or cry with loud wailings. Whatever he does, he should show the action of crying realistically and be appropriate to the moment. If the singer remains composed and displays no sad emotion at all but simply sits absentmindedly without any movement, making only the sound of a lament, he will have failed in his craft by separating singing from drama. Has not p'ansori lost its spirit when the audience feels neither moved nor sympathetic at all?
>
> Let us say one is to sing, "A bamboo stick in hand and hempen sandals on his feet, he ventures into a thousand leagues of rivers and mountains." In describing the motion of entering upon a thousand, even ten thousand leagues—unbending from a crouch while slowly lifting his body and while indicating the way with his hand—both the singing and the descriptive movement must tally precisely with each other.[41]

Training and Transmission

According to what we learn from Chŏng No-shik, the training of a kwangdae usually began in his youth, before adolescence, under a relative or neighbor. During this first stage, the novice learned the basic techniques of interpretation and performance but did not necessarily develop the characteristic vocal quality of the mature kwangdae. After this first stage, the novice usually left his home and family to study with a famous master or practice alone in the mountains, frequently at a Buddhist temple. This second period of study, physically the most demanding, would typically last as long as five years. This was a period of deprivation, of punishing efforts to ac-

quire a "voice," one of the major elements on which his professional reputation was to depend. Chŏng No-sik's biographical sketches frequently tell
of learners who not only sang themselves hoarse, but who vocalized in the
wilderness or challenged the sound of a waterfall to produce voices of great
power, often pushing themselves to the point of spitting up blood in the
process.

After years of solitary practice, a new kwangdae generally began his
professional life as an itinerant performer. He might become one of the few
who managed to make his debut at some competition, banquet, or other
major festivity, thus taking the first step toward the fame and reputation for
which he would be remembered in the oral genealogies of succeeding generations. A kwangdae's career entered its last stage when he retired from
giving regular performances and devoted himself to the training of disciples.

We have access to the details of training and professional growth of a
traditional p'ansori singer through the experiences of such living "intangible
cultural treasures" as Kim So-hŭi and others who were born early enough
to be trained by masters who were of the nineteenth-century school. Kim
So-hŭi was born Kim Sun-ok on December 1, 1917 in Hŭngdŏk-ni, Hŭng-
dŏk-myŏn, Koch'ang-gun, North Chŏlla Province.[42] Koch'ang had been home
to many a great singer, including the great female singers, Chin Ch'ae-sŏn,
Hŏ Kŭm-p'a, and Kim Yŏ-ran. She told a magazine interviewer in 1984 that
she was given the name "So-hŭi" by her maternal aunt and that it was a
matter of "inevitable fate" that she "followed the path of a 'So-hŭi' rather
than that of a 'Sun-ok.' "[43] She adds that this "fate" may have been coaxed
along by hearing the spectacular voice of the female p'ansori singer Yi Hwa-
jungsŏn (1897–1943) when young. Another influence could have been her
father, who loved the arts and could play both the Korean flute and oboe
quite well. By her own account, she had had a personality and temperament
quite different from the other girls.

She began her p'ansori study at the age of twelve, while still attending
higher common school.[44] Her first master was the famous Song Man-gap,
who lived near her neighborhood. Song was an early-twentieth-century representative of an unbroken p'ansori lineage reaching back to his grandfather's elder brother, the great Song Hŭng-nok.[45] The first work that Song
Man-gap had Kim So-hŭi learn was the "Song of Shim Ch'ŏng," which he
felt was more appropriate for a young girl to learn than other songs, like
the "Song of Ch'un-hyang," that dealt with relations between the sexes.

Kim was one of the many students studying with Song Man-gap at the
time. Sometimes twenty or thirty students would perform group exercises

together with him. In addition to these large classes, Kim also received private instruction from Song for about three hours each day, polishing what she had been taught in class and learning melodic lines that had not been taught to the group as a whole. The master and his pupil did not start from the beginning of the "Song of Shim Ch'ŏng" but, rather, from a point midway through the first half. Learning and polishing this one section of about 500 lines—one quarter of the whole song—took one year. The next year was spent on the beginning of the first half, and the following year on the second half of the song. At the same time, however, she was also beginning to learn other songs.

Though she did not feel qualified to appear as a professional in her own right until after ten years of study, Kim was already performing sections of the "Song of Shim Ch'ŏng" soon after she learned them. In the city of Namwŏn, North Chŏlla Province, at age thirteen, she made her first public appearance and placed first among some eighty competitors. "I soon became famous as a 'baby star'!" she recalls. Kim asserts that a basic requirement for a p'ansori performer is to develop a good singing voice and control. For this reason, she moved to a Buddhist temple in 1934 to devote two years to further study and to broadening her abilities.

Not only is the "Song of Shim Ch'ŏng" the work with which Kim began her studies and the first piece she performed in public, but it is also the one for which she is most famous today. As Chŏng Pyŏng-uk of Seoul National University once noted, "Whenever someone says 'Kim So-hŭi,' we find ourselves immediately thinking of the 'Song of Shim Ch'ŏng.' "[46]

Kim later extended her study of the "Song of Shim Ch'ŏng" under other masters: "We learn from these teachers of different artistic lineages in order to incorporate their individual treatments."[47] As she now sings it, the song is more heavily influenced by the style of Pak Yu-jŏn than by that of her first master, Song Man-gap. She studied the two halves (divided at Shim Ch'ŏng's plunge into the Indang Sea) under two different teachers, each of whom traced himself back via different professional lineages to an original disciple of Pak. As a result, while both halves of Kim So-hŭi's treatment descend from Pak Yu-jŏn, they show clear differences in technique and interpretation.[48] Figure 2 shows the lines of transmission.

We are fortunate to have a close approximation of the tradition which one of these masters received and passed on to Kim So-hŭi. This is the performance by Yi Ch'ang-yun (fl. ca. 1880) of the Separation Episode, as reconstructed by the contemporary scholar of p'ansori, Pak Hŏn-bong (for a translation of the entire episode in the Wanp'an text version, see ff. 1:25b–1:26a in Chapter Eight below). By juxtaposing Yi's interpretation with two

FIGURE 2. Transmission of the "Song of Shim Ch'ŏng" from Pak Yu-jŏn to Kim So-hŭi

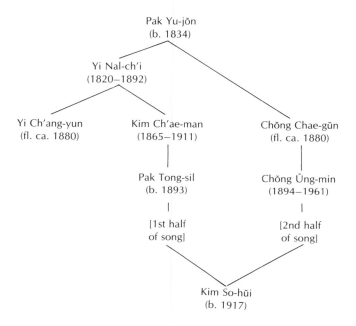

Source: Pak Hwang, *P'ansori sosa,* p. 44.

recordings of the same portion of the Separation Episode made by Kim So-hŭi in 1969 and 1974, we observe not only the results of transmission over a long period of time, but also the changes than can occur between performances by the same singer within a much briefer span.

At first glance, there appear to be considerable differences between Yi's and Kim's versions; but these prove to be more the result of adding and dropping than of outright changes in the transmitted text. This can be substantiated by conflating the texts of Kim's two performances and comparing the results with the reconstruction of Yi's version.

For example, consider the following passage, which occurs when Shim Ch'ŏng confesses to her father that she has sold herself as a sacrifice to ocean merchants for three hundred sacks of rice (text in italics was added by Kim in 1974; text in brackets was dropped by her in 1974). Yi sang in the *chajin mori* rhythm and Kim in *chung chung mori,* but the words are closely parallel.

YI CH'ANG-YUN
1880

KIM SO-HUI
1969/1974

Blindman Shim, hearing these words,
His white eyes dancing giddily,
Leaps up then sits back,
Not knowing what to do.
He cannot speak for some time.
"Alas! This is a disaster!
How in the world can you
Say such words as these?
Now, look here, my Ch'ŏng!

Blindman Shim, hearing these words,

Leaps up *and falls back down:*

"*Ha, ha, child! Ch'ŏng! Ha, ha.*
"How in the world can you
Say such words as these?
[Now, look here, my Ch'ŏng!]
Have you done as you please,
Never asking your father?

Oh, my thoughtless little thing![49]

Oh, my thoughtless little thing![50]

Here as elsewhere in the text, comparison reveals very little substantial invention on Kim's part. Indeed, most passages that appear in her version, but not Yi's, can be found in performances by her contemporaries. Furthermore, passages included by Yi but not Kim may still be assumed to be available to her in her personal inventory, ready for use on another occasion. In conversation, Kim has confirmed this lack of invention and the retention of a "text" common to all singers, although she suggests a written, literary source for her oral tradition: "We never change the words; we always sing them just as written!"

Nevertheless, Kim does make changes of her own from time to time. Based upon an extended comparison of her two recordings, one may say that she makes the most extensive changes in *aniri* passages, as, for example, early in the Separation Episode when Shim Ch'ŏng makes her confession to her father:

1969 RECORDING

1974 RECORDING

"Father! Father!"

"Father! Father!"

She has fallen in a swoon.
Blindman Shim, who had been sitting comfortably, suddenly starts.

"I say, child! Ch'ŏng!

"Child, my Ch'ŏng! What has happened?

"I say, have you seen something that has frightened you, my child?

"Ha, Ha. This morning's side dishes were too good! It was something you ate that gave you indigestion! Child! Eat some salt. Eh?

"Child! Child! I say, did someone taunt you for being a blind man's daughter?

"Child! Child, child! Alas, what is this, child?

"Calm yourself and speak to me!"

"Alas, father!"

"Baby, baby!"

"Were this morning's side dishes so very rich that something you ate gave you indigestion? Child! Eat some salt. Salt.

"I say, this isn't a swoon!

"Child, my Ch'ŏng! Did someone taunt you for being a blind man's daughter?

"Calm yourself and speak to me! Little thing, child, my Ch'ŏng!"

Shim Ch'ŏng barely regains her senses:

"Alas, father!"

"Yes, speak to me."

We find fewer changes in the more rapid *ch'ang* (such as those in the *chung chung mori* rhythm), and fewest of all in *ch'ang* set in the slow and deliberate *chinyang cho* rhythm. Although some of her changes involve segments as short as the Parry-Lord formula, most of them involve the addition or deletion of established sequences the length of couplets or small thematic units, that is, from two to ten lines in length. With the exception of her idiosyncratic treatment of *aniri*, it is clear that Kim does not compose freely during performance in the manner of Lord's Yugoslav singers.

The age of genuine oral composition in Korea has passed. What we hear today is the result of faithful transmission, through a series of masters and disciples, of established routines that appear to have originated in a now-lost art of formulaic oral composition. We can assume that this art succumbed to the pressures for standardization exerted by the major schools of p'ansori that emerged during the first third of the nineteenth century. Only the greats of the later nineteenth century, like Song Man-gap, would appear to have fought the constraints of school-bound tradition and managed to achieve a degree of individual creativity. According to Chŏng No-shik, Song's innovative style of composition and singing departed so sharply from his family's tradition that his father even tried to poison him in retribution.

오시는 못 오시는
불상훈 신우리
父親 장님잔치
에 오시 노가

THREE

THE SONG OF
SHIM CH'ŎNG

7
P'ansori on Paper

It was only in the second half of the nineteenth century that written and printed Korean language texts of p'ansori began to appear. Extant p'ansori libretti in Korean fall into three categories according to the physical type of the record: manuscripts, woodblock imprints, and typeset editions. The woodblock editions were commercial ventures, issued for profit early in this century. The earliest typeset editions, dating from the first decades of the twentieth century, drew upon the woodblock editions; but many printed versions appearing since the 1960s are transcriptions of modern performances.[1] A list of texts consulted for this study is appended to this chapter.

Koreans today frequently use the term, "p'ansori novel," to designate any and all printed versions of p'ansori, whether woodblock or typeset. In so doing, they distinguish these printed versions as constituting a genre apart from the oral tradition. Implicit here is the misperception that both woodblock and typeset editions are literary adaptations done by individual authors, even though no woodblock edition has ever been attributed to an author. Recent research into the bibliographic history of the "Song of Shim Ch'ŏng," however, sheds new light on the relationships among the oral tradition, kwangdae scripts, woodblock editions, and typeset paperbacks.

Yi Hae-jo issued his typeset edition of the "Song of Shim Ch'ŏng" as *Kangsangyŏn* (Lotus on the river) in 1912. Textual analysis shows that this is based on a Wanp'an woodblock edition, which, in turn, was based upon the oral tradition of the River and Mountain School.[2] The typeset edition cannot be said to have superseded the earlier forms, however, for the year 1912 fell right in the middle of a publishing boom in woodblock editions of the "Song of Shim Ch'ŏng," which ran from 1905 to 1916.[3] It did, however, serve as a basis for other, later paperback editions. In other words, the expression, "p'ansori novel," does not make a useful distinction. It wrongly suggests a rupture in the evolution of p'ansori literature; and, at the same time, it implies a direct relationship between the oral tradition of p'ansori and the written basis of the novel genre in Korea, which cannot be substantiated.

Extant Texts of the "Song of Shim Ch'ŏng"

As of the early 1990s, more than one hundred known texts of the "Song of Shim Ch'ŏng," ranging in date from 1873 to 1991, have been introduced and discussed in scholarly circles.[4] This large number includes woodblock imprints, manuscripts, typeset editions, field transcriptions, and translations; and it is, of course, subject to change as new materials are uncovered and introduced. Indeed, the count has been growing steadily since 1962, when the first modern study of the variant editions of the "Song of Shim Ch'ŏng" listed some twenty items.[5] Nevertheless, in spite of the large total, they can be considered in several groups from a bibliographical point of view. Before turning to a full discussion of the Wanp'an text that is translated in the next chapter, we shall quickly review these various basic groups.

Some sixty manuscripts and a dozen or so woodblock editions capture p'ansori in its late-nineteenth-century heyday. These range in date from 1873 to 1920 and probably represent a far larger but as yet unreported body of materials. Some are kept in the National Library in Seoul, and in the libraries of Korea University, Yonsei University, Seoul National University, and the Academy of Korean Studies; and others are found in the private collections of Kim Dong-uk, Kim Kŭn-su, Kim Ki-dong, Kang Han-yŏng, Cho Yun-je, and others. Outside Korea, traditional manuscripts and woodblock editions are held by the Tōyō Bunko and Tenri University libraries in Japan, the British Museum, and the Harvard-Yenching Library at Harvard University.

With the exception of Shin Chae-hyo's work and kwangdae family materials, p'ansori manuscripts are all copies taken from woodblock editions or other manuscripts. They are useful for the corrections and rephrasings they contain and for their occasional use of Chinese characters, which never appear in the woodblock editions. The most valuable and yet most inaccessible manuscripts, which are *not* copies of woodblock editions, are those kept by the families of the singers themselves. Their existence is confirmed by the references of Chŏng No-shik and Pak Hŏn-bong.

Shin Chae-hyo Manuscripts.   The earliest version in Korean script came from the brush of Shin Chae-hyo in 1870–1873. The Shin family manuscript of the "Song of Shim Ch'ŏng," which exists in two similar versions (one kept by the family and one in the collection of Kang Han-yŏng), is the basis of a typeset and annotated edition issued by Minjung Sŏgwan Publishing Company in 1971.[6] A third Shin manuscript, distinguished by its use of Chinese characters and slight differences in spelling and vocabulary, is preserved in the Karam (Yi Pyŏng-gi) Collection of Seoul National University.

Hashimoto Manuscripts.   Among the manuscripts consulted for this study, the oldest and most interesting, philologically, are two which were copied from other texts by one Hashimoto Shōbi, the first in 1894 and the second in 1897. According to his endnote, Hashimoto copied the first one in 1893 from a version owned by one Ch'ŏn Sŏg-yŏ and emended it in 1894. At that time, Hashimoto locates himself in Pusan at an institution called the "Yonghwa-wŏn" of the "Tonghwa-gwan." The spelling incorporates features of dialect, and the text is distinguished by personal and place names that do not appear in any other version. The second manuscript, which shows an improvement in Hashimoto's han'gŭl calligraphy, was copied while he was in Chŏlla Province, in October 1897. Its content is close to, but does not coincide with, that of the Wanp'an text. Both of these manuscripts are in the collection of the Harvard-Yenching Library of Harvard University. Since the dating of these manuscripts rules out woodblock editions as their source, we may suspect that they are close to kwangdae family texts, which were the probable basis for the later woodblock editions.

Seoul Woodblock Editions. The Seoul woodblock editions were published in the capital prior to 1920; they are characterized by brevity, laconic style, paucity of dialogue, and a preference for written rather than spoken forms of the language. Their businesslike texts move quickly, rarely pausing to develop a character or describe a scene. Stylistically, they are the furthest removed from the oral tradition of any existing texts. One representative Seoul text was reproduced in an Ewha Women's University anthology of "old novels," which was published in four volumes between 1958 and 1961.[7]

Wanp'an Woodblock Editions. Although Seoul was the major printing center of the country, the largest number of woodblock editions of p'ansori texts were produced in the city of Chŏnju, capital of North Chŏlla Province, the heartland of p'ansori. These are known as "Wanp'an" editions (*p'an* means "edition") after Wansan, an old name for the city. The Wanp'an editions of the "Song of Shim Ch'ŏng" are not only the lengthiest written sources but also are stylistically the closest to the oral tradition (River and Mountain School). The Wanp'an editions consulted for this study were all printed between 1905 and 1916 and are nearly identical in content, distinguished only by occasional engraver's errors and differences in spelling. See below, under "The Translator's Wanp'an Text," for information on the specific text that was translated for this study.

Ansŏng woodblock editions. Another printing center, the city of Ansŏng (fifty miles south of Seoul), has contributed its own distinct woodblock edition, which is preserved at the Tōyō Bunko Library in Tokyo. This short version shares the style and much of the content of the Wanp'an editions but lacks many of their episodes.

Modern typeset editions. These modern materials are of three sorts: popularizations based on Yi Hae-jo's 1912 *Lotus on the River* (Kangsangyŏn); performance-based texts; and foreign-language translations. Typeset paperback editions of p'ansori begin to appear just after the turn of the twentieth century. The first were popularizations done in 1912 by the early modern novelist Yi Hae-jo, who made few changes in his source texts, except for such things as cutting out obscure passages, modernizing outmoded phraseology, and tacking on new openings. However, he left intact the stylistic features that distinguish sung from spoken passages, an essential characteristic of the p'ansori oral form.

The works of Yi Hae-jo's successors continue to be widely available in popular bookstores. Chang Chi-yŏng in 1964 published an annotated edition of one such example, the same that had been used by the North Korean scholar Yun Se-p'yŏng for his annotated edition of 1955.[8] The early-twentieth-century master singer Yi Sŏn-yu (b. 1872) transcribed and published the five songs in 1933, complete with rhythm notation.[9] Pak Hŏn-bong, long associated with the School of National Music Arts, combined his knowledge of the kwangdae oral tradition and his ready access to their family manuscripts to produce an anthology of conflated texts in 1966.[10] Chŏng Kwŏn-jin (1927–1986), heir to a family kwangdae tradition dating back to Chŏng Chae-gŭn (fl. ca. 1880), was the late twentieth century's living embodiment of Pak Yu-jŏn's River and Mountain School of interpretation and singing. Designated an "intangible cultural treasure," Chŏng recorded his "Song of Shim Ch'ŏng" for the Bureau of Cultural Properties in 1968. The text of that performance has been published in various locations.[11]

The "Song of Shim Ch'ŏng" has been translated into English, French, and Japanese. The first of these, by the American missionary and diplomat Horace N. Allen in *Korean Tales* in 1889,[12] appears to be based on a Seoul woodblock edition. His brief treatment was followed by an 1893 version in French, *Le Bois Sec Refleuri,* by the Korean Hong Tjyong-ou (Hong Chong-u), a fanciful adaptation of the Seoul edition, which he embellished with imaginative subplots.[13] Hong's effort later reappeared in a faithful English translation by Charles M. Taylor, published in Boston in 1919 as *Winning Buddha's Smile.*[14]

While two Japanese translations of the "Song of Shim Ch'ŏng" were issued in the 1920s, it did not appear in translation again until after the Korean War, this time as the English version of a North Korean operatic libretto in 1958. Since then, it has appeared only occasionally in summary form in foreign-language surveys of Korean folklore. An English translation of a modernized ch'anggŭk libretto, however, has been published by Alan C. Heyman.[15]

The Translator's Wanp'an Text

The orthography of the Wanp'an version of the "Song of Shim Ch'ŏng" that was translated for this study illustrates the disorderliness which had crept into the Korean writing system by the early twentieth century, after some four hundred years of growing confusion. Over these years, certain changes had occurred in the spoken language to which the writing system had not been adjusted, such as palatalization, monophthongization, and a shift of vowel sounds. What changes did find their way into the script and orthography were only random, reflecting no systematic adjustments to language change. The state of Korean orthography in the early twentieth century, before the introduction of a unified system in 1933, is reminiscent of the anarchy of English spelling in the late sixteenth century.

The translation in the next chapter is based on a Wanp'an edition from the Kim Dong-uk collection, which has been reproduced twice.[16] Although it is undated, Kim Dong-uk placed it near 1916, the year of a dated Wanp'an edition (Chŏnju, Taga sŏp'o, 1916) that shares many of the same printing blocks (identified by unique engraver's errors and damage to the surface of the blocks).[17]

The text is printed in large, clear letters in a square script; the mixed provenance of its printing blocks is reflected in minor differences in the dimensions of the borders which surround the text, the calligraphic style, and certain ornamental features; and the book itself is divided into two sections of thirty and forty-one folio pages, respectively, bound as one volume. The pagination of the original is noted in the margin of my translation: a colon separates the section of the text ("1" or "2") from the page number, and a letter indicates the side of the folio page ("a" for *recto* and "b" for *verso*). For example, 2:13a is the *recto* side of folio page 13 in the second section and 2:13b is the *verso* side of the same folio.

With the exception of the division into two sections and the occasional use of ornamental marks to set off lines of quoted poetry, nothing interrupts the flow of the approximately 39,700 syllabic clusters that make up the text. There are no graphic features that separate sung (*ch'ang*) from spoken (*aniri*) passages or set off the individual lines of verse; syntax and content are the only guides.

Since there is no indication given in the woodblock editions of the rhythm in which a passage is sung, my translation incorporates rhythmic specifications from a transcription of a performance by Chŏng Kwŏn-jin, whose family maintained the interpretation of the River and Mountain School, on which the Wanp'an editions are based. These rhythms are given parenthetically at the head of each passage. They are, in rhythmic order from slow to fast, *chinyang cho*, *nŭjin mori*, *chung mori*, *chung chung mori*, *chajin mori*, *hwi mori*, *ŏt mori*, and *ŏt chung mori* (the last two being relatively rare). In addition to these, the notation *aniri* marks a spoken passage.

Each physical line in the following translation is roughly equivalent to a hemistich in the Korean original. In p'ansori, a hemistich is the smallest freestanding prosodic unit and it is typically *but not always* matched by another hemistich to form a full line. My representation was chosen in order to place emphasis on the hemistich—as does the singer in performance. Furthermore, since English translation frequently takes more words than the original Korean, my convention of basing physical lines on the hemistich also helps to maintain a clear visual distinction between spoken *aniri* (set full width) and sung *ch'ang* passages (set in narrow columns). Since the continuously flowing text of the Wanp'an edition provides no punctuation marks, my division into hemistichs for this translation was done on the basis of rhythm, sense, and comparable texts.

Unless otherwise attributed, the following interpretation of the Wanp'an text draws upon explanations given to me by the late Professor Kim Dong-uk, formerly of Yonsei University, without whose generosity this undertaking would never have been possible.

Texts Consulted in the Preparation of This Study

The decade of the 1980s produced several important studies that are de-voted wholly to the "Song of Shim Ch'ŏng" and append extensive bibliog-raphies of primary textual materials: Ch'oe Un-shik, *Shim Ch'ŏng chŏn yŏn'gu* (A study of the "Tale of Shim Ch'ŏng"); Ch'oe Un-shik, *Shim Ch'ŏng chŏn* (The "Tale of Shim Ch'ŏng"); and Yu Yŏng-dae, *Shim Ch'ŏng chŏn yŏn'gu* (A study of the "Tale of Shim Ch'ŏng"). The thirty texts consulted in the prep-aration of this study are listed below in the five categories of manuscript, woodblock edition, typeset edition, modern performance text, and transla-tion.

MANUSCRIPTS

Hashimoto (1894): "Shim Ch'yŏn kya." Manuscript (32 folios). Copied by Hashimoto Shōbi in 1894 from a text dated 1893. Harvard-Yenching Li-brary. Described but not cited in this study.

Hashimoto (1897): "Shim Ch'yŏng chyŏn." Manuscript (36 folios). Copied by Hashimoto Shōbi in 1897 from a text dated 1896. Harvard-Yenching Li-brary.

Pihl: "Shim Ch'yŏng chyŏn." Undated manuscript (48 folios). Collection of Marshall R. Pihl. Closely related to Wanp'an text.

Shin Chae-hyo: "Shim Ch'yŏng ka." Undated manuscript (45 folios). Tran-scribed by Shin Chae-hyo, 1870–1873. Reproduced in Kang Han-yŏng, *Shin Chae-hyo p'ansori chŏnjip* (Seoul: Yonsei University, 1969); and in Kang Han-yŏng, *Sin Chae-hyo p'ansori sasŏl chip* (Seoul: Minjung sŏgwan, 1971). The latter, a typeset edition, is thoroughly annotated.

WOODBLOCK EDITIONS

Ansŏng: "Shim Ch'yŏng chyŏn." Undated woodblock (21 folios). Published in Ansŏng. Tōyō Bunko Library, Tokyo.

British Museum: "Shim Ch'yŏng chyŏn." Undated woodblock (26 folios). British Museum. Nearly identical to Seoul Text.

Karam (1911): "Shim Ch'yŏng chyŏn." Woodblock (30 + 41 folios). Issued by Sŏgye sŏp'o in Chŏnju, 1911. Karam Collection, Seoul National University Library. A Wanp'an edition.

Karam (1916): "Shim Ch'yŏng chyŏn." Woodblock (30 + 41 folios). Issued by Taga sŏp'o in Chŏnju, 1916. Karam Collection, Seoul National University Library. A Wanp'an edition, very close to Wanp'an text.

Karam (n.d.): "Shim Ch'yŏng chyŏn." Undated woodblock (30 + 41 folios). Attributed to Taga sŏp'o in Chŏnju. Karam Collection, Seoul National University Library. A Wanp'an edition close to Wanp'an text.

Seoul (Kyŏngp'an): "Shim Ch'yŏng chyŏn." Woodblock (24 folios). Issued by Hannam sŏrim, 1917. Reproduced in Son Nak-pŏm, ed., *Kan'guk kodae sosŏl ch'ongsŏ*, vol. 1 (Seoul: Ewha Women's University, 1958), pp. 229–276.

Wanp'an: "Shim Ch'yŏng chyŏn." Woodblock (30 + 41 folios). Attributed to Taga sŏp'o in Chŏnju ca. 1916. From the collection of Kim Dong-uk. Reproduced in Kim Dong-uk, ed., *Kososŏl p'an'gakpon chŏnjip* (Seoul: Yonsei University, 1973), pp. 179–193. The translator's text.

TYPESET EDITIONS

Chang Chi-yŏng: "Shim Ch'ŏng chŏn." Annotation by Chang Chi-yŏng in *Hong Kil-tong chŏn—Shim Ch'ŏng chŏn* (Seoul: Chŏngŭm sa, 1964), pp. 81–252.

Chang Tŏk-sun: "Shim Ch'ŏng chŏn." Adaptation by Chang Tŏk-sun in *Han'guk kojŏn munhak chŏnjip,* vol. 3 (Seoul: Hŭimang ch'ulp'an sa, 1965), pp. 127–173.

Chŏn Kyu-t'ae: "Shim Ch'ŏng chŏn." In Chŏn Kyu-t'ae, ed., *Han'guk kojŏn munhak taejŏnjip,* vol. 1 (Seoul: Sejong ch'ulp'an kongsa, 1970), pp. 197–236.

Sech'ang: *Shim Ch'yŏng chyŏn.* Typeset paperback (60 pages). (Seoul: Sech'ang sŏgwan, ca. 1915).

Taech'ang: *Shim Ch'yŏng chyŏn.* Typeset paperback (64 pages). (Seoul: Taech'ang sŏwon, 1919). Additional 25 pages titled *Shim puin chyŏn.*

Yi Hae-jo: *Kangsangyŏn.* Typeset paperback (75 pages). Adaptation from a Wanp'an edition by Yi Hae-jo (Seoul: Sin'gu sŏrim, 1912).

Yi T'ae-guk: "Shim Ch'ŏng chŏn." Adaptation by Yi T'ae-guk in Kim Ki-dong, et al., eds., *Han'guk kojŏn sosŏl sŏn* (Seoul: Saegŭl sa, 1965), pp. 61–147.

Yun Se-p'yŏng: *Shim Ch'ŏng chŏn.* Typeset paperback (194 pages). Annotation by Yun Se-p'yŏng of "Hŭidong sŏgwan edition." (Tokyo: Hagu sŏbang, 1955). Reprint of 1954 P'yŏngyang edition.

MODERN PERFORMANCE TEXTS

Chŏng Kwŏn-jin: "Shim Ch'ŏng ka." Mimeo (77 pages). Transcription of performance by Chŏng Kwŏn-jin (Seoul: Munhwajae kwalli kuk, 1968).

Pak Hŏn-bong: "Shim Ch'ŏng ka." In Pak Hŏn-bong, ed., *Ch'angak taegang* (Seoul: Kugak yesul hakkyo, 1966), pp. 221–288. Based on traditional interpretations of famous kwangdae, individually attributed.

Shaman: "Shim Ch'ŏng chŏn." Transcription of performance by shaman Yi Kŭmok in Shin Tong-il, *Shim Ch'ŏng chŏn yŏn'gu* (Seoul: Seoul National University, 1969). Unpublished M.A. thesis.

Shinsegi: "Shim Ch'ŏng ka." Transcription of performance in Yi Hye-gu et al., eds., *Kugak taejŏnjip* (Seoul: Sinsegi Record Co., 1968), pp. 355–387.

Yi Sŏn-yu: "Shim Ch'ŏng ka." Mimeo. In Yi Ch'ang-bae, *Kayo chipsŏng*, rev. ed. (Seoul: Ch'ŏnggu kojŏn sŏngak hagwŏn, 1961). Based on performance of Yi Sŏn-yu (b. 1872).

TRANSLATIONS

"Shim Chung, The Dutiful Daughter." In Horace N. Allen, tr., *Korean Tales* (New York, G.P. Putnam, 1889), pp. 152–169. Republished in Horace N. Allen, *Korea: Fact and Fancy* (Seoul: Methodist Publishing House, 1904), pp. 109–120. Based on the Seoul Text.

Le Bois Sec Refleuri. Translation by Hong Tjyong-ou [Hong Chong-u] with original subplots added (Paris: Ernest Leroux, 1893). Based on the Seoul Text. This was retranslated into English by Charles M. Taylor as *Winning Buddha's Smile* (q.v.).

"Shin sei ten." Japanese translation by Cho Kyŏng-ha in Hosoi Hajime, ed., *Tzūzoku Chōsen bunko*, vol. 9 (Tokyo: Jiyū tōkyū sha, 1922). Republished in Hosoi Hajime, ed., *Chōsen bungaku kessaku shū* (Tokyo: Hōkō kai, 1924).

"The Story of Shim Ch'ŏng," tr. Alan C. Heyman, *Korea Journal* 30.3:50–67 and 30.4:57–67 (March and April 1990). Translation of a ch'anggŭk script prepared by the National Theatrical Compilation Committee.

"The Tale of Shim Chung." Operatic libretto from D.P.R.K. (P'yŏngyang: Foreign Languages Publishing House, 1958).

Winning Buddha's Smile. Charles M. Taylor, tr. (Boston: Richard G. Badger, the Gorham Press, 1919). English translation of *Le Bois Sec Refleuri* (q.v.).

A Note from an Imperfect Translator

When I cannot comprehend the meaning of a passage in the Wanp'an woodblock edition and cannot replace it with a corresponding passage from another text, I note the gap by a short elipsis mark for several words or a line-length elipsis in the case of an entire line. However, when I make an educated attempt to wring meaning from a particularly reluctant passage, the asterisk at the end of the resulting line of English confesses my lack of confidence.

8

The Song of Shim Ch'ŏng

The Tale of Shim Ch'ŏng[1]

송나라말년에 In the last years of the Sung dynasty there was a man in Tohwa Ward of Hwangju:[2] his family was the Shim and his name was Hak-kyu.[3] As a family with many generations of official service they had enjoyed great renown but their fortunes turned and they became impoverished. Before he was twenty, Shim Hak-kyu went blind: a career of advancement to the capital with official rank[4] was denied him and the glory of gold seals and purple ribbons[5] became an empty dream. With a lot so harsh—not only blind but living in a corner of the countryside without relatives of any degree nearby—how could it be that no one gave him protection? But, still, being of yangban descent, with his unwavering principles and virtuous behavior, he earned the reputation of a gentleman and the praise of all.

aniri

His wife, Kwak-ssi,[6] was good and wise. She had the virtue of T'ai Jen or T'ai Ssu, the beauty of Chuang Chiang, and the constancy of Mu Lan.[7] There was nothing she did not know in the *Book of Rites, Family Rituals,*

Home Rules, or *Book of Songs.*[8] She was on good terms with their neighbors in the village, kind but firm with slaves, and able to manage all the details of household affairs. While their poverty was like that of Yen Hui,[9] she maintained the loyal integrity of Po I or Shu Ch'i.[10] In their one-room house with few family possessions, they lived from hand to mouth on a simple diet of vegetables and water. They had neither a plot in the fields nor a servant to live by the gate. The pitiful, good Kwak-ssi, disregarding her health, sold her labor for a living.

Doing needlework to earn an income: *chajin chung chung mo*
Formal robes and overcoats, scholars' gowns, officials' robes,
Military cloaks, soldiers' uniforms and battle dress,
Coats for elder gentlemen, outer wear for men and women;
Close quilting, hemstitching, horse-hair plaiting,
Puckered quilting and piped hemming;
Doing washing, starching, bleaching;
Tops and bottoms for summer clothing,
Plaited inner-hats and folded chin-straps,
Waistcoat buttons, outer cuffs, and stockings,
Anklets, purses, pouches, cuff-ties,
Sashes, medicine pouches, and mufflers,
Hoods, peaked and fur-lined caps, baby blankets,
All sorts of bedding, pillowcases
Embroidered with pairs of mandarin ducks,
Black silk crowns and belts, embroidered crests of office.

Weaving silks and damasks, brocades and gauzes:
Kongdan, suju, and *saengch'o;*
T'onggyŏn, t'oju, and *kapsa*—
Every weave of cloth in cotton, hemp, and ramie.

Making food for weddings, funerals, and other feasts:
Shinsŏlo, cookies, cakes, and pastries,
Decorating with paper lotuses and phoenixes,
Stacks of fruit and cake dyed in red, green, orange, and brown.[11]

Three hundred sixty days a year
Each day without a moment's rest;

She wears her fingers to the bone,
And sells her labor to get some savings.

She saves each *p'un* to make a *ton*,
And saves each *ton* to make a *yang*.[12]
At daily, short, and long-term interest
She lends it out to honest neighbors
Who all comply without a fault.

In observing memorials in spring and fall
And honoring her sightless husband,
And with clothing for the seasons and dishes for his table
And special foods to suit his taste,
And in harmonizing faithfully to his humors—
From beginning to end she is ever constant.

Neighbors in the upper and the lower villages all praised Kwak-ssi for   *aniri*
her gentleness.

One day, Blindman Shim said, "Pay me heed, good wife!"

"Yes?"

"Since men of yore, who has been born into this world and not had a mate? But, by some blessed affinity in a former life, we became man and wife in this world. With a blind husband like me, you never rest for even a moment; but, burdened day and night, you care for me to the utmost as you would a baby—preparing food and clothing at their proper times, anxious lest I'm hungry or lest I'm cold. I ought to be comfortable but, rather,   [1:2b] all the hardship you endure as my wife makes my heart unquiet. From this day forward, be done striving thus for me and let us just live life as it comes.

"Nevertheless, since we have reached the age of forty without even one child at our knees, it is likely that the worship of our ancestors will end with us. Even when I'm dead and gone to the netherworld, what face will I have to present to our ancestors? And, considering our own lot, who will there be to bury and mourn us, observe the first two anniversaries, and then offer up even a bowl of rice and some water on that day in the years that follow? If your devotions to the gods of the great mountains and famous temples could bring us the fortune of a child, be it a boy or a girl— even a blind one—my life's sorrow would be dispelled. Please pray with all sincerity."

Kwak-ssi answered, saying, "It is said in an ancient text that the worst of three thousand unfilial acts is the failure to produce an heir.[13] That we are without a son is all my fault. Though, rightfully, I should have been driven away, it is through your generosity that I have been kept on this long. My wish to bear a child is as fervent in day as night and, with every effort made,[14] could I not do so? However, with our poor lot and my ignorance of your rightful heart, I could not speak right out. But since you have spoken first, I shall pray with all sincere devotion."

She sells her labors,
Offers up her every treasure,
And does every kind of good work:

chung m

At great mountains, famous temples, and holy shrines,
Ancient altars, wayside temples, and village shrines;
For the many buddhas, bodhisattvas, and the Maitreya Buddha,
Ursa Major,[15] Five Hundred Arhat, and the Sovereign Sakra,
The guardian spirit of the Flower Sutra and the spirit of the road.

She donates clothing to monks, oil for temple lanterns,
Paper for temple windows, and every sort of gift.
On days when she stays at home,
She offers devoted rites to the
Spirits of the kitchen, house, and earth.
How could a tower of such effort collapse
Or a tree of such pains be broken?

On the eighth day of the fourth month of the year *kapcha*[16]
She has a certain dream:
As an auspicious air coils up within the void
And the Five Colors shine brilliantly all around,
A fairy mounted on a crane
Descends from the skies.

She is wearing many-colored clothing
And, on her head, a flowered crown;
From her belt hang moon-shaped jade pendants
That chime against each other,
And in her hand she holds a sprig of laurel.

She bows to Kwak-ssi, fingers pressed together,
And then approaches and sits down at her side:
It is as if the pure essence of the moon
Has entered into her embrace,
As if the Goddess of Mercy herself
Has risen again from the sea.
Her mind and body are swept by an ecstasy
She finds difficult to quiet.

Then the fairy speaks:

"I was the daughter of the Queen Mother of the West.
I was on my way to present the Sacred Peach[17]
When I met the concubine Yü-chen[18]
And the two of us fell to chatting.
With my lateness I had committed
A sin against the Jade Emperor[19]
And he had me banished to the human realm.

"I had no idea where to turn until
The Old Gentleman of Mount T'ai-hang,[20] the Earth Spirit,
The many buddhas and bodhisattvas, and Sakyamuni
Directed me toward your house.
Hence have I come and pray you take pity."

With this, the fairy enters her bosom
And Kwak-ssi wakes with a start
To find it all a passing dream.[21]

Forthwith she woke Blindman Shim to talk about the story of her dream: *aniri*
they had both had the same dream. By reason of something they did that
night, there were signs of pregnancy starting that month. Kwak-ssi, with
goodness in her heart,

Takes care not to sit in a seat improperly arranged, *chajin mori*
Nor eat food improperly cut,
Nor listen to unclean talk, [1:4a]
Nor look at ugly things,

Nor stand on one leg or lie on her side.[22]
When the tenth month is reached,
One day the signs of childbirth are clear.

"Oh, my stomach! Oh, my back!"

Though Blindman Shim is, in one way, happy,
He is also, in another, alarmed.
He carefully spreads a handful of straw,
Sets out a low table, and on it
Offers a bowl of pure water.[23]
Then he kneels reverently before it.

"I pray. Lo, I pray.[24]
I pray before the Three Givers of Life.[25]
Kwak-ssi, with child at her late age:
Please let her deliver as easily as
A cucumber seed slips through an old skirt."[26]

Suddenly, fragrance fills the room and
He is encircled by vapors in the Five Colors.
In this bewildering midst the birth occurs.
Indeed, it is a daughter!

See now what Blindman Shim did![27] He separated the baby from its
sack and laid it down, his heart full of gladness.

Just then Kwak-ssi recovered herself and asked, "Pay me heed, blind
husband. Which is it, a boy or a girl?"

Blindman Shim laughed heartily and felt between the baby's legs. His
hand slipped through without a pause like a ferry on its crossing.

"It seems as if the old clam has produced a fresh one!"[28]

Kwak-ssi, saddened, spoke, "After my prayers and deeds this child I
bear in late years is but a daughter, you say?"

Blindman Shim responded, "Good wife! Cease that talk! Most important
is that you have had a smooth delivery. With a child so well born, even
though a daughter, would you trade her for just any son? Let us raise this
girl with care, teaching her proper etiquette from the start, and all of needlework and weaving. Then let us choose a fit husband for our gentle and

virtuous daughter. If they are happy, hearten each other, and produce throngs of progeny, cannot their sons remember us in their rites?"[29]

He quickly prepared the first soup and rice[30] and, offering it on the altar to the Three Givers of Life, adjusted his clothing and headgear and prayed with his two hands raised, saying,

비
나
이
다
"I pray. Lo, I pray.   *chajin mori*
I raise my prayer before the Thirty-three Heavens,
The Western Paradise, and Indra.
I pray that the Three Givers of Life become as one
And bend down to look upon me.

"The child we are given in our fourth decade
Was a drop of dew in its first and second months;
In the third month its blood took form;
In the fourth month it took on human shape;
In the fifth month the five organs were formed;
In the sixth month the six feelings appeared;
In the seventh month the frame took shape
And the forty-eight thousand hairs grew;   [1:5a]
In the eighth month she had received her full burden;
The Diamond Gate gently opened
And she had an easy birth.[31]
Was this not due to the Three Givers of Life?

"Although not a son but a daughter,
Pray give her the long life of Tung-fang Shuo,
The virtuous behavior of T'ai Jen,
The filial piety of the Emperor Shun and Tseng Ts'an,
The faith of Ch'i Liang's wife,
The talents of Pan Ch'ao,
And for fortune, the wealth of Shih Ch'ung.[32]
May she have the blessing of an unbroken lineage.
I pray you let her grow apace
Like a cucumber or wild reed
And mature by the day and month,
Avoiding the many ills of childhood."

After serving up a bowl of hot soup and rice and feeding the baby's   *an*
mother, he sang by himself as he fondled the child.

"Rare as gold and fair as jade!   *chung chung m*
Oh, ho, my perky daughter!
Has Sukhyang of the P'yojin River
Been reborn in you?[33]
Has the Weaving Girl taken your form
And come down to earth?[34]

"Had I fields to the north and south,
Could they give me greater joy?
Had I pearl and coral for my use,
Could I be more pleased?
Where have you been
That now you come to be mine?"

And in this way he enjoyed himself. But then, unexpectedly, Kwak-ssi   *a*
developed secondary complications. Before the first seven days[35] had passed   [1:
after birth, the wise and gentle Kwak-ssi was exposed to a draft and fell ill.
"Oh, my stomach! Oh, my head! Oh, my chest! Oh, my legs!"
Her whole body was racked with unremitting pain. Blindman Shim,
dumbstruck, felt all over where she hurt.
"Pull yourself together and speak to me! Is it indigestion? Have the
Three Gods found fault with us?"
As her condition grew more and more serious, Blindman Shim became
frightened. He brought over Mr. Song, the *saengwŏn*,[36] from the next village,
who checked Kwak-ssi's vital signs and prescribed medicines. They tried
asparagus root, lilyturf root, lizard-tail plant, orange peels, cassia bark, fu-
ling mushrooms, beefsteak plant leaves, willow root, thoroughwax leaves,
cinnamon, apricot pits, and peach stones. Just as the Emperor Shen Nung[37]
had tasted the hundred herbs, so they, too, gave her medication and doc-
toring. But there is no medicine for a fatal illness.
Her condition became more and more critical until there was no prospect but death. Kwak-ssi, too, knew she could not survive.

She takes her husband's hand.   *chinyang*
"Ah! Blindman!"
She gives a long sigh.

"The two of us met each other
And pledged to grow old together.
But in our life of poverty
Any carelessness of mine   [1:6a]
Could easily have caused distress
To a master who cannot see;
So I accepted all your wishes
And tried to honor them.

"Heedless of wind or cold or heat or damp,
Selling my labors in villages north and south,
I got us rice and other foods.
I ate cold rice myself
And offered warm to you—
Caring respectfully that you
Not go hungry nor be cold.

"Be it simply Heaven's will
Or the cleaving of our destinies,
There is nothing we can do.
How can I close my eyes and go?
Who will mend your clothing now?
And who will press good food on you?

"Once I have died,
My dim-eyed husband will be alone
Without kin in any direction
And with no one to rely upon.

"Carrying a gourd in one hand
Grasping a cane in the other,
Going out at mealtimes
Only to fall into some ditch
Or stumble over some rock
And there bemoan his lot—
As if seen with my very eyes.

"Going 'round from gate to gate,
With his sad cry for food—
Heard as if jangling in my ears.
Though dead and but a shade,
How could I bear to see and hear?

"Does this mean I am to die
Without once nursing at my breast
Or really knowing the face of this child
I bear at forty after offering prayers
At famous mountains and great temples?   [1:6b

"And this young one,
For some sin in a former life
Born into this world only to be motherless,
At whose breast will she nurse and grow?
While you cannot cope alone,
How can you manage her as well?
What will you do with such a lot?

"How can I, overcome by tears,
Set out for the distant Yellow Springs?[38]
The way is dark—how can I go?

"I have entrusted ten *yang* of cash
To the family of Master Yi across the way.
Will you get that ten *yang*
And use it to defray the mourning costs?
And in the chest I had set aside
Some rice for my recovery.
But now I am to die without it—
So imminent draws my time.
Please keep it for provisions
After the mourning days are over.

"When I couldn't embroider all the crest
On a set of robes of Inspector Chin,
I wrapped them in a scarf

And put them in the bottom chest.
When he comes to fetch them,
After I die and the mourning is done,
Please don't fret but give them to him.

"Kwidŏk's mother in the next village
Has been a friend to me and used to visit;
If you took the baby in your arms
And asked her to nurse it,
She surely would not refuse you.

"If this child, with Heaven's grace,
Doesn't die but lives to grow
And walks on her own two feet,
Then have her guide you as you ask the way
And, seeking out my grave,
There, teach her, saying,
'This is the grave of your mother, who is dead.'
If you brought this mother and daughter together,
Though a spirit, I would be freed of anguish.

"There is no way to deny the will of Heaven.
With you, blind husband,
I leave the young one
And make this last parting as I go.

"Do not let your precious health
Suffer in grieving for me,
But take good care of yourself in every way.
We shall meet again to live out together
The unfinished destiny of this life.

"Oh, Oh! I had forgotten!
As a name for the child,
Give her that of 'Shim Ch'ŏng.'
The jade ring I used to wear
Is kept in the small box;
When Shim Ch'ŏng has grown
Please give it to her as if to me.

[1:7a]

chung mori

"I also made her a pretty red wool purse
With knotted red silk drawstrings
To which I tied the royal coins
Engraved, *Perfect Peace and Comfort,
Longevity, Happiness, Health, and Peace.*
Please give this to her wear as well."   [1:7b]

She suddenly dropped his hand, which she had been holding, and lay   *aniri*
back, sighing deeply. She then drew the baby to her and clucked her tongue
as she rubbed its face against her own.

"The world is heartless and the gods are cruel.   *chung mori*
Were you only born a little earlier
Or were I to live a little longer!
But I die as soon as you are born.
And now it is for you to know
Unending and profound sorrow.

"A dying mother and a living child:
For what sin are we separated by life and death?
At whose breast will you nurse and grow?
In whose arms will you sleep?
Oh, my child!
Nurse at my breast this last time
And grow, grow quickly!"

Tears in two streams wet her face.
The wind, heaving sighs,
Murmurs mournfully;
The rain, forming tears,
Falls plaintively;
The sky hangs low,
Thick with heavy clouds.

Birds crying in the woods
Pause lonely to vent their passion;
Water turning in the streams,
Makes a piteous sound and

Sobs as it flows along.
With this, how can people not be sad?   [1:8a]

She hiccoughs two or three times.
And her breathing suddenly stops.

Blindman Shim knew at last that she was dead.   *aniri*

"Oh, no! Oh, no! Wife!   *chajin chung chung mori*
Have you really died?
What is this?"

He beats his breast, bangs his head,
Gets up and and down, prostrates himself,
Falls on his back, and stamps the floor
As he suffers in his agony.

"Oh, wife, pay me heed!
Were you to live and I to die,
Then you would raise the child;
But now I live and you are dead—
How will this child be raised?

"Oh, no! Oh, no!
Were we to live out our hard life
What would we eat to live?
Were we to choose to die together,
What would the youngster do?

"Oh, how shall I clothe and care for her
Against the cold winds of winter?
After moon-down in my gloomy, empty room
When she begs a breast to nurse,
At whose breast will she nurse and live?

"Oh, I beg you! Don't die, I beg of you!
It has been my lifelong hope that
We would die and lie together.
Where is this netherworld

For which you abandon me in death,
Leaving the child behind?

"If you leave us now, when will you return?
Will you follow the spring and   [1:8b]
Come home again in its good company?[39]
Will you come back with the moon
That has shone who knows how long in blue heaven?[40]
Flowers fall then bloom again,
The sun sets to rise again;
But has my wife gone whence she cannot return?

"Has she followed the Queen Mother of the West
To her Feast of the Sacred Peaches at Yao Lake?
Or has she joined Heng-o of the Lunar Palace
And gone aloft to grind medicines?[41]
Has she gone to Huang Ling Shrine
To share her thoughts with Nü Ying and O Huang?[42]
Has she gone in search of Lady Sa
Who cried to heaven from Hoesa Pavilion?[43]
Of whom am I to go in search?
Oh, no! The pain of it!"

As Blindman Shim lamented like this, the people of Tohwa Ward—   *anir*
men and women, old and young alike—gathered and shed tears as they
spoke.

"Alas, wise and gentle Kwak-ssi is dead! How sad. We are more than
one hundred families; let us each give a share and see to her funeral!"

The consensus was expressed as if from one mouth. They selected a
spot for her on a sunny slope. They carefully dressed and blanketed the
body and laid it in a double coffin.[44] Then on the third day,[45] as the cortege
set forth, they sang a dirge.

"Wŏnŏ wŏnŏ![46]   *chung mor*
Wŏnŏlli nŏmch'a wŏnŏ!   [1:9a

"They say the Pei-mang Hills are far,[47]
But yonder hills are they!

Wŏnŏ wŏnŏ!
Wŏnŏlli nŏmch'a wŏnŏ!

"They say the Yellow Springs are far,
But here they are, outside the door!
Wŏnŏ wŏnŏ!

"How sad it is, the Lady Kwak-ssi!
Her conduct was so gentle,
Her talent was so rare!
She was neither young nor old,
But has forever left this world!
Wŏnŏ wŏnŏ!
Wŏnŏri nŏmch'a wŏnŏ!
Ŏhwa nŏwa wŏnŏ!"

Now see what Blindman Shim does
As they wend their way across.
The little baby, wrapped in swaddling,
He leaves in care of Kwidŏk's mother;
And, wildly grabbing his cane,
Cuts across the paddies and fields to catch up.
He hangs onto the back of the bier
But cannot cry loudly for his hoarseness.

"Heed me, wife! Let me die!
It is you who must live
And raise our little baby!
Most cruel of wives in all the world!
Left to live with you dead,
How can I in my blindness raise
This baby not yet seven days old?
Alas, alas!"

With Blindman Shim sadly crying, they arrived at the grave. After Kwak-ssi was laid to rest and the earth was mounded up over her grave, the blind man joined the ceremony, composing and reciting a eulogy with a heavy heart.

aniri

[1:9b]

"Ah, sad lady! Ah, sad, lady!   *chanted*
I had met this graceful gentlewoman;
Her manner lacked nothing of the ancients!
We had pledged ourselves one hundred years,
But suddenly you die and your soul departs.
You have left behind this child forever—
How am I to raise it up?
Oh, Heaven of no return!
Will you ever come back to me?

"In your home of pine and catalpa,[48]
You are lain as if asleep.
The face and voice I think of now
Are remote for me—so difficult to see or hear.
Tears flow, flow and wet my collar
And the soaking tears become blood.
My heart is anxious and I am estranged;
There is no way for me to live.

"The person whom I cherish lies therein.
Though I yearn, what use is it?
Now that I have buried you,[49]
To whom can I turn?
As the moon falls behind the aspens,
The mountains grow desolate and the night profound.
Whispers of sorrow fill my ears,
But what appeal have I?

"Our worlds are set apart on different roads.
Who will comfort her?
Were we to ever met again,   [1:10a]
The sorrows of this life would fade.
May you be sated, ere you depart,
With the wine, fruit, dried meats,
And salted fish of our simple offering."

He wildly recited the eulogy and then, his eyes crossing, cried out,   *anir*
"Alas! Alas, what is all this?   *chinyang ch*
Go! Go!

> What use is there in lamenting
> A wife who abandons me?
> There are no inns
> On the road to the Yellow Springs.
> At whose houses will you sleep as you go?
> Tell me where you are going!"

Blindman Shim wailed without restraint until he was calmed by the   *aniri*
funeral guests and taken home.

집
이
라
들
어
가
니
Blindman Shim enters his house   *chung mori*
To find the kitchen desolate
And the rooms deserted.
He hugs the little baby to him
And lies alone in the utterly empty room,
As lonely as a crab dropped by a jackdaw
Deep within the T'aebaek Mountains.[50]
How can he be at peace?

He stands up suddenly,
Feeling the blankets
And groping for the pillows.
The bedding which always covered them
Is there as ever
But with whom will he be covered
And sleep, alone in this empty room?

He pounds on the clothes chest
And gropes wildly at the sewing box.
He throws her comb box
Spinning into the air   [1:10b]
And runs his hands over
The small dining table
Where he took his meals.

Heading for the kitchen,
He calls out uselessly
And goes next door to ask in vain,

"Did my wife come over here?"
He clasps the baby to his chest.

"Your mother couldn't stay with us.
She died and left you behind!
You managed to get nursed today
But to whose house shall we go tomorrow
To find a breast to nurse you?
Alas, alas! Some cruel and heartless god
Has taken my wife away!"

Blindman Shim lamented in this way but then began to reconsider his *anir*
plight.
"The dead cannot be revived—there is nothing to be done about it.
Better that I should raise this child well."
So he came to make the rounds of houses with babies, asking for nursing breasts to feed on. Though his eyes were dim and he could not see, he
could guess by his sharp ears: after he sat in wait, day would dawn and,

Hearing sounds by the well,   *chajin mor*
He goes out quickly.

"Heed me, ladies!
Listen here, girls!

Won't you please nurse this child?   [1:11a
Could you look upon me and be cold-hearted?
Could you think of the goodness when she lived
Of my dead wife and yet be harsh?
How could you not have pity
For this motherless baby?
Please give her a little of the milk
Left after nursing your own babies."

Who would not nurse the child?
In the sixth and seventh months,
He seeks women resting from their weeding
Who give their breasts with pity.
Sometimes, when he finds his way

To the river where they do the washing,
A woman asks him for the child
And there she kindly nurses it.

"Come again some other day!" she says.
Sometimes another one says,
"I've just now nursed our baby
And have no more milk to give."

When Shim Ch'ŏng gets a lot of milk
And her baby stomach is quite full,
Blindman Shim is happy:
At the foot of a sunny slope,
He sits himself down
And fondles the child.

"Baby, baby! Are you sleeping?
Baby, baby! Are you laughing?[51]
Grow up quickly and, like your mother,
With her wisdom and loyalty,
Become your daddy's treasure!"

[1:11b]

Did Shim Ch'ŏng have a grandmother to look after her or have in-laws   *aniri*
to be left with? Some days, with no one to look after the child, Blindman
Shim would have her nursed and put to bed.

Then he slings a double sack from his shoulder   *chung mori*
To gather cooking rice in one end
And unmilled rice in the other.

At the six markets every month,
He tours the shops
And, begging one *p'un* here and two *p'un* there,
Gets enough to buy some sea mussels
Or a *p'un* of dark taffy for the baby's gruel.

So pass their days.
The Blindman sees to Kwak-ssi's rites

Always on the first and fifteenth every month
And on the first and second anniversaries of her death.[52]

And Shim Ch'ŏng,
Treasured by the gods and spirits of
Heaven and earth
And blessed buddhas and bodhisattvas,
Grows without illness
And, walking on her own two feet,
Survives the trials of her infant years.

Pitiless time flows like waves
And, suddenly, she is six or seven.
Her face is of unparalleled beauty.[53]
And, in etiquette, filial love, intelligence,
Natural benevolence, and affection,
Shim Ch'ŏng is a prodigy.

Who would not praise her ability
To prepare and serve her father's meals
And attend to her mother's rites,
All according to propriety?

[1:12a

One day she said to her father,

anir

"If such small things as crows
Know enough to feed their
Parents in the lonely twilight forests,
Could not a human being do so well
As such very little creatures?

p'yŏng chung mor

"Father, since you are blind, you are
Apt to fall and hurt yourself while begging
If careless on some height,
In a hollow, or on a narrow path.

"Or, possibly, on some bad day,
When it's frosty or a rainy wind is blowing,

You could catch cold and fall ill.
These concern me day and night.

"I am now seven, nearly eight years old.[54]
If I cannot now return the generosity of my parents,
Who bore and raised me,
Then how could I repay it in lamentations
In days after they have died?

"Starting from today, Father,
If you will watch the house,
I shall go out and beg the rice
And lessen your worries over our daily meals."

Blindman Shim laughed and replied, "Your words are indeed admirable!   *aniri*
But how could I possibly send a youngster like you off and then sit at home,
taking the food with an easy heart? Do not speak of this again."
Shim Ch'ŏng responded, saying,   [1:12b]

"Tzu-lu was a sage who carried rice   *p'yŏng chung mori*
One hundred *li* to feed his parents.[55]
And even T'i-jung, still a little girl,
Offered herself as a government slave[56]
To atone for the crime of her father,
Who was imprisoned in Lo-yang.

"When I think of these events,
I ask if there are differences
Between people then and now?
Please don't be so unyielding!"

Blindman Shim knew that she was right.   *aniri*
"You're remarkable, my daughter! You're a filial child, my daughter!
You may do as you have said."

Shim Ch'ŏng from this day forward   *nŭjin chung mori*
When she goes out to beg the rice—
As the sun shines on the distant mountains
And smoke appears in the village yonder—

She binds old hemp pants at the cuffs
And, over a hemp skirt with just the waistband intact,
Binds on a jacket with no front,
This way and that way.

She pulls a blue cotton cap over her head,
Bares her stockingless feet,
And puts on sandals without heels.
She tucks an old gourd under one arm
And carries a pot by some twine bound onto it.
On the snowy days of deepest winter
She is oblivious to the cold.

She steps inside the gates of this house and that
With her pitifully begging words:

"That my mother has forsaken this world
And that my father, dim of eye,
Cannot see, who does not know?
Ten spoons make one meal, it is said.[57]
If you eat one spoon less and give it,
My father, whose eyes are dim,
Would avoid being hungry."

The people who see and hear her
Are moved at heart;
Bowls of rice with pickles and sauce
They do not stint in giving her.
Sometimes they say, "Stay and eat!"
But Shim Ch'ŏng then replies:

"My old father in his cold room
Will surely be waiting.
How can I eat by myself?
I must go right back quickly
And eat together with father."

[1:13

When she begs her rice in this way
Two or three houses are enough.
She hurries quickly back
And goes into the door of their room.

"Are you not cold, father?   *chajin mori*
Are you hungry, father?
Have you been waiting, father?
It has happened that I am late."

After having seen his daughter off, Blindman Shim,
With nowhere to lay his heart, had lamented.
But now, quickly cheered to hear her voice,
He throws open the door to her.

He grasps her two hands.
"Are your hands cold?"
Touching them to his mouth, he blows.
"Your feet are cold, too!"
He massages them.
As he clucks his tongue, tears form.

"Alas, alas!
How pitiful your mother!   [1:13b]
How merciless my lot!
Eating the rice I make you beg for me—
Is that how I am to live?
Alas! Do I eke out this hard existence
Just to cause my child distress?"

Shim Ch'ŏng, with great filial love,
Consoles her father, saying,

"Please don't say such things, father!
That parents are to be cared for
And accept their children's love
Is in keeping with the Law of Heaven
And a proper thing in human affairs.

Please don't be so troubled.
Simply have your meal!"
She speaks and takes her father's hand.
"These are pickled vegetables.
And this is the soy sauce.
Since you are hungry, please eat well!"

In this fashion, Shim Ch'ŏng cared for him and, throughout the   *an*
four seasons of spring, summer, fall, and winter, she was the beggar of
the village.

One year, two years, four-five years passed. She was nimbly talented and her needlework was skillful. By taking in sewing for the village, they received payments for her labors and did not depend on
handouts. Saving this, she provided clothing and side dishes for her
father. On days when she had no work, she would go out to beg food.
Thus they managed to survive.

The years and months flowed like water and Shim Ch'ŏng reached fif- [1:14
teen. Her face was surpassing, her filial behavior outstanding, her gaze gentle,
and her etiquette uncommon. Her grace was heaven-sent. Could it have
been taught her? She was a princess[58] among women, a phoenix among
birds.

Rumors of this were on the lips of people near and far. One day a
serving girl from the house of Minister Chang in the village of Murŭng[59]
across the fields came on instructions from Lady Chang to fetch Shim
Ch'ŏng.[60] Whereupon, Shim Ch'ŏng spoke to her father:

"Since an elder has called, I shall go with the servant to visit. If by some
chance I should be late, I have prepared you some leftover rice and vegetables and set them out with chopsticks on the table. If you become hungry,
please eat them. Please take care while you wait for me to return."

As she follows the servant,   *chinyang c*
She looks toward a place
Indicated by the girl with her hand.
The grand and luxurious willows
Growing at the gates
Bespeak a Ch'ai-sang Village.[61]

As they enter the main gate,
Clear dew falls in drops from the

Sultan's parasol plant on their left
And startles cranes from their reveries;   [1:14b]
Broad pines growing on the right
Undulate like ancient dragons
In the fresh breeze that blows.

They enter the middle gate.
Among the flowers planted by the windows,
Fresh, inner leaves poke out from the
Phoenix-tailed foliage of the sun-warmed plantains;[62]
In the lotus pond in front of a pavilion,
Gulls swoop with joy
And lotus leaves like great coins
Buoy high up in the water.
Broad-winged ospreys rise in pairs,
Golden carp roll and gambol.

They enter the inner middle gate.[63]
The structure is imposing
And the brocaded doors and windows are elegant.

The lady, over fifty years of age,   *tan chung mori*
Is attired with restraint.
Her flesh is full and beautiful.
And her good fortune is abundant.
She gazes at Shim Ch'ŏng and then
With pleasure takes her hand.

"Are you really Shim Ch'ŏng?
You are exactly what I have heard of you!"
After proffering a cushion and seating Shim Ch'ŏng,
She consoles her on her pitiful life
And then carefully looks her over.
It is clear that this face
Of unparalleled beauty is heaven-sent.

Shim Ch'ŏng takes her seat with care,
Like a sparrow that has bathed and then alighted

After a fresh rain on a clear stream's white stones
Only to be startled at the sight of men.

That glowing face of hers
Is the moon risen to its zenith
And reflecting on the waters.   [1:1̃
She lifts her autumn-water eyes with a twinkle:
They are like morning stars
Sparkling in the dawn-clear skies.

The lovely color of her cheeks
Is like the newly-opened lotus,
Red as autumn sunset in the mountains.
Her fine eyebrows
Are like new moons and
Her lustrous black hair
Glistens like a new-grown orchid.
The hairs at her temples are cicadas' ears.

When she opens her mouth to smile,
She is a peony blossom
Just blooming to the life-giving dew
Left during the night just passed.
When she opens her pearly teeth to speak,
She is the very Parakeet of Lung-shan.[64]

Lady Chang, full of praise, speaks:

"Know you nothing of your former life?
You are a fairy for sure!
When you were exiled to live in Tohwa Ward,
The fairy in the Lunar Palace lost a friend!
As I look on you today
I know this is not an accident!

"I live here in Murŭng Village
And you appear in Tohwa Ward;
Spring comes to Murŭng
And a flower blooms in Tohwa!

You were born embodying the very essence of heaven,
You uncommon child!
Listen now to what I say.

"The minister left the world too soon,
Leaving me with three sons.
They have all succeeded in the capital
And I have no other children or grandchildren.

[1:15b]

"I have neither pleasure at my knees
Nor friends before my eyes.
Each daughter-in-law
Pays her respects each day[65]
But then goes about her tasks.

"Thus, in this empty room,
I am faced by just a candle
And all I look upon is ancient books.

"When I think about your lot,
Descendant of a yangban
Living in such straits,
How can I not feel pity?

"If you would become my adopted child
I could teach you letters and a woman's arts.
Raising you as if my own,
I would find joy in later years.
What mind have you of this?"

Shim Ch'ŏng rose and bowed. She spoke.   *aniri*
"When, according to harsh fate, my mother forsook the world within
seven days of my birth, I managed to survive as my blind father begged
milk with which to feed me. While I don't even know my mother's face at
all, there will never be a day when my lamentations for her will cease.
Hence, with thoughts of my own parents, I can also respect the parents of
others. Your calling me here today, Lady Chang, means you will treat me [1:16a]
as a daughter and not reckon me low. I am moved with awe, as if I had
met my own mother again. Had I nowhere at all to entrust my heart and so

were to follow what you say, this person would know rank and nobility. But who would continue providing my blind father's meals morning and evening and his clothing in the four seasons? Everybody benefits from his parents' succor but my case is unusual: I cherish my father even as a mother, and my father trusts me even as a son. If it were not for my father, I would not have lived until now; and if I were gone, my father would have no way to live out his remaining years. We shall continue to rely upon each other in our poverty and I shall stay by his side as long as I am able."

When she finished speaking, tears wet her jade face, just as fine rain borne by a spring breeze gathers on peach blossoms and then falls, drop by drop.[66] Lady Chang, for her part, was moved to pity and, patting Shim [1:1 Ch'ŏng on the back, spoke.

"You are a filial daughter, a filial daughter! Such words you speak! You're surely right. My dotard's words were ill-considered."

They passed the time this way and that until the day darkened.

Shim Ch'ŏng spoke, saying, "Blessed with your gentle kindness, I have kept your company this whole day long. But, while I have enjoyed much honor, the day has ended and I should hurry back to console my father's waiting heart."

Lady Chang, unable to dissuade her and with a heart full of affectionate thoughts, gave Shim Ch'ŏng plenty of silk, dress cloth, and provisions before sending her off in the company of the serving girl.

"If you were not to forget me but kept between us the intimacy of a mother and daughter, that would be this old person's good fortune!"

Shim Ch'ŏng answered, saying, "So noble is your intent that I shall surely learn from it."

She bowed and withdrew in an abstracted state of mind.

At this time, Blindman Shim had been sitting alone waiting for Shim Ch'ŏng.

He is so hungry his belly touches his back   *chinyang*
And the room is so cold his teeth are chattering.
As birds fly back to their nests,   [1:1
He hears the sound of a distant temple bell
And can guess the sun is setting.
He says to himself,

"Could my daughter Shim Ch'ŏng
Be so engrossed in something

That she doesn't know the sun is setting?
Does the lady have her so engaged
That she cannot come away?
Has she become involved with some friend
Along the darkening road?"

At the sound, on the snowy wind,
Of dogs barking at passers-by:
"Is that you, Shim Ch'ŏng?"
He listens happily, but in vain!
A falling leaf, carried by the wind,
Comes to strike the window.
"Could that, by chance, be Shim Ch'ŏng?"
He says, rising hopefully.
"Shim Ch'ŏng are you back?"
But there isn't a sound in the empty yard.
"My eager heart was quite deceived!"

He finds and grabs his cane,   *chajin mori*
Then goes out the brushwood gate;
But, at a drainage ditch crossed by the road,
He falls as if he has been pushed.
His face is covered with mud
And his clothing is icy.
Though he leaps up, he only sinks further;
When he tries to get out, he only slips back.
There is no hope—he is done for.

No matter how he cries out,
Who could there be to pull him out
On this hazardous twilight path?

[1:17b]
In truth, Buddha, Savior of Man, abides in every place. For, at this time,   *aniri*

An alms-gathering monk[67]   *ŏt mori*
Has come down from Mongun Temple,
A subscription book slung from his shoulder,
To collect gifts for rebuilding at the temple.

The green hills have fallen dark
And the moon has risen over the snow
As the monk is returning to the temple
Along the slanting, stony path.

Then, on the wind, he hears a cry.
"Help! Someone save me!"

With a merciful heart,
The monk seeks out the place
From where the sound has come.
A man has fallen into the ditch
And now is nearly dead!

Alarmed, he throws his staff down on a rock,
Raising a clang with its iron rings.
He takes off his hat
And shucks his black-dyed cassock
With its tasselled waist-cord still left tied.
With floppings and flutterings
He quickly removes his six-strapped sandals,
Leggings, anklets, and stockings.

He hastily hikes his quilted pants and jacket well up
And abruptly leaps into the ditch.
There he grabs Blindman Shim's pepper-shaped topknot
And pulls him out with a heave-ho.
It is Blindman Shim, whom he has seen before!

When the blind man had recovered his wits, he asked, "Who are you?"
The monk answered, "I am an alms-gathering monk from Mongun Temple."

"Indeed! Veritable Buddha, Savior of Man! You have rescued me from the brink of death. I shall never forget your mercy though my bones be bleached to white."[68]

The monk carried Blindman Shim back into his room,[69] seated him, and then asked how he came to fall into the ditch. Blindman Shim be-

moaned his lot and then told the monk his history. The monk responded
to the blind man.[70]

"How unfortunate! The Buddha of our temple is very effective. There
has been no instance of a prayer going unanswered; whenever one seeks his
help, he responds. If you were to offer up three hundred sacks[71] of sacrificial rice to the Buddha and worship him with all sincerity, your eyes would
surely open and you, becoming a whole man, would see all the things of
heaven and earth."

Blindman Shim gave no thought to his circumstances—he was bewitched by the talk of regaining his sight.

"All right, then, mark me down for three hundred sacks."

The monk laughed.

"See here, in view of your household, how could you manage three
hundred sacks?"

Blindman Shim responded with anger.   [1:18b]

"Now *you* see here! What fool would make a pledge to the Buddha with
empty words? Set about regaining my sight only to be made a cripple? Have
you only contempt for a person? Don't you worry. Note it down!"

The monk spread open his sack. On the first red sheet, he wrote, *Shim
Hak-kyu—White Rice, Three Hundred Sacks.* With that, the monk took his
leave. After seeing the monk off, Blindman Shim began to reconsider.

"For me to ask for aid   *chung mori*
Without any way to provide
A three-hundred-sack offering of rice
Will surely bring me retribution!
What am I to do about this?"

This woe, that woe,
Old woes, new woes,
Well up all together.
Unable to endure it, he cries out,

"Alas, alas! Such fortune!
I am so foolish and it's all my own doing!
The Will of Heaven being just,
There is no partiality.
But for what reason did I become blind
And even live in poverty,

With no way to make out things
As bright as the sun and moon,
And unable to see kin as close as wife and child
Though I could even touch them?

"If my dead wife were still alive,
There would be no worry about daily meals.
But I must send my nearly grown daughter
Out to villages in the four directions   [1:19a
To sell her labors and beg rice
So that we can eke out a living.
And yet I grandly put myself down
For a rice offering of three hundred sacks!

"Though I think one hundred ways,
I can find no plan.
Though I tilt the empty crock,
There would barely be a *toe* of rice.
Though I search the clothing chest,
Why should there be a single *p'un* of cash?
Though I think to sell this little house,
Who would ever want to live here
Since it can't even block the wind and rain?
Though I were to sell myself,
I would not be worth a single *p'un:*
Even I would never buy!

"There are those men of good fortune
Whose eyes and ears are sound,
Who are provided hands and feet,
Who grow old with their wives,
Whose grandchildren fill their halls,
Whose grains flow endlessly,
And whose treasures are abundant.
No one forbids them to make these theirs;
They may be used and not exhausted.[72]
They want for nothing.

"But alas, alas! My fortune!
Could there be another like me?

One may call a hunchbacked cripple sad
But he can see his parents, wife, and children.
One may say a speechless mute is sad
But he beholds all things of heaven and earth!"

[1:19b]

aniri

Blindman Shim lamented thus for some time.

Shim Ch'ŏng arrives in haste.[73]
She looks at her father's appearance
And, startled by what she sees,
Stamps her feet in frustration
But then massages him all over.[74]

chajin mori

"Father! What is this about?
Did you come out in search of me
Only to suffer this hardship?
Did you go visiting next door
Only to have this mishap?
How cold you must be!
How distraught you must be!
The old lady at the minister's house
Held on to me and wouldn't let me leave
So I suddenly found myself late."

She called the minister's serving girl.
"Load up the firebox[75] with that wood in the kitchen!"

aniri

Making the request, she gathered up her skirts and wiped away the traces of his tears.

"Please eat, father! I've brought you some warm rice. First, take some soup."

She took his hand and guided him.

"Here are some pickled vegetables. This is salted fish."

Blindman Shim's face was covered with worry and he had no desire at all to eat.

"What's wrong, father? Is it because you hurt somewhere? Are you this angry with me for being late?"

[1:20a]

"No, no. There's no need for you to know."

"Father! What kind of talk is that?   *p'yŏng chung mo*
What faults could there be
Between parent and child?
Father, you have trusted just in me
And I have trusted only you.
We have always talked things over, large and small.

"But today you say to me,
'There's no need for you to know.'
The worries of the parent
Are the worries of the child.
No matter how unfilial I may be,
I am saddened that you will not tell me."

Blindman Shim finally spoke.   *an*
"Would I ever deceive you about anything? But I couldn't speak for fear your heart would be filled with worry once you knew. While I was waiting for you earlier, I grew very uneasy when the sun set and you hadn't come. So I went out to find you but fell into a ditch crossed by the path. I was sure to die but, luckily, an alms-gathering monk from Mongun Temple pulled me out and saved my life. He told me that my eyes would be opened in this life and I would see all the things of heaven and earth if I donated three   [1:20 hundred sacks of rice with a true heart! In a moment of passion I put myself down for it but reconsidered after I had sent the monk away. Now I regret it. When I haven't even a single piece of money, where are the three hundred sacks to come from?"

Shim Ch'ŏng listened in good humor and consoled her father.

"Please don't worry, father. Do eat your rice. If you give in to regret, you cannot keep a true heart. Father, if you wish to open your darkened eyes and see all the things of heaven and earth, then I shall get together three hundred sacks of rice somehow or other and present them to Mongun Temple."

"But, no matter how you try, what can be done in our straits?"

Shim Ch'ŏng replied,

"Wang Hsiang broke the ice[76]   *chung n*
And caught a carp through the hole.
A man by the name of Kuo Chü[77]
Had set out dishes for his parents,

But his son sat and ate
At the head of the table.
As he tried to bury him alive,
He unearthed a jar of gold
And with it served his parents.

"Although I cannot match
These men of old in filial service,
I believe that Heaven is moved
Whenever one is sincere.
The sacrificial rice will be obtained
In the natural course of events.   [1:21a]
Please don't worry yourself so deeply."

She consoled him in every way. Starting that day, she made herself   *aniri*
clean in body and mind, cut her fingernails and arranged her hair, swept
and cleaned the house, and

In the back garden she builds an altar.   *chinyang cho*
When Ursa Major tilts across the midnight sky[78]
And all is desolate and silent,
She lights a lamp brightly
And offers toward the north
A bowl of pure water with prayer:

"On this particular day[79] Shim Ch'ŏng
Bows and reports with all respect.
Sun, moon, stars, and planets of the heavens;
Gods of the earth and mountains in this realm below!
Village spirits, gods of the rivers in all directions!
Sakyamuni, Eight Diamond Kings,[80]
Eight Guardian Generals, Ten Great Kings,
Holy Emperor, and Kangnin Spirit!
I beg you pray for us!

"God has placed the sun and moon
In heaven for the sight of man;
If they were not there
What could we discern?

My father, born in the year of *muja*,[81]
Became blind within thirty years[82]
And cannot see anything.
I beg you let this body of mine, instead,
Bear my father's flaw
And then brighten my father's eyes!"

And thus she prayed without end. One day[83] Shim Ch'ŏng heard that
some men from a trading ship out of Nanking were trying to buy a fifteen-
year-old maiden. Pleased to hear this, she sent Kwidŏk's mother as a go-
between to ask the particulars of their intention to buy a person.

"We are sailors from Nanking. If we make a sacrifice when we pass the
waters at the Indang Sea, we can cross the boundless seas without incident
and make our fortunes. So, if there is a maiden who will sell herself, we
will not begrudge her the price."

Shim Ch'ŏng was delighted to hear of this and spoke to them.

"I am a person of this village. My father is blind; but if he serves the
Buddha sincerely with a sacrifice of three hundred sacks of rice, it is said
his eyes will open and he will see. However, we are destitute and utterly
without the means to make an offering, so I intend to sell myself. What do
you think of buying me?"

Hearing this, the sailors replied, saying, "Your filial piety is profound
but you are desperate."

They acceded and immediately delivered three hundred sacks of rice to
Mongun Temple.

"The ship leaves on the fifteenth day of the third month of this year,"
they said, and left.

Shim Ch'ŏng spoke to her father.

"The three hundred sacks of sacrificial rice have already been delivered
so please don't be worried any more."

Blindman Shim was startled.

"What does this mean?"

How could such an inherently filial daughter as Shim Ch'ŏng deceive
her father? But it was unavoidable under the circumstances. She replied
using a clever trick to deceive him for the nonce.

"The old lady of Minister Chang's household asked last month to take
me as her adopted daughter. I couldn't possibly have agreed then. But now,
with no way to arrange for the three hundred sacks of sacrificial rice, I

explained the situation to the old lady. So I have sold myself as her adopted daughter for the gift of three hundred sacks of white rice."

Blindman Shim, not knowing the true color of events, listened with pleasure.[84]

"That would be an admirable thing to do! That lady is the wife of a national minister and so is perhaps no common person. They must have enjoyed plentiful reward and therefore their three sons command great authority in the official life. Still, it does sound strange to say that you have sold yourself as a child to a yangban. But, in that you sell yourself as an adopted daughter to the household of Minister Chang, should I be concerned? Just when are you going?" [1:22b]

"They say they will take me on the fifteenth of next month."

"Ah, how well this has worked out!"

From this day on, Shim Ch'ŏng was plunged deep into thought.

To be separated by death forever
From her dim-eyed, white-haired father
And to be born into the world
Only to die at the age of fifteen:
Such thoughts leave her senses stunned.
She has no heart for household tasks
And gives up eating altogether.
Having passed the time in melancholy,
She thinks matters over and over again.

chinyang cho

"This is water that has been spilt,
An arrow that has been set in flight.
The day draws slowly closer—
This will not do!
As long as I remain alive
I shall see to father's clothing and laundry."

After lining his spring and autumn clothing
And stitching up his summer suits,
She irons them and sets them aside.
She pads his winter clothing
And puts it away in the chest, wrapped in a cloth.

She rolls blue cotton chin straps for hats,
Which she hangs up on the wall;
And, fashioning inner hats,
She attaches their ties and hangs them up.

She reckons the day of the ship's departure
And it is only one night away.
It is the third watch of the desolate night
And the Milky Way has turned.

[1:23

Facing just her lonely candle,
With both knees bent up under her,
And her butterfly eyebrows lowered;
She draws a long, deep sigh.
No matter how filial a daughter,
Can her heart be calm?

"I'll sew up father's stockings
For this last time," she thinks.

She slips thread into a needle;
But her breast is seized with feeling,
Her eyes are dim and her spirit is dazed.
Endless tears well up from her very heart.
But, for fear her father will be woken,
She cannot cry aloud.
Weeping with hoarse sobs,
She touches her face to his
And caresses his hands and feet.

"How many more days will you know me?
Once I am dead and gone,
In whom will you trust as you live on?
Oh, sad, Father!
After I came of age,
He gave up begging;
But even from tomorrow on
He'll become the village beggar.
How he will be spurned!

How he will be contemned!
By reason of what flawed destiny
Did my mother die in the first seven days
And am I parted even from my father?

"Could this have happened to another?

"When Su T'ung-ch'ien was separated from his mother:
The sun set at Ho-liang and tears welled up within the clouds.[85]
When separated from brothers on Lung Mountain:
There was one less to put dogwood in his hair.[86]
When friends were separated at Wei-ch'eng:
There were no more old friends west of Yang Gate.[87]
And when the beauties of Wu and Yueh were separated from their
      men:
For the traveler on Kuan-shan, how long his road?[88]

"There have been many such partings.
For people who have parted while they live
There comes a day to hear of news
And there comes a day for them to meet again.
But when my father and I have parted,
On what day will I hear his news
And at what time will we two meet again?

"Mother, who is dead and gone,
Has journeyed to the Yellow Springs;
And now that I have come to die,
I shall go to the Water Palace.[89]
How many thousand *li* does it take to journey
From the Water Palace to the Yellow Springs?

"Though my mother and I try to meet again
How would my mother know me
And how would I know my mother?
If perchance I ask the way and find my mother,
On the day when we two meet again
She will surely ask for news of father.
With what words would I answer?

"If only I could bind tomorrow morning's sun   [1:24
To the branches of the Fu-sang Tree
As it rises from this night-long stay in Hsien Lake,[90]
Then I could care a little longer for my poor father.
But sad! Who could stay
The sun and moon in their transit?
Alas, alas! How sad!"

The world is heartless,   *chinyang c*
For soon the rooster crows.
Shim Ch'ŏng is helpless.

"Rooster! Rooster! Still your cry!
I beg of you, be still!
I am not Meng Ch'ang-chün[91]
At the midnight frontier gates of Ch'in!
If you cry, day will dawn
And when day dawns, I die.
It is not sad that I die.
But how can I go, forgetting my father
Who has no one to depend upon?"

Before she realized, the east had grown bright and Shim Ch'ŏng knew   *a*
she must set about preparing and serving her father's rice for the last time.
When she opened the door and stepped outside, the sailors were standing
beyond the brushwood gate.

They spoke to her, saying, "This is the day the boat sets sail. Please let
us go then, quickly."

As Shim Ch'ŏng listened to these words, the color drained from her
face, the strength disappeared from her limbs, her throat grew tight, and
her senses, dazed. She barely managed to call the sailors to her.   [1:2

"Please heed me, sailors. I also have already realized that today the boat
sets sail. But my father does not yet know that I have sold myself; and
when he comes to learn of it, there is going to be some trouble. So, I beg
you hold off just a while. After I have made father's rice for the last time
and he has finished eating, I shall tell him and prepare myself to leave."

The sailors answered, "Please do so."

Shim Ch'ŏng went back inside and, while in tears, made rice and offered it to her father. Sitting across the small table from him, she did all she

could to see that he ate well. She broke off pieces of seasoned fish and put them into his mouth; she wrapped rice in dried seaweed and put it on his spoon.

"Please eat a lot."

Blindman Shim was quite unaware.

"Ah! Today's side dishes are very tasty! Were there memorial rites at somebody's house?"

Blindman Shim had dreamed a dream that night about the relationship of parent and child. There was portent to the dream.

"Child, child! It's a strange thing. Last night I had a dream. You were riding a large wagon and seemed to go on without end. The wagon would [1:25a] be something ridden by a noble person; perhaps there will be some happy event at our house! If not, perhaps it was a palanquin from Minister Chang's house to take you there!"

Shim Ch'ŏng guessed it was a dream of her death[92] but replied falsely.

"That is a good dream!" she said, and moved the food table away. After she lit her father's pipe for him, she turned to the table to eat. But tears boiled up from within her heart and poured from her eyes. As she thought of her father's situation and the fact that she was going to die, her senses became dazed and her body trembled. She could not eat.

After removing the food table, Shim Ch'ŏng washed her hands again and went into the family shrine in order to take her leave. She opened the door of the shrine with care and there paid her last respects.

> "This unworthy descendant Shim Ch'ŏng   *chinyang cho*
> Has sold herself to be taken
> As a sacrifice at the Indang Sea
> In order to reopen her father's eyes.
> Though this burning of incense
> For our ancestors may cease,
> I shall bear them in my heart forever."

[1:25b]

chajin mori

> After withdrawing tearfully
> And closing the door of the shrine,
> She goes back to her father
> And, catching hold of him with both hands,
> Falls into a swoon.
> Blindman Shim is alarmed.

"Child, child! What is this?
Calm yourself and speak to me!"

Shim Ch'ŏng speaks.

"I am an unworthy daughter;
I have deceived you, father.
Who would there be to give me
Three hundred sacks of sacrificial rice?
I have sold myself
For a sacrifice at the Indang Sea
To sailors from Nanking
And today I am to depart.
Behold me for the last time!"

Blindman Shim, having heard this: an

                                                                chung chung m

참
말
이
나
참
말
이
나

"Is this true? Is this true?
Oh, no! No! What do you mean?
You can't go! You can't go!
Have you done all of this on your own
Without even asking me?
It would be well and proper
For you to live and me regain my sight,
But could I possibly endure
Having killed you to reopen my eyes?

"After your mother bore you late in life
And then died within the first seven days,
This dim-eyed old thing
Carried you in his arms
As he went from this house to that,   [1:
Saying words too difficult to say
And begging milk for you to drink.
Thus have you grown this far.
No matter how blind I have been,
I have known you as my eyes;

And slowly, since your mother died,
Things have become as they were before.

"But now, what is this you tell me?
Don't do it! You can't do this!
With a wife dead and a daughter lost
For what would I have to live?
Let's you and I, then, die together!
I would sell my eyes to buy you;
Though I sold you to open my eyes,
What would I open my eyes to see?
By reason of what cruel fate
Did I become a widower?

"Hey, you! You fellows there!
It's all right to do your trading
But where have you seen a human being
Bought and then killed in rites?
With God's benevolence
And the clearness of the spirits' hearts,
Would you escape your retribution?
Have you lured away without my knowledge
Then paid a price and bought
The only daughter of this blind fellow—
Young child, unknowing of the world?
I don't want rice, nor do I want money!

"Louts! You common fellows!
Don't you know the ancient texts?
During the great seven-year drought
When people prayed with human sacrifice,
The Emperor Ch'eng T'ang had compassion: [1:26b]

What I pray for now
Is for humanity.
If you must kill people to pray,
Then take my body in their place!

"Making a sacrifice of himself,
He wrapped his body in white grass,
Cut his hair and fingernails,
And prayed in Shang-lin Gardens:
Then came great rains to cover
Thousands of *li*, it is said.

"Since such a thing once happened
How would it be for me
To be taken in her place?
Look here, villagers!
Do you only stand and watch such louts?"

Shim Chʼŏng catches hold of her father   *chung mori*
And consoles him tearfully.

"Father, there is nothing we can do.
Though I die first, father,
Please let your eyes be opened
And see the bright, wide world.
Find yourself a good person
And, bearing sons and daughters,
Send down your progeny
Without thinking of this unworthy daughter.
Live a long, long, healthy life!
Since this is the will of heaven
What good is our regret?"

When the sailors took in this sad spectacle, their leader conferred with   *anir*
them.
"In view of the maiden Shim's filial piety and Blindman Shim's situation
in life, how would it be if we devised a plan to see that he went neither   [1:27a
hungry nor ill-clothed?"
"Yes, what you say is proper."
They brought into the village two hundred sacks of rice, three hundred
yang of money, and one bolt each of cotton and hemp cloth. They called
the villagers together and made arrangements.
"Give the two hundred sacks of rice and three hundred *yang* of money

to a diligent man to increase it well without interest and so provide food for Blindman Shim. Give him twenty of the three[93] hundred sacks as a year's provisions; and if you put out the remainder each year, taking long-term interest, he will be amply provided for. And, with the cotton and hemp, prepare his clothing for the four seasons. Have our intentions published by the local magistrate and conveyed to the village."

When the sailors had made all arrangements and asked Shim Ch'ŏng to go, the lady of Minister Chang's household in Murŭng Village finally heard of this and quickly sent her serving girl to call for Shim Ch'ŏng.

> The maiden follows after the servant.   *chinyang cho*
> The minister's lady dashes out the gate
> And, grasping the maiden's hand, cries,
>
> "Oh, you thoughtless person!   [1:27b]
> I had thought of you as my child,
> But you do not know me as a mother!
> To sell yourself and face your death
> For three hundred sacks of rice
> May be ultimate filial piety,
> But can it be the same as
> Staying in this world and being filial?
>
> "If you had only consulted with me,
> I would have assisted at once!
> Now, I am going to provide you
> Three hundred sacks of white rice—
> Give it back to the sailors
> And cease this silly talk!"

The maiden Shim responds, saying,

> "Though now I may regret
> Not speaking at the outset,
> What is there that can be done?
> In begging help for father,
> How could I presume upon another's treasures?
> And, even if I gave back

The three hundred sacks of rice,
It would be untoward for the sailors.
That, also, is a difficulty.

"For me to promise myself to them,
Only to go back on the agreement,
Would be the act of an unworthy person.
In this I cannot obey you.
How dare I lift my face
And what words could I say
Months after receiving payment?   [1:28a]

"I shall repay the favor of
Your kind words and great benevolence
After going to the netherworld,
As the old man repaid Wei K'o
By binding his enemy's legs."[94]

Tears soak the collar of her jacket.
The lady looks once more
And sees that Shim Ch'ŏng means her words.
With no choice in the matter,
She can neither try to dissuade Shim Ch'ŏng
Nor can she let her go away!
Shim Ch'ŏng, in tears, speaks to her:

"Lady Chang, in a former life
You were my parent.
When shall I again attend you?
I shall compose a poem
To express for you my feelings;
Hence you can divine them
When you look upon it."

Lady Chang happily gets out   *chung mor*
The paper, brush, and ink.
As she lifts up the brush and writes,
She lets flow tears of blood
That fall one by one and blossom

As flowers on a picture scroll.
They hang it in the main hall
And the lines of poetry read:

Birth and life, death and return are but the passing of a single dream;
Why should this draw forth our feelings, inundating us with tears?
But in life there is a moment—most heartbreaking of them all:
As the southern bank of the Yang-tze greens, and someone there does not [1:28b]
    return.[95]

Again and again Lady Chang
Tries to detain Shim Ch'ŏng.
But then, seeing the poem, speaks:

"You are surely not
A person of this world!
Your poetry is truly a fairy's work!
Clearly the cycle of destiny is finished
And the Jade Emperor calls you back.
How can you avoid it?
I shall also write a poem
To harmonize with yours."

Wind and rain, unbidden, come darkly in the night.
A famous flower, borne on the wind—at whose gate will it fall?
Heaven surely must have pity for one exiled in this world;
And so breaks the strong ties between a father and his child.

Shim Ch'ŏng pressed the poem to her bosom and separated tearfully   *aniri*
from Lady Chang. One could not have borne to watch.

Shim Ch'ŏng returned and went to take leave of her father. Shaking [1:29a]
with agony, he took hold of her.

"You're leaving me for dead! You can't just leave! Take me with you!
You can't go alone!"

Shim Ch'ŏng consoled her father.

"Do I break the bonds between parent and child because I want to
break them? Do I die because I want to die? That our way is blocked by

misfortune and that there is a time to live and to die are solely matters of Providence. What use are lamentations? In our hearts, there will be no day of parting."

Shim Ch'ŏng gave her father into the hands of the villagers and followed the sailors.

> As she lets loose painful wails,   *chung m*
> She tightens her waistband,
> Hugs up her trailing skirts,
> And lets her disheveled hair
> Fall loose below her ears.

> The tears that fall like rain
> Soak into her clothing.
> Stumbling back and forth,
> She grasps for support as they go
> And looks toward a house across the way.

> "Older daughter of the house![96]   *chinyang c*
> With whom will you do   [1:29
> Your hemstitching and embroidery now?
> Do you perhaps remember
> When we played together after swinging
> Last year on Tano Day?[97]

> "Younger daughter of the house!
> We were going to pray together
> On the seventh day of the seventh month.[98]
> But now it's all in vain!
> When shall I see you again?
> You all were born to good fortune;
> Stay well and take good care of your parents!"

> The villagers, men and women, old and young alike, *chung m*
> Cling to each other and cry
> Until their eyes are swollen.

> God in Heaven might well understand:
> For after the parting at the village wall,

The bright sun disappears
And somber clouds gather densely;
The green mountains seem to frown
And the sound of the river is a hoarse sob;
Languid flowers, once colorful and fair,
Seem to wither now and lose their hue,
And even the deep green willows droop sadly.

As spring birds, full of feeling,
Make a hundred cries, one of them asks:
"Nightingale there!
From whom have you parted
That you come crying for your friend?"

Suddenly a cuckoo cries, letting blood.
No matter how you cry from that branch—
Somewhere within the empty, moonlit hills—
Your heart-rending plea, *Oh! To go home!*[99]
How can that body whose price is paid
Ever once again come back?

[1:30a]

A flower, borne on the wind,
Brushes against the jade-fine face;
She picks it up and gazes on it.
They say the spring wind takes no one's part;
But why does it blow a flower my way?[100]
Princess Shou-yang of the Emperor Wu of Han
Had a crown of flowers;
But a person on her way to die—
For whom will she adorn herself?
Do blossoms falling in the springtime mountains
Fall because they want to?

The course of events is beyond us:
Whom do we hate? Whom do we fault?
Looking back at one step
Crying at a second step,
She arrives at the river's head.

By a gangplank laid at the bow   *chajin mori*
They lead Shim Ch'ŏng aboard;
And, after placing her in the passengers' tent,[101]
They weigh anchor and hoist sail.

The sailors raise their oaring chant,
Ŏgiya, ŏgiya!
Ŏgiyang, ŏgiyang!

To the *tung-dung* beating of a drum, they worked their oars to row the   *aniri*
boat.
The story changes.[102]   [2:1a]

They move into the mainstream waters:[103]   *chinyang cho*
The vast and remote oceans,
The monumental waves.

A sea gull from the water-chestnut verge[104]
Soars into an embankment red with smartweed;
And a wild goose from the banks of the Three Hsiang
Returns to the waters of the Han.
Above the harmonious sound of water
A fisherman's flute is clear:
The song ends but no one is seen;
Countless peaks alone show green.[105]

In the sound of rowing lies the agony of yore[106]
Are words that surely speak of me.

Passing by Ch'ang-sha—
The Royal Tutor, Chia I, is gone without a trace.[107]
Gazing on the waters of the Mi-lo—
Ch'ü Yuan's faithful spirit within the stomach of a fish:[108]
Would he be at peace?

Arriving at the Yellow Crane Pavilion—
The sun slips into dusk, but where are my gates of home?
Smoke swells above the river's flow and makes men sad.[109]
The traces of Ts'ui Hao.

Arriving at the Phoenix Terrace—
Three mountains half-dropped from an azure sky;
Two rivers set apart by White Heron Island: [110]
Here Li Po once gamboled.

Coming to the Hsin-yang River—
Po Chü-i is now gone
And the sound of the lute is ended. [111]
Does the Red Cliff River just flow on?
Though the moon and breeze where Su Tung-p'o once played
Remain as they were of old,
Where now is Ts'ao Ts'ao, hero of his age? [112]

As crows cry deep in the night after moon-down,
They tie their boat at Ku-su Fort.   [2:1b]
The sound of the Han-shan Temple bell
Reaches to the traveler's boat. [113]

Crossing over Ch'in-huai River—
The wine girls know not the sorrow of a kingdom's ruin
As smoke veils the cold water and moonlight covers the sands:
They only sing of Courtyard Flowers. [114]

Entering the Hsiao and Hsiang Rivers—
The towering structure of the Yo-yang Pavilion
Floats above the lake.
Gazing to the south and east,
The Wu Mountains are a thousand ranges and
The waters of Ch'u are ten thousand furrows.

The Eight Sights of the Hsiao and Hsiang [115]
Stretch out before one's eyes
And are clear to see on every side.

The skies above the river are vast and far
And the dribbling, trickling rains
Are the tears of O Huang and Nü Ying. [116]
On the wetted branches of the bamboo

Spot after spot takes shape:
Is this not *Night Rain on the Hsiao and Hsiang?*

Over the vast clear waters of Tung-t'ing Lake
Rises an autumn moon.[117]
Above and below, the skies shine blue;[118]
The old fisherman sleeps
While a lonely cuckoo flies above:
Is this not *Autumn Moon over Tung-t'ing Lake?*

On broad waters, Wu to the east and Ch'u to the south,[119]
The trading ships that travel back and forth
Hoist sails into a favoring wind;
As the beating drums reverberate,
The sailors cry, *ŏgiya, ŏgiya:*
Is this not *Returning Sails from Distant Shores?*

From two or three houses of a river village on the far bank [2:2
Smoke rises where the rice is being cooked;
A stone wall, half submerged, reflects the sun[120]
Like a mirror's face unveiled:
Is this not *Sunset at Wu Mountain?*

. . . .
. . . .

Wild geese cry and rise
And gather round in flocks:
Is this not *Evening Clouds at Ts'ang-wu?*

At the heaped verge by boundless blue waters,
Unable to endure pure sorrow,[121]
A wild goose approaches on the wing.
A reed held in its beak,
It slowly rises into flight
With the cry, *kkilluk-kkilluk:*
Is this not *Wild Geese Lighting at P'ing-sha?*

In tears, I head for the Hsiang, where
The old shrine stands unchanged.

The two sisters who traveled south,
Though spirits, are surely here;
Tears form at the mention of them:
Is this not the *Double Shrine of Huang-ling?*[122]

The call of a sunrise bell
Mixes with the sound of wind chimes;
On the approaching boat
The heavy sleep of distant travelers
Is shattered as they wake.
Before an altar the ancient monk
Chants his prayer to Amitabha:
Is this not *Evening Bell at Han Temple?*

After having seen all Eight Sights,   *aniri*

행
선
을
하
려
할
제

As the boat is about to sail away,   *chung mori*
A fragrant wind arises.
And the sound of jade pendants is heard.   [2:2b]
From the midst of a bamboo grove
A certain pair of ladies
Wearing high their fairy crowns,
Purple aprons over pomegranate robes,
And shod in slippers, come forth.

"Over yonder, Mistress Shim!
You probably do not know us.
Only when the Ts'ang-wu Mountains crumble
And the River Hsiang runs dry
Can the tears upon the bamboo disappear.[123]
For myriad years
We've had no place to make appeal!
But now we come forth to honor
Your ultimate filial piety.

"Thousands of years after Yao and Shun,
Whatever reign it now may be,
Has the Nan-feng poem for the five-stringed harp[124]

Been passed on even until today?
On the far, far waterways
Take care as you make your journey!"

They speak and suddenly are gone.
Shim Ch'ŏng thinks within her heart,
"Those were the Two Queens!"

Upon arriving at Hui-chi Mountain,
The wind and waves grow heavy,
Cold vapors whine drearily
And dark clouds surround them.
A man appears.
A face as large as a wheel
And eyebrows wide and full,
His body is wrapped in leather
And both his eyes are tightly closed.
He calls out to Shim Ch'ŏng.

"How sad! Our King of Wu,
Heeding the calumny of Po P'i,
Gave me the Chu-lou Sword
And, after I cut my throat and died,
Had my body wrapped in leather
And thrown into these waters!

"But to my bitter sorrow,
I foresaw with such clarity
The destruction of Wu by armies of Yueh,
That I disgorged my eyes
And, hanging them on East Gate,
Did really see that thing!
But there is no one to remove
This leather that enshrouds me
And to my sorrow I have no eyes."

If you ask what man this was
He would have been Wu Tzu-hsu,[125]
The faithful minister of Wu.

[2:3

As the winds let up and the clouds move on,
The sun and moon shine clear
And the waves are calm and peaceful.
But then two men
Emerge at the bank.
One man, who is standing at the fore,
Has the bearing of a prince;
His dark face is full of worry
And his clothes are only tatters.
He is clearly a "prisoner of Ch'u."[126]
Tears fall as he speaks.

"How sad and mortifying
To be deceived by the State of Ch'in![127]
For three years at the Barrier Gate of Wu
I gazed upon my native land
Then died to become a homeless spirit!
To my endless sorrow
I had become another lonely cuckoo![128]
When then with joy I heard the Po-lang bludgeon,[129]
I danced an empty dance   [2:3b]
Under the pitiless Tung-t'ing moon."

Behind him is yet another man
Whose expression is dejected
And whose features are emaciated.[130]

"I am Ch'ü Yuan of the State of Ch'u.
I had served Prince Huai,
But when I met the calumny of Tzu-lan,
I threw myself into these waters
To wash my sullied body.
How sad, our Ruler!
I had hoped to serve him even after death
But have come to this place and so attend him.

" 'Li Sao,' which I have written:[131]

"Scion of the High Lord Kao Yang,
Po Yung was my father's name.
I thought how trees and flowers were fading and falling,
And feared that my fairy's beauty would fade too.[132]

"Among the men of letters of this world,
How many have recited this?
You, to serve your father,
Die with filial love;
And I for loyalty,
Did my very all.
You and I are one in loyalty and love,
And thus I come consoling you.
O'er ten thousand leagues of distant seas
I pray you go in peace."

Shim Ch'ŏng thinks,

"The soul of one some thousand years dead
Remains to be seen by the eyes of a mortal—
Then this also is a spirit.
It is a sign that I am to die!"

She laments sadly: *chinyang c*

"How many nights am I to sleep on the water?   [2:4
How many days am I to eat on this boat?"
Unnoticed, four or five months
Have passed away like the waters.

The autumn wind gusts and evening rises;
Jade heaven opens, wide and lofty.[133]

Thinning mists and a lovely ibis take flight together;
Autumn waters and endless skies together are one color.
A line composed by Wang Po.[134]

Leaves drop boundlessly—falling, falling;
River runs endlessly—flowing, flowing.
Is a line that Tu Fu sang.[135]

Oranges fill the riverbank
Like scatters of yellow gold;
Rush blossoms fly the wind
Like blizzards of white snow.[136]

Falling fronds of slender willows in fresh winds:
How lonely in the pearly dew and chilly breeze![137]

How lonely! In the fishing boats
They hoist their lanterns up on high
And chorus to the Fisherman's Song.
They, too, have their worries.

Green mountains by the seaside
Standing like knives, peak on peak—
They are a curtain of embroidery.

Sun sets at Ch'ang-sha and autumn fills the distance,
But I don't know where to mourn the queens of Hsiang.[138]
Could Sung Yü do better with his "Autumn Sorrow"?[139]

Is this the Ch'in emperor's boat that sought elixir
With three thousand boys and girls on board?
Since the adept Hsu Shih is not here, then
Is this the Han Emperor Wu's boat that sought elixir?[140]

Even if she thinks to die early,
The sailors keep close guard   [2:4b]
That she may make the trip alive.
Her homeland is so very far behind.

They come upon a certain place   *ŏt mori*
Where they lower sail and drop anchor.
This is the Indang Sea.

Wild winds rage
And the seas turn over
As if the dragons are aroused
And the thunders are stirred up.

In the midst of the high seas
A boat bearing one thousand sacks:

The oars lost and the anchor cut,
The rigging broken and the rudder gone;
The wind howling and the waves billowing,
The fog dense and mixed with rain.

The way ahead stretching yet
One thousand, ten thousand leagues;
Growing dark on all sides, heaven and earth now quiet,
The foam rising in the distance.[141]

With hull thundering and mast crashing,
The moment is a dangerous one.
The chief boatman and all his crew
Are beside themselves with fear—
Their spirits quit their bodies.

Preparing to carry out their rites,
They cook a sack of rice and,
A crock of wine at hand, catch a large ox.
They quarter it and consecrate
Whole limbs and whole head.
They catch a large pig and boil it whole.
Skewering it on a large knife,
They lay it out as if crawling.

Three colors of fruit and five of candy,
Fish to the east and meat to the west,
Dried meat to the left, pickled fish to the right,
Red fruits to the east and white to the west,
And so stacked up by points of the compass.

[2:5

They have Shim Ch'ŏng bathed
And dressed in white clothing.
After seating her at the head of the table
Now see what the chief boatman does.
While beating on a drum, *turidung-duridung*,[142]
He recites his supplications:

"We cast our eyes up—Thirty-third Heaven!   *chajin mori*
We drop our eyes down—Mansions of the Sky! [143]
Cosmic void and heavens beyond thought!
Three Emperors, Five Rulers, Heaven of Indra!
Ten great kings of the netherworld
Who have established their reigns!
Great Jade Emperor of Heaven!
Yellow Emperor Hsien Yuan of the lands below
Who ruled the twelve earthly kingdoms!

"The Four Sages[144] have given us the Doctrine,
Sakyamuni established Buddhism,
The Great Emperor Fu Hsi
Made the Eight Signs of divination,
The Emperor Shen Nung tasted one hundred herbs
And made the first medicines.[145]

"Hsien Yuan gave us the boat[146]
So we could cross where there was no way.
Later men have followed his example:
Gentlemen, farmers, artisans, and merchants,
Each doing his own life's work.
Was this not a meritorious deed?

"Hsia Yü during the Nine Year Flood
Rode a boat to rule his realm;
He established the Five Domains[147]
And toured the nine provinces.   [2:5b]
When Wu Tzu-hsu fled to the Wu state,
He crossed over to a rowing song.[148]
The general who fell at Kai-hsia[149]

Returned to the River Wu,
Where he moored his boat and waited.

"Chu-ko Liang, with surpassing skill
Conjured up a southeast wind;
Then attacked with fire by land and sea
Ts'ao Ts'ao's hundred thousand troops.
How would they have fared without ships?[150]
When T'ao Ch'ien came back to the countryside
And Chang Han returned to the east of the river,
Here, too, they went by boat.[151]

"In autumn's seventh month in the year *jen-hsu,*
Trusting his reed-boat to drift as it might,[152]
Su Tung-p'o enjoyed himself.
Returning with moonlight filling the empty boat[153]
To the chant, *chigŭkch'ŏng-ŏsahwa,*
Is a pleasure for the fisherman.
Down the river's reaches by cinnamon mast and orchid oar:
Pretty maidens of Wu and Yueh in their lotus boat.[154]

. . . .[155]

"Year in and year out
Is it not the trading ships?

"Our band of twenty-four comrades,
With trading as their livelihood,
For fifteen years have plied the tidal flows
And wandered the waters of the West Lake.
As a sacrificial offering
To the Dragon King of the Indang Sea
We consecrate the filial daughter Shim Ch'ŏng,
Who is fifteen years of age
And lives in Tohwa Ward of Emerald-land.[156]
We pray the Dragon King of the Four Seas
Accept her with tenderness.

"Amyŏng, God of the East Sea!
Kŏsŭng, God of the West Sea!

Ch'ugyung, God of the South Sea!
Onggang, God of the North Sea!
Dragon King of Ch'ilgŭm Mountain!
Dragon King of Chagŭm Mountain!
Dragon King of each and every island!
Great spirit of the Pratyeka Buddha!
Lotus Spirit of the afterdeck!
Spirits of the bow and stern!
Bend down to us, we pray!

"In our distant, thousand-league ocean course
Open us a tunnel through the winds;
Even out the waters by day
As if spread upon a tray.
For this boat, let it be flood tide.
For this anchor, let it be flood tide.
From crow's nest to anchor line, let it be flood tide.
Let it be so! We pray of you.

"Assure our boat may never sink,
Avert the loss of stores and cargo,
And bring us profits beyond reckoning!
Let us fly the phoenix pennant from our mast
And, with laughter, enjoy harmony
As we celebrate our luck with dancing.
We pray you let this be so!"

While beating the drum, *turidung-duridung:*

"Time is short, Shim Ch'ŏng!
Quickly, quickly into the water!"

See now what Shim Ch'ŏng does.   *chung mori*
She presses both hands together and,   [2:6b]
Rising up, she prays these words
Before God:

"I pray. Lo, I pray.
I pray before God!

That Shim Ch'ŏng dies
Is not sorrowful in the least;
But, since I meet this death
With hope to ease, while he still lives,
My blighted father's deepest sorrow,
I pray Fair Heaven be moved
To open brightly once again
My father's darkened eyes!"

Her tears fall as she speaks:

"Sailors and tradesmen, gentlemen!
May you go in peace
And reap profits beyond reckoning!
Then, when next you pass these waters,
Call forth my soul and give me water and rice." [157]

Without a change in countenance
She steps to the gunwales and looks.
The torrential blue waters
Cap and crash, *wŏllŏrŏng-k'wallŏng,*
And the bubbling foam is old and yellow.

Shim Ch'ŏng is stunned.   *chajin*
She sinks back suddenly
But then grasps the gunwales once again
Only to fall forward in a swoon.
One cannot bear to watch the sight.
Shim Ch'ŏng gathers her wits once more
And, helpless, pulls herself up.
She draws her limbs up close together   [2
And wraps her skirts above her head.
With quick steps she moves back
And, then, giving herself to the vast sea:

"Alas, alas!
Oh, father! I die!"

One foot slipping on the gunwale,
She falls head over heels—*p'ung-dung!*

She went under. *aniri*

An apricot blossom follows the wind and waves. *chinyang cho*
A bright moon sinks into the ocean gate.
Of such has been said:
An infinitesimal grain in the vast sea![158]

Like the quiet of a dawning day,
The waves grow calm,
And the wild winds become diminished
As dense fog and thin clouds settle in.
The mists dissolve into blue heaven,
Like the east when a new day begins,
And the day is clear and bright.

The chief boatman spoke. *aniri*
"After holding rites we have fair weather for a smooth passage. Is this
not due to the goodness of the maiden Shim?"

All assembled were of one mind. They ended the rites, each drinking a
cup of wine and smoking a pipeful of tobacco.

"Let's get under way!"

"Yes. Let's do!"

To a chorus of their working chant, *ŏgiya-ŏgiya*, they hoisted the rough
cotton sails and, hanging them out to both sides, headed toward Nanking.
They slipped like a slender arrow through the whirlpools and rapids and
arrived at Nanking in a twinkling; like tidings from across the North Sea in [2:7b]
a letter tied to the leg of a wild goose.[159]

At this time Shim Ch'ŏng had given herself to the boundless seas and
believed that she was dead. But colorful clouds glowed brightly and unfa-
miliar fragrances filled her nostrils. When the clear sound of a jade flute
faintly touched her ears, she let her body rest and hesitated.

Then the Jade Emperor[160] spoke on high, issuing a command to the
Dragon King of the Indang Sea, the Dragon Kings of the Four Seas, and
each of the kings of the nether regions.

"Tomorrow, the innately filial Shim Ch'ŏng will go to that place.[161] See that not one drop of water wets her body! For failure to give her escort, I shall visit heaven's punishment upon the Dragon Kings of the Four Seas and banish the kings of the nether regions! You shall escort her to the Crystal Palace and for three years feed and clothe her properly before returning her to the world!"

Thus he commanded. The Dragon Kings of the Four Seas and the kings of the nether regions were all struck with awe. Innumerable generals of the rivers and soldiers of the springs and ponds gathered together.

원
참
군
별
주
부

The Great Terrapin Bailiff and minor terrapin officials,
The Seabream Royal Secretary, octopus from the border office,
The Carp Inspector, the Salmon Trout Counselor,
A Hallim Academy carp, the Horned Pout Leader of the Guard,
The Catfish Messenger, sea robins, pollacks,
Mackerels, cutlass fish, crabs,
Every naval official—one million scales and shells—
All stand by with countless fairies,
A white jade palanquin in readiness,
Waiting for the moment.

The jade-fair Shim Ch'ŏng had actually leapt into the water. The fairies received her and raised her up onto the palanquin. Whereupon Shim Ch'ŏng gathered her wits and spoke.

"As a vulgar human from the Dusty World, how could I ride a palanquin of the Dragon's Palace?"

The various fairies replied to her, "The instructions of the Jade Emperor are very strict. If you do not take the palanquin, our Dragon King will not be able to avoid punishment! Please do not demur but ride the palanquin, we beg of you!"

Shim Ch'ŏng, unable to put them off, finally accepted the seat high up on the palanquin.

Eight fairies shoulder the palanquin,
Six dragons offer escort;
The river general and soldiers of the springs and ponds
Guide her on the left and right;
And two boys mounted on blue cranes

Lead the way ahead,   [2:8b]
Forming a passage through the ocean waters.
As they make their entrance to elegant music,
Heavenly angels and fairies,
Hoping to see Shim Ch'ŏng,
Stand in lines to either side.

The T'ai-i Fairy is mounted on a crane[162]
And the immortal Ch'ih Sung-tzu rides a cloud.[163]
The lion-mounted magician Ko Hsien-weng,[164]
Boys in blue robes and boys in white robes,
Flute-playing pairs of palace girls,
Heng-o of the Lunar Palace and the Queen Mother of the West,
The fairy beauty Ma Ku, the fairy Fu Fei of the Lo River,[165]
And the eight fairies of the Lady of Nan-yueh,[166]
All gather together.
Their lovely clothing and fine ornaments,
Fragrances that are strange indeed.

Elegant music leads the way:
Wang Tzu-ch'iao's phoenix flute,
Hermit Kuo's bamboo drum,
Ch'eng Lien-tzu's harp,
Chang Liang's jade clarinet,
Hsi K'ang's fiddle,
And Juan Chi's whistling.[167]
To these are mixed strains of the airs
Piping and Drumming, Old Topers' Bower,
Icy Waves, Treading the Void,
Feathery Robes, and *Picking the Lotus.*[168]
The sounds of this music
Reverberate through the water palace.

They enter into the Crystal Palace:
It is like another world.
Then King Kwangni of the Southern Sea,
Wearing a royal crown

And carrying a white jade mace,
Enters with heroic brilliance.   [2:9
The Inner Three Thousand and the Outer Eight Hundred,[169]
With all the great ministers of the water palace,
Stand in ranks to serve the king
Outside the gates of Yŏngdŏk Palace.
They raise the cry, "Long Live the King!"

Behind Shim Ch'ŏng,
Lü Yen riding a white heron,
Li Po mounted on a whale,
And Chang Nyo on a blue crane
Are flying in the heavens above!

Looking round at the ornamentation:
It is refined and grand.
Excellent mirrors hang from the walls,
Their radiance like the morning sun;
And auspicious emanations coil in the void.
Palace of pearls and towers of shells
Like radiant bodies of heaven;
Embroidered skirts of angel's dress—
Things of unearthly beauty!
Screens of coral and vases of tortoise shell
Are brilliant in their splendor,
And curtains of mermaid-patterned silk
Hang in the heights like clouds.

Looking to the east:
Great rocs fly in the heavens and
Mermaids and indigo waters
Swirl around the jeweled turrets.
Looking to the west:
Thin waters and quicksand stretch afar
And pairs of *ch'ing-tao* birds soar above.[170]
Looking to the north:
Myriad mounts are green as jade.
Looking above: [3

The auspicious sun and clouds shine red
Over the three thousand worlds on high and the nine lands below.

Looking round at the banquet:
It is not the food of our world!
In cups of glass with amber saucers,
On crystal trays and agate tables—
Fairy liquor and thousand-day wine,
With charqui of unicorn as appetizer.
In gourd carafes, both honeyed posset
And sugared water are stored.
Sacred peaches are set
Amongst dew and nectar wine on jade and coral tables;
And, in the very middle, three-thousand-year peaches
Are stacked in circles.
These are incomparable fairy tastes;
For Shim Ch'ŏng's visit to the Crystal Palace
Is at the order of the Jade Emperor.
Would they be careless with his commands?

Each of the Dragon Kings of the Four Seas
Pays his respects morning and evening
By sending his ladies-in-waiting.
Taking turns, they greet and court her.
Brocades, damasks, gauzes, colorful silks—
Fair and graceful, lovely beauties.
Each of them strives to charm:
Ladies laughing as they flirt,
Ladies endeavoring to be gentle,
Ladies charming to the utmost!
These graceful ladies
Care for her day and night.

They give her a small feast every third day
And a large banquet on the fifth.
At the palace, one hundred bolts of silk;
And in the lower chambers, three baskets of pearls.
In so caring for her,   [2:10a]
They take every precaution
Lest they fail in the proprieties.

각
설
이
때
The story changes.[171] At this time, Lady Chang of Murŭng Village, hav-   a
ing hung Shim Ch'ŏng's poetry on the wall, watched it daily for meaningful signs; but there had been no change in its color.[172] But, then one
day, water flowed on the scroll and the color changed, darkening it.
Does this mean Shim Ch'ŏng has gone into the water and died? she wondered.
She lamented continuously until, soon, the water disappeared and the colors turned bright again. Thinking it strange, Lady Chang wondered, *Has
somebody saved her and does she live?* She was full of conjecture but how
could such a thing easily happen? Lady Chang that night made preparations
to go out to the river bank and there, calling forth Shim Ch'ŏng's spirit,
hold rites to comfort her. With her maid attending, she arrived at the river
moorings.

The night is deep at the third watch.   *chung r*
Mists that rest in layer upon layer
Sink deep into the mountains,
And waves of haze have billowed up
To cover the surface of the water.
She rows the little bobbing boat
Out to float in midstream.
She sets a Spirit's Place within the boat   [2:]
And with feeling pours a cup of wine.
Sobbing hoarsely,
Lady Chang calls to Shim Ch'ŏng
And comforts her, saying,

"Oh, how sad, the Maiden Shim!   *chinyang*
Enjoying life
And not wanting to die
Is true of human nature.
In death she would repay
The goodness of her father's
Constant heart and loving care;
And so by her own decision
Cut short her only thread of life.

"When a lovely flower is strewn
Or a butterfly enters the flame,
How can that not be sad?

I comfort you with a cup of wine:
If your soul is not present,
It surely will not disappear.
Come quickly and receive this offering, I pray."

She scatters tears as she wails.   *chung mori*
Can even the smallest creatures
Of heaven and earth remain unmoved?
Even the clear, bright moon
Withdraws behind unstirring clouds;
Even the wind blowing over the water
Becomes silent now.

Even if dragons are there,
The river's heart is still;
Even the gulls that play on the banks
Thrust their necks far out,
To cry, *kkŭlluk-kkŭlluk*.
And the usual fishing boats
Now pause with their sails furled.

Unexpectedly, in the middle of the river,   [2:11a]
A wisp of pellucid essence
Coils up before her boat
Only to fade after a moment
As the day grows bright and clear.
Lady Chang rises and looks:
The cup she poured brim full
Is now half gone or more.
She can, indeed, feel Shim Ch'ŏng's presence!

One day, at word that Lady Yü-chen of the Kuang-han Palace[173] was   *aniri*
coming, the Water Palace seemed in an uproar. The Dragon King was in a
state of trepidation and every quarter bustled. This lady originally had been
Kwak-ssi, the wife of Blindman Shim, who died and then became Lady Yü-
chen of the Kuang-han Palace. Having heard that Shim Ch'ŏng had come
to the Water Palace, she had obtained permission from the Jade Emperor to
come and meet with her daughter. But Shim Ch'ŏng, not knowing who she
was, only stood and watched from a distance.

Colorful clouds appear: *chinyang cŏ*
A five-colored palanquin
Is mounted high on jade unicorns
With blossoms of the pear and cinnamon
Fixed in rows on the left and right;
Girls from every palace give escort
As blue cranes and white cranes
Lead the way ahead;
Phoenixes perform a dance   [2:11
And parakeets spread the news.

Shim Ch'ŏng has never seen such before.   *chajin mŏ*
Then, descending from the palanquin
And alighting on a stepping-stone,
The lady calls out,

"My daughter, Shim Ch'ŏng!"

She knows this is her mother
And goes flying to her.

"Mother, my mother!
Who bore me and died
Within the first seven days!
Now, at fifteen, I don't even know your face!
I thought no day would see the end of
My sorrow as boundless as all creation.

"Had I known that we would meet today,
After coming to this place,
And had I told my father
On the day when I set forth,
He would have had some comfort
Against the sorrow of my loss.
Happy as it is for
Mother and child to meet—
Whom can my lonely father
Take joy in looking on?
Oh! Thoughts of father come anew to me!"

Lady Yü-chen cries as she speaks:

"Now I have died to become immortal and
My thoughts of man have grown remote.
Your father brought you up and
You came to trust in one another.
But now even you have left his side:
How intense his feelings must have been
The day that you came here!
Now that I have seen you   [2:12a]
My heart, indeed, is glad.
But against the sorrow of your father's loss
Can it be compared?

"Let me ask you.
Your father lives amidst difficulty,
How does he seem to be?
He must have aged a lot.
Over these tens of years
Did he ever remarry?
And Kwidŏk's mother from the back village,
Has she not been generous?"

She touches her face to Shim Ch'ŏng's
Then rubs her hands and feet
And looks at her white ears and neck.

"You are so very like your father!
With such lovely hands and feet,
How could you not be my daughter?
You still have the jade ring I wore.
And, Oh! You are even wearing
The pretty red wool purse
With knotted green and red silk drawstrings
And royal coins engraved on each side,
Perfect Peace and Comfort
Longevity, Happiness, Health, and Peace!

"Separated from father to meet mother again,
Unable to have us both together:
This is the pain and joy of humankind.
But when you part from me today
There is no way for you to know
Whether you will see your father again.

"Among the works of Kuang-han Palace
I am given so many tasks
It is difficult to stay away for long   [2:12]
And, hence, must leave you once again.
Though you lament sorrowfully,
It can be to no avail.
For all your grieving, what can be done?
We shall meet again another day
When there will be time for joy."

She shook herself loose and rose. Shim Ch'ŏng could neither stay her   *an*
nor had any way to follow after. Having tearfully bid her mother farewell,
she remained at the Crystal Palace.

At this time, Blindman Shim, without his daughter,   *chinyang*
Is unable to forsake his life of hardship
And barely manages to endure.
The people of Tohwa Ward,
Moved to thoughts of pity—
Since Shim Ch'ŏng died her watery death
Out of absolute filial love—
Set up the Monument of Falling Tears
And there write words they have composed.

Thinking only of her father's sightless eyes,
This filial sacrifice to the Dragon's Palace!
Myriad misty leagues forever deep and blue;
Fragrant grasses every year while our sorrow never ends.

Not one traveler passing by the mooring
Can read this message without tears.

And when thoughts of his daughter come to him,
Blindman Shim embraces the stone and cries.

The people of the village turned a profit with Blindman Shim's cash *aniri*
and grain so that his wealth increased each year. [2:13a]
     In this village there was a woman known as "Ppaengdŏk's mother," who
was quick to take on lovers and went about with reddened eyes like some
dog that copulated day and night. Knowing that Blindman Shim had much
cash and grain, she came to live with him as a volunteer wife. Her habits of
speech, indeed, were like those of her crotch; she was a wench who was
not about to rest for even a moment.

Trading food for cakes to eat, *chajin mori*
Selling hemp to raise wine money,
Napping by day underneath an arbor,
Having the neighbors cook her rice,
Speaking rudely to the villagers,
Picking fights with woodcutters,
Getting drunk in the middle of the night
And crying out suddenly,
Carrying an empty pipe in her hand
And asking for whatever tobacco she sees,
Tempting bachelors and collecting
All sorts of evil diseases—

So she carries on. But, all the while,
Blindman Shim, who has hankered several years,
Now has the pleasures of his bed
And so is fully unaware that
His estate is slowly being ruined.

Blindman Shim couldn't figure these things out. *aniri*
     "See here, mother of Ppaengdŏk! Others used to whisper that we were [2:13b]
in good, sound condition. But recently for some reason we have gone bank-
rupt and, worse, are on the brink of begging for our food again. Even if I
tried to beg again at my age, the villagers would be embarrassed and we
would surely be impoverished. Where could I go and yet hold my head
up?"
     Ppaengdŏk's mother answered, "Blindman Shim, what have you been

eating lately? You have had wine for your hangover before each meal, and that has taken eighty-two *yang* of cash. Lord, how frustrating! And now, pregnant with that child not yet born and raised, I want so much to eat apricots! The cost of the apricots is seventy-three *yang*. Oh, so frustrating!"

Blindman Shim laughed falsely as he smoldered within.

"Ah, you've eaten too many apricots! But, they say, 'What a woman eats is as lost as if a rat had eaten it.' But what good does that do? Let's sell all our household goods and move to some other place."

"Yes, let's do that."

So they sold off their ordinary household goods and, carrying their [2:1] possessions on head and back, set out to drift from place to place.

One day the Jade Emperor gave an imperial order to the Dragon Kings of the Four Seas.

"The time draws near when the maiden Shim should be matched with a husband. See that she is returned to the Indang Sea and so does not miss this propitious moment of her life!"

His instructions were most strict and the Dragon Kings of the Four Seas set about sending off the maiden Shim. She was escorted by two ladies-in-waiting who attended her in a huge flower blossom. Provisions for daily meals and many embroidered brocades and treasures were loaded in. When they were carefully placed into a jade vessel and moved toward the Indang Sea, the Dragon Kings of the Four Seas came forth in person to see her off. The ladies-in-waiting of every palace and the Eight Fairies spoke to her.

"Maiden, when you go back to the human realm, we pray you enjoy a long, long life amid riches, honor, and royal favor."

The maiden Shim replied, "Having been blessed by the goodness of the various kings, this body that was to die now returns to life in the world again. I cannot forget this benevolence. And for every lady-in-waiting I share deep feelings, too. I am saddened at this departure; but our roads are different, above and below, and I must leave you behind. Though I leave, I pray that you precious beings of the Water Palace be forever in peace." [2:1]

She took her leave and turned around. As if in a moment's dream, they rose to the Indang Sea in a twinkling where the surface of the water became clearly brilliant—a wonder of heaven, by the divine power of the Dragon King. Though winds blow, could it be budged? Though rains came, could it be swept away? Colorful clouds filled the interior of the flower as it rode high up in the water.

The sailors, who had been to Nanking and turned a profit beyond reckoning, were returning to their home country when they arrived at the Indang Sea. There they anchored their boat and, neatly preparing their sacrifices, offered rites to the Dragon King. They appealed with prayers:

우리일일행수십명
"The tens of men in our sailor band   *p'yŏng chung mori*
Have escaped the many bodily ills
And found our small requests, as asked,
Given their fulfillment.
We offer up with true sincerity
A cup of wine for the benevolence
Of the generous Dragon King.
Become one mind with us, we pray,
And accept the fragrance of our sacrifice."

Rearranging their offerings,
They call forth the spirit of the maiden Shim
And console her with sad words.

"Maiden Shim, the heaven-sent filial daughter,
Of a rosy-cheeked sixteen years,   [2:15a]
Who looked upon death as if going home!
You became a lonely soul in the watery kingdom
In order to open the eyes
Of your noble, white-haired father.
How could this not be wretched?
How not pitiful?

"We band of sailors,
Through your intervention,
Turned a profit at our trading
And are now returning home.
But, spirit of the maiden!
On what day will you return again?
On our way, we shall visit Tohwa Ward
To garner knowledge of your father;
Whether he is there, whether living or dead.

"But still we console you with a cup of wine.
If, perchance, you are aware,
We beseech you accept our sacrifice!"

They undid their offerings, wiped their eyes,
And gazed out toward a certain place:
There was a single blossom,
Floating buoyantly on the sea.
The sailors thought this strange and
Conferred among themselves.

"Perhaps the maiden Shim's spirit
Has become a flower and floated up."

They went close to see and, indeed, it was
Where the maiden Shim had gone into the water.

Moved at heart, they pulled the flower out of the water and placed it   *anir*
on board to see. In size it was as big as a wagon wheel—two or three men   [2:15b]
could have sat in it with ease. Such a flower did not exist in the world and
appeared so very strange to them that they preserved it carefully and left
the place.

The ship sped like an arrow. A course taking four or five months to
follow they completed in only several days. This, furthermore, seemed strange
to them.

When their huge treasure of profit was divided among them, the captain for some reason turned down his treasures and took only the flower.
When he made a platform in a neat corner of the garden of his house and
placed the flower there, fragrances filled the place and colorful clouds surrounded it.

At this time, the Sung Emperor, having lost his Empress, did not choose
another spouse but sought, instead, his flowering plants. He filled his garden, the Shang-lin Park,[174] and also planted flowers here and there in the
courtyard of the Huang-chi Palace.[175] He sought the most exotic and gave
rank to the best of them.

Such plants indeed abound.   *chung chung mor*
The August lotus looking lordly:
Red lotus on brimming autumn waters.[176]
Deep fragrance floats in hazy moonlight:
The news conveyed by a flowering plum.[177]

All planted after Liu Lang left:[178]   [2:16a]
The reddening blossoms of the peach.
Red is the moon when the cassia flowers:[179]
A cinnamon blossom in the wasteland.
The nails of lovely, sleek jade fingers:
Gold-dusted face of the garden balsam.
Drinking at Lung-shan in September:
A chrysanthemum laughs at me.[180]
Gamboling with noble youth in the flowering shade:[181]
Riches and nobility are the peony.
Pear blossoms cover the ground but no one opens the door:
The flower of the pear in Ch'ang-hsin Palace.[182]
Where Confucius' seventy disciples discoursed:
Apricot flowers in the spring wind at Hsing-t'an.[183]
Upon entering the T'ien-t'ai Mountains:
Peonies that opened on both sides.[184]
Unable to overcome the sorrow of Shu:
Azalea, flower of the cuckoo that cried blood.[185]

October, white, and Shu chrysanthemums,[186]
Buckwheat flowers, orchids, and quince blooms,
Roses and sunflowers,
Phoenix flowers and knotgrass,
Flowering willows and morning glories,
Red and purple mountain azaleas,
Royal rhododendrons and Indian lilacs,
Irises, plantains, and rare incense.

In the middle: needle firs and walnut trees,
Pomegranate trees and weeping cypresses,
Plum, crab-apple, and peach trees,
Schizandra, mandarin orange, and citron trees,   [2:16b]
And the vines of grapes, berries, and clematis.

As they flutter in many colors,
He plants them bank on bank;
And, following the seasons, comes out to look.
When the fragrant breezes stir,
The flowers toss playfully

And then hang down colorfully;
Bees, butterflies, birds, and beasts
Dance dances and sing songs.
The Emperor takes delight in this
And every day comes out to look.

At this time, the sailor from Nanking heard this news of the court and   *anir*
suddenly thought, "Men of old would turn their backs on rank in consideration of their emperor. Shall I, also, present this flower to the Emperor
and so express my sincerity toward him?"

With the flower found at the Indang Sea resting in its jade vessel, he
arrived at the gates of the palace and his intent was reported to the throne.
The Emperor, pleased, took the flower in and then placed it in front of the
Huang-chi Palace to appreciate.

Its colors are brilliant,   *tan chung mor*
Radiant as the sun and moon;
Its size is without equal,
And its fragrance is pre-eminent.
Surely not a flower of this world!

The shadow of the red cassia on the moon
Still shows clearly: ·
This cannot be a cassia bloom.
Is it not three thousand years   [2:17a
Since Tung-fang Shuo plucked
The jade peach of Yao Lake?[187]
This cannot be the flower of that peach.
Can the seed of a lotus from the West[188]
Have fallen to become this flower,
Then floated hither on the ocean?

Bestowing it the name of Descendant Fairy,
He then examines the flower closely.
It is filled with red vapors
And auspicious emanations coil about.
The Emperor is greatly pleased
And moves it to a flower terrace.

As the peonies and lotuses all fall in rank,
The plums, chrysanthemums, and balsams
Are all named as courtiers.
For all the Emperor now cares,
Other flowers have been dismissed
And, for him, there is only this flower!

One day, the Emperor, following the ancient custom of the T'ang dy-   *aniri*
nasty, gave orders to the women of his court and bathed in the Hua-ch'ing
Pool.[189] The Emperor, himself, then followed the moon to stroll about in
the flower garden.

A bright moon fills the garden   *tan chung mori*
and gentle breezes waft.

The blossom of the Descendant Fairy
Suddenly trembles, gently opens, and
Seems to emit some sound.
The Emperor conceals himself and
Watches with care.

A lovely maiden from the Dragon's Palace
Lifts her face half up and   [2:17b]
Peers slightly outside the flower.
But seeing the traces of human beings about,
She ducks back down inside.

The Emperor's mind and body
Are swept with sudden ecstasy.
He is full of curiosity;
But no matter how long he stands,
There is no further movement.

He moves up close and
Carefully opens the blossom to look.
One maiden and two beauties.
The Emperor, delighted, inquires,

"What are you, spirits or humans?"

One beauty promptly steps down and,
Prostrating herself, speaks,

"I am a lady-in-waiting from
The South Sea Dragon's palace.
Giving escort to the maiden,
I have come out onto the ocean
And now violate your majesty's presence.
I am profoundly awed."

The Emperor thought to himself, "The Jade Emperor has sent me good   *ani*
fortune. *When one does not take the gift of Heaven—Time! Time! It never comes
again!* I should settle upon her for my spouse."
    The Emperor made his final decision and had the court astrologer select   [2:18a
the proper date. It was the day *kapcha,* the fifth day of the fifth month. He
conferred upon the maiden the title of Empress and had her escorted to the
residence of the Prime Minister. Later, when the auspicious day had come,
he commanded,
    "This event is something unknown even in ancient times. Promulgate
the particulars of our decision to observe all the proprieties of a state ceremony!"
    Indeed, it was the first occasion of such solemn majesty in the present
age. What is more, there had never been greater even in the days of yore.
    The Emperor emerged and stood at his place. Then, the two ladies-in-
waiting from inside the flower came attending the maiden, each supporting
an arm. The interior of the palace was as dazzling as if the attendants of
Ursa Major had themselves lined the way. It was difficult to gaze upon
directly.
    Being a cause for national joy, an amnesty was ordered and, in partic-
ular, the captain of the ship that had been to Nanking was given rank by
the Emperor and appointed Prefect of Mujang. The assembled officials to
the court raised up the cry, "Long live the Empress!" and all the people of
the country raised threefold cries of congratulations.
    The Empress Shim's benevolence was so rare that year after year of
abundance followed and the age of Yao and Shun was seen again: it was
the government of the T'ang!

Empress Shim had attained ultimate riches and nobility but a constant concern within her heart was none other than thoughts of her father. One [2:18b] day, when her anxiety was more than she could bear, she went out with her maid [190] and leaned against the jade railing.

추월은밝아

The autumn moon is bright   *chinyang cho*
And illuminates the coral curtains;
Crickets cry sadly,
Their sound floats in to her.[191]

Little by little she lets rise
Her boundless concerns.
All the while, in the sky above,
A solitary wild goose
Comes flying with a cry.
The Empress, her heart gladdened,
Looks toward it and speaks:

"You, wild goose, pass you hither?
Pray stay a moment
And listen to what I say.
Are you the wild goose that carried a letter
From Su Wu across the North Sea?[192]
Are you the goose that could not endure pure sorrow
At the heaped verge by blue waters and bright hills?[193]

"Has my father in Tohwa Ward
Tied a message to your leg
That you come hither?

"In the three years apart
I have heard no news.
I shall now write a letter
And send it on by you.
Please, please be my messenger!"

She goes into her chambers where
She quickly opens up her writing box
And cuts writing paper from a roll.

She lifts a brush to write the letter [2:19a]
But her tears fall first before she can.
The letters turn to running ink
And all the words become entangled.

"Since I left your side, the year has changed three times and the sorrow   *aniri*
that surrounds and overcomes me is as profound as the rivers and the seas.
Prostrate with respect, I wonder if Father's health since then has been steadily untroubled? My heartfelt thoughts are full of concern for you.[194]

"When this unfilial daughter, Shim Ch'ŏng, followed the sailors away, I
wanted each day to die twelve times—once at each of the watches.[195] But
somehow I found no chance and so slept on the waters for five or six
months until, finally coming to the Indang Sea, I went under as a sacrifice.
Helped by the Heavenly Emperor and rescued by the Dragon King, I returned to the world and have now become Empress to the Emperor. I have
obtained the ultimate riches, nobility, and glory; but, because of a sorrow
that penetrates my very marrow, this richness and nobility has no meaning
and I have no desire to live. If I were to be at your side and see you once
again, I could die that day without regret.

"I was keenly aware of your thoughts as you sent me off and stood [2:19b]
leaning on the gate, your heart barely enduring the course of events. But
worse, in death my spirit was stifled and in revival I am choked with anguish. Thus we are split apart. During the three years past I pray your eyes
have been opened, that the cash and grain left with the village is intact and
cared for, and that you have well protected your precious health, father. My
myriad prayers are to see you, father. My myriad prayers are thus."

Quickly writing   *chinyang cho*
The year, month, day, and hour,
She brings the letter outside
Only to find the wild goose is
Gone without a trace.

Beyond boundless clouds,
The Milky Way tilts above.
The moon and stars
Alone shine bright
And the autumn wind
Whistles coldly.

She folds the letter and,
Crying silently,
Puts it away in the box.

At this time, the Emperor entered the inner palace and looked upon   *aniri*
the Empress. Her brows were knit with care, like dark mountains sunk in
twilight; her face, traced by tears, was like a flower wilting in the sun.   [2:20a]

"What worry leaves these traces of tears? On all the earth you are the
most noble and you have the wealth of the Four Seas. You are the richest
of all. What could have happened to make you sad?"

The Empress replied, "Actually, your wife has a great desire but dares
not speak to you of it."

The Emperor responded, "I pray you tell me in detail what sort of great
desire it is."

The Empress kneeled and spoke.

"Your wife is not really a person from the Dragon's Palace. I am a daughter
of the blind man, Shim Hak-kyu, who lives in Tohwa Ward of Hwangju. In
order that my father might open his eyes . . . ."[196]

She explained to him in detail how she sold herself to sailors and came
to sink into the waters at the Indang Sea. Having heard, the Emperor spoke.

"In that case, why did you not speak of it earlier? This is not a difficult   [2:20b]
matter. I pray you not be too concerned."

The next day, after his morning audience, he held a discussion with all
the court officials.

"Send notification to Hwangju that Shim Hak-kyu is to be readied and
sent here with the title, Father of the Empress."[197]

The local officials sent their report to the throne which, when opened,
was found to read, "Indeed, in Tohwa Ward of this province there had been
a blind man, Shim Hak-kyu, but he set out wandering several years ago and
his whereabouts are unknown."

The Empress heard this and, unable to overcome her grief, cried pi-
teously and heaved great sighs. The Emperor consoled her generously.

"If he has died, there is nothing we can do. But, if he is alive, the day
will surely come when you will meet. How could it be that you will not
find him?"

The Empress was suddenly inspired and spoke to the Emperor.

"There is, actually, one plan that I pray you follow. All the country's
citizens and officials are, indeed, subjects of the Emperor. Among the

people, the most pitiful are the Four Unfortunates—widowers, widows, orphans, and the childless. Even among them, those of unsound body are to be pitied. But worse, even among the unsound, there are the blind. I ask [2:21a] that you gather together the blind men of the realm and hold a feast. I pray you lessen for them the regret they suffer as they look upon but fail to see heaven and earth, sun and moon, stars and planets, black and white, long and short, mother and father, or wife and children. If so, then in their midst perhaps your wife would meet her father. This would not only bring fulfillment to your wife's hope but also bring harmony to the state. What could you do about this?"

The Emperor, full of praise, spoke.

"You are, indeed, a Yao or Shun [198] among women. Let us do as you say."

The Emperor promulgated his command to the realm.

"Without discrimination among officials, gentry, and commoners, if any is a blind man let his name and residence be recorded; let each township in its turn send them hither. Cause them to participate in a feast; and if there be even one blind man who, ignorant of this command, is unable to attend, every high and local official of the province in question will be severely punished."

As it was a command issuing from the Emperor, every province and town in the realm was struck with awe and carried out the instructions like shooting stars. [2:21b]

At this time, Blindman Shim, taking Ppaengdŏk's mother with him, had been wandering about when, one day, he heard that in the imperial capital a blind men's feast was being arranged. Blindman Shim spoke to Ppaengdŏk's mother.

"Being born into this world, one should once have a look at the capital! But I cannot go alone on the long, long, thousand-league road to the capital. What about your going with me there? Can we not go along the road and then, at night, do what we would?"

"Yes, let's go. Let's do that."

That very day they set out on the road, Ppaengdŏk's mother leading the way. Traveling several days, they reached a certain post station and slept there.

Now, there was in that neighborhood a blind man known as Blindman Hwang but he was only half-blind and lived comfortably. He had heard that Ppaengdŏk's mother enjoyed sex and was quick to take on lovers. Hearing the rumors being passed around the neighboring districts, it had become his heartfelt desire to try her one time.

He heard that she was coming with Blindman Shim and talked it over
with the innkeeper, who set about luring Ppaengdŏk's mother, reasoning   [2:22a]
with her in all sorts of ways. Ppaengdŏk's mother also had her thoughts.

"Even though I went along with him, in the end, there would be no
joining the feast for me. Even after coming back, our life would be worse
than before and our livelihood would be at an end. But, rather, if I went
along with Blindman Hwang, the lot of my declining years would be most
comfortable."

She made a firm promise and decided to wait until Blindman Shim had
fallen asleep and then slip out. They spread out the bedding[199] and, when
Blindman Shim was sound asleep, she escaped and ran off without a second
word.

At this time, Blindman Shim woke from his sleep and, with a wicked
thought, felt at his side. Ppaengdŏk's mother was not there. He pushed
himself up by his hands.

"Say, mother of Ppaengdŏk, where have you gone?"

But there was no movement at all. In an upper corner of the room,
where a sack of red pepper had been left, a rat was gnawing noisily. Believing only that Ppaengdŏk's mother was making sport, Blindman Shim got up
with his two arms outstretched.   [2:22b]

"You want me to crawl after you?" he said and groped about.

The rat, frightened, jumped aside.

Blindman Shim laughed, "Ah, you thing! Here I come!"

He ran about from corner to corner and the rat scooted clean away.
Blindman Shim sat down quietly and thought things over.

"My eager heart has been thoroughly deceived! She has already gone off
to set her ass up for Blindman Hwang, who has what she likes so much!
How could she be here? Say there, innkeeper! Has my wife gone in there?"

"No, she hasn't!"

Blindman Shim at last realized she had run off, and lamented alone.

"See here, mother of Ppaengdŏk!   *chinyang cho*
Where have you gone, abandoning me?
You cruel and evil bitch!
On the long, thousand-league road to the capital
Whom will I take as my friend?"

He cries, then has a thought.   *chajin mori*
And, scolding himself,
Flails the air with his arms.

"Be done! Enough!
I am a silly old bastard[200]
To be concerned about you!
I foolishly fell for that slattern
Who squandered my estate away
And left me here for ruined.
All of this is my destiny;
Who is there for me to hate or blame?

[2:23a]

"My wise and gentle Kwak-ssi—
I saw her die but still I live on;
My loving daughter Shim Ch'ŏng—
We parted living and then she drowned,
I saw her die but still I live on.
And now, on top of that,
To concern myself over such a tramp—
I would be the son of a dog!"

He mumbled uselessly all alone as if he had someone to talk to. Then *an[*
the day brightened and it was time to leave again.

At this time, the season being that of the fifth and sixth months, the
heat was intense and his sweat flowed, soaking his back. By the edge of a
river, he took off his hat and clothing and laid down his sack. But when he
bathed and came out, his hat, clothing, and traveling gear had disappeared
without a trace. The sight of him groping here and grasping there all about
the river bank was like that of a hunting dog that had caught the scent of a
quail. For all his groping here and there, was the clothing likely to be somewhere? Stuck and with nowhere to go, Blindman Shim lamented loudly. [2:23*]

"Alas! Alas! How am I to go *chung mo[*
To the capital, one thousand leagues away?
Hey you, wretched, petty thief!
Do you take away my things
And leave me to do what I can't?

"In so very many rich men's houses
The treasures they've left over
Are for you to take and use;

Are you satisfied just to take away
The goods of this poor blind fellow?

"With no laundry maids about
To whom can I go to beg my food?
Having nothing now to wear
Who is there to give me clothes?

"Deaf fellows and crippled men
Are all of them called pitiful;
But they see all that's under heaven—
Sky, earth, sun, moon, stars, planets,
Black and white, long and short.

"By what ill-starred destiny
Did I become a blind man?"

For some time he cried and lamented thus. *aniri*

At this time, the Prefect of Murŭng, who had been up to the capital, was on his way back down.

"Hey there! Turn around and step aside! Oho! Ho! Hey there, fellows, keep a bright eye out! Watch the scattered rocks, watch the rocks!"[201]

They had continued their progress for some time, clamoring like this. [2:24a] Blindman Shim was delighted to hear the warning cries of the attendants.

"Right! Somewhere down the road an official is approaching. Let's see what persistence will do!"

He sat down with his head stretched forward. Then, at last, they drew near. Grasping his cock and balls in both hands, he waddled out on the road. The patrol soldiers pounced upon him and pushed him aside. Blindman Shim spoke as one who felt insulted.

"Hey, you fellows! Look what you did! I am a blind man now on his way to the capital. Tell me immediately what your names are and what official's procession this is!"

They had quarreled like this for a while when the Prefect of Murŭng spoke.

"You! Listen to me! Where do you come from, blind man? How did you become undressed? What is it you want to say?"

Blindman Shim responded.

"I am Shim Hak-kyu who lives in Tohwa Ward of Hwangju. On the   *chant*
way toward the capital the day grew extremely hot. Thereupon,
unable to go further, I thought to take a bath before proceeding.
After I had bathed a moment and came out, I discovered that some   [2:24
heartless petty thief had made off with my hat, clothing, and my
sack. Indeed, I am as shameless as a daylight ghost but am stuck,
unable to move on or go back. I pray you help find my hat, clothing, and sack or

"Arrange some special treatment.   *chung m*
If you do not do so,
I shall be helpless, unable to go on.
I pray that you, sir, an official,
Grant me special consideration."

The prefect listened to these words and was moved to pity.   *a*
"From what you have said, you seem intelligent. Prepare and present
your petition. Thereupon I shall give you hat, clothing, and travel expenses."
Blindman Shim replied, "Though I can compose a little, my eyes are
dim. If you assign your secretary to me, I shall write by dictating."
The prefect ordered his secretary, "Write!"
Blindman Shim called out his petition. He did not hesitate but composed fluently and then had it handed it up. The prefect received and studied it.[202]

I am one of cruel destiny, received from Heaven at my birth.
Though there is nothing brighter than the sun and moon, these dim eyes   [2:2
    cannot distinguish them;
And, though there is no greater happiness than that of man and wife, since
    she has gone to the next world it is lamentable that I cannot know
    such joy.

I had early cherished dreams of official life but now, in old age, I have
    become just a white-haired pauper.
Tears, never drying, soak my collar without end and boundless sorrow for-
    ever knits my brow.
My body declines by the day, and that decline can be seen in my flesh.
. . . .

The reigning Emperor, high officials, and officers of the court
Have ordered a feast for blind men; like the springtime sun, this news has
*   reached the furthest valley.*

· ·

The way is far and for that I have only my one cane;
And, since I am poor in household possessions, the only thing I carry on my
*   person is a simple gourd.*

. . . Following the model of Tseng Tien, I stopped to bathe.[203]
Then I lost my hat and clothing at the riverbank;
I have not been able to recover my traveling money and sack from amongst
*   passers-by.*
Considering my lot, I am like a fenced-in sheep.
In my nakedness, I am shameless as a daylight ghost.

· [2:25b]

I beg you quickly save me as you would a bird injured by an arrow or a
*   fish whose water is drying up.*
. . . I should praise your help as if given rebirth!
Ah, that you should see clearly and act!

Full of praise, he called a runner and had him open the clothes chest
and hand over a suit of clothing; he called a yamen slave and had him take
down a hat hanging on the back of the palanquin and give it to him; he
called a clerk and had him give traveling expenses. Blindman Shim spoke
again.

"I cannot go without shoes. Is there anything that can be done about
shoes? How about giving me a pair of servant's shoes? Curse it! Am I to go
barefoot?"

In the entourage there was a groom who handled his horse so skillfully
that he easily threatened money out of his mounted passengers; and if the
price of the horse gruel was one *ton*, he would up it to twelve *nip*; and even
when his shoes were whole, he would claim they were run down and,
always upping the price of shoes, buy a pair and hang them from the horse's
rump.

The prefect, who looked upon this fellow's greed as insolence, finally
said, "Take those shoes down and hand them over."

The yamen slave dashed over quickly, took them down, and presented [2:2€ them.

After Blindman Shim accepted the shoes and put them on, he said, "That wicked thief took away my pipe, which had an engraved nickel bowl and a Kimhae-style bamboo stem that drew freely. As I go along today, I'll have no pipe to smoke."

The prefect said, "In that case, what is it you want us to do?"

"Well, it's just that it's so."

The prefect laughed and gave him a black bamboo pipe. Blindman Shim received it.

"I am awed. But it might be nice to have a taste of some good, P'yŏng-yang tobacco."

He called the houseboy and had him provide tobacco. Blindman Shim then took his leave and went along toward the capital, lamenting to himself in a loud voice.

"On the road I met the benevolent prefect and obtained clothing but there is no one to guide me on the road. How am I to find my way?"

And so he lamented as he went. He came to a certain place.

> The green shade is luxuriant   *chung m*
> And sweet grass is bending over.
> Willows by the front stream—a circling green curtain;
> Willows by the back stream—a circling yellow curtain.
> As one they hang down low;   [2:2€
> As one they spread out and, then,
> Droop down long and round.

In such a place, Blindman Shim turned toward the green shade and   *ar* there he rested. Every kind of bird flew thither. Suddenly, flocks of birds in flight formed in pairs to answer spring; together, on the wing, they would come and go.[204]

> Parakeets that talk so well,   *chung chung m*
> A pair of cranes that do a dance,
> Two crested ibis make a pair,
> Wild geese over blue rivers,
> Sea gulls and sparrows;
> Every one of them flies thither.

The cock pheasant's cry, *kkilkkil,*
The pheasant hen's flutterings;
The greenfinch's jingle,
The kingfisher's cry, *sururuk.*
All sorts of birds fly thither.

A mountain dove by the well-treed gate,
And yonder cuckoo cry their cry;
Going toward this mountain,
Ssukkuk, ssukkuk!
Going toward that mountain,
Ssukkuk, ssukkuk!

Then yonder nightingale cries;
She, with head combed pretty, pretty,
Will cross the waters for a mate.
And yonder raven cries;
Coming hither, *kalgok!*
Going thither, *kkaok!*
Now yonder garden dove cries,
Catching a bean in his beak.
Male and female embrace, *ŏruru;*
Two tongues emerge to kiss,
And they fondle, *kuruu-guruu.*   [2:27a]

Blindman Shim went on a little further. Then, unexpectedly, some   *aniri*
shepherd boys, holding sickles in their hands and drumming on the legs of
their wooden back-racks, took up a shepherding song. Seeing Blindman
Shim, they mocked him.

" 'Midst myriad mountain folds   *chung mori*
High peaks rise as thick as hair:
Green mountains and blue waters,
Full, and boundless deep.
Here is heaven-in-a-vessel[205]
And earth like vast, full oceans.
Holding a walking stick by the handle,
He enters leagues of hills and streams.

With high skies and bountiful earth,
A land worth traveling in.

"We sing our verse atop eastern hills,
Compose our poems afloat clear streams;
The vigor of the hills and streams is good
But the prospect of the southern sea is vast.
Unable to endure the long, long, narrow road,*206
He draws his knife and holds it high;
In the shadow of blue water and green hills,
Looking out about, he wanders to and fro.
Strolling about, he sees the sights
Of hills and streams—east, west, south, and north.

"Two-three mountain village houses near and far
Are sunk in fading mist and evening smoke.
Where is the hermit of the mountain depths?
It is difficult to ask the way.
Yonder cloud, quite unconcerned
Floats over countless peaks and autumn waters.
A solemn raven
Comes and slips inside the verdant mountains.

[2:27

"Where is Yellow Mountain Valley?
The Village of Five Willows is there.207
Ning Ch'i rode an ox and
Meng Hao-jan rode a donkey.208
Tu Mu went down for a look
By the Po-lo River bank;209
Chang Ch'ien took a raft and
Lü Yen rode a white heron.210
Meng Chiao went down to the broad fields
At the Wo-lung foothills;211
The land-shrinking tactic of the Eight Arrays—
Is this only the work of Chu-ko K'ung-ming?212

"It is clearly Blindman Shim
Who has come into the mountains.
While rambling about hither and thither,

He quite enjoys himself the whole day long.
With the pleasure here of the hills and waters
He can embrace the Four Great Virtues.
Wind in the pines serves for a harp
And a waterfall for the drum.
When done with pettiness*
And given way to pleasure,

"He makes his lunch and with it drinks
The wine that woke him in the morning.
In his hand he takes a Hwangch'ong flute*
To play the "Gromwell Flower Song."
With the Four Grayheads of Mount Shang,[213]
Counting me, then we are five.
With the Seven Sages of the Bamboo Grove,[214]
Counting me, then we are eight.

[2:28a]

*"The sound of the midnight bell
At Han-shan Temple by Ku-su Fort is here.*[215]
Yonder old monk, ringing his bell
At the Hall of the Ten Great Kings,*
Preaches rebirth at Paradise Hall.*
He recites with all sincerity:
Amit'a-bul, kwanseŭm-bosal.[216]
He strives to calm his heart
And think of men of yore.

"Chief Counselor Chiang of Chou[217]
Went fishing in the waters of the Wei;
For the sagely Liu it was Chu-ko Liang
Who tilled his fields in Nan-yang clouds.[218]
. . . .
. . . .[219]
Blindman Shim, too, awaits his moment,
Having entered into these mountains."

Thus had the shepherd boys mocked him. Blindman Shim parted from *aniri*
the shepherd boys and moved on from village to village, gradually drawing
nearer to the capital. He quickly passed over Naksu bridge and entered into

the green trees of the old capital.[220] At one place there was a miller's house where several girls were polishing rice at the mill. To escape the heat, Blind- [2:28 man Shim sat and rested in the shade of the miller's house.

Some of the girls saw Blindman Shim and said, "Oh, is that blind man another of them coming to the feast? Have you had it in the blind man's style lately?[221] Don't sit like that yonder, come and work the pestle a bit!"

Blindman Shim finally explained to himself, "If they're not the house slaves of nobles, then they're the bedmates of commoners! I'll have a little fun with them."

He answered, "You ask a traveler from a far distant place to work the pestle like you would the man of your house. If you'll give me a little something, I'll work it."

"Oh, my! That blind man's a tricky one! Give you something? What would we give? Why don't you just have lunch?"

"I shall work the pestle to get lunch but, then, what are you going to give me?"

"We'll give you meat or something."

Blindman Shim laughed.

"This is meat, too! It's meat.[222] Though easy to give, how do I know whether to give it?"

"Well, just work the pestle and then we'll see."

"Right! That word was half the promise!"[223]   [2:2

He climbed up on the pestle and, as he worked it with a *ttŏlgudŏng-ttŏlgudŏng*, he mumbled to himself, "I can sing a good milling song, but who's to let them know?"

Some of the girls heard that and urged him on. Blindman Shim, giving in, sang a milling song.

> "*Ŏyua! Ŏyua! Pangayo!*[224]   *chung chung m*

> "Sage ruler of ancient times,
> With wood and virtue reigned!
> Is this the wood
> With which he ruled?[225]

> "*Ŏyua! Pangayo!*

> "Yu Ch'ao bound wood
> To make a shelter![226]

Is this the wood
With which he built his house?

"*Ŏyua! Pangayo!*

"Shen Nung took wood
To make a plow! [227]
Is this the wood
With which he made a plow?

"*Ŏyua! Pangayo!*

"This rice pestle—
Whose pestle is it?
A fleshy pestle
For every serving girl? [228]

"*Ŏyua! Pangayo!*
Ttŏlgudŏng-ttŏlgudŏng, hŏch'ŏm-hŏch'ŏm;

"Was this pestle
Made by Counselor Chiang? [229]

"*Ŏyua! Pangayo!*

"This pestle was made
By cutting wood in mountain wilds;
But when we look at how it's formed,
It is strange, very strange indeed!
Was it made to mock the human form,   [2:29b]
Two legs stretched and spread?
The hairpin of a pretty girl in mind,
The pin is driven through the waist!

"*Ŏyua! Pangayo!*

"With slender, narrow hips,
Is this the spirit of the beauty Yü? [230]

I'll work the pestle
The way a beauty stands upon the swing![231]

"Ŏyua! Pangayo!

"When its head is lifted up,
It seems an angry old dragon of the sea;
When its head is lowered down,
Is it King Wen of Chou bowing low?[232]

"Ŏyua! Pangayo!

. . . .
"After Minister Po-li Hsi died,[233]
The sound of the pestle was stilled.
With our emperor's gracious reign
The country's peaceful and the people well;
And, what's more, our blind men's feast
Was never known to men before!
So let us sing a milling song
Of great peace in an age of wisdom.

"Ŏyua! Pangayo!

"While stepping up high with one leg,   *chajin m*
Then up and down it pounds.
And, inside the "clam," the rice[234]
Twitching and quivering and frothing!

"Ŏyua! Pangayo!

"Joyful! Joyful!
All sing praise!"

[2:3

He sang loudly, carried away by his enthusiasm. The girls, hearing him,   *a*
giggled and spoke.
"Oh, blind man! What kind of talk is that? You certainly know all the
details! You were probably born through there!"[235]

"It's not a matter of being born through there. I've had experience."

They all clapped and laughed loudly as he worked the pestle this way and that. He got lunch to eat and tucked some wine away inside his traveling gear. Then, after picking up his cane, he spoke.

"Well, ladies, enjoy yourselves! I go well fed."

"My, that blind man's not a bore—and he's a good heart, too. Goodbye! And drop by again when you come back from the capital!"

Blindman Shim took his leave and eventually made his way into the capital. The metropolis was so thick with blind men that they were colliding with each other, making it difficult to get about.

He passed a place where a certain woman, stepping from a gate, spoke to him.

"Yonder blind man! Are you Blindman Shim?"

"Who could that be? There's no one here who knows me. Still, is someone looking for me?"

"Hello over there! Aren't you Blindman Shim?"

"It's true then. I wonder what it's about?"   [2:30b]

"I have good reason. Please stop for a moment."

She then came and guided him into a guest parlor where she had him seated and presented him a tray of food.

Blindman Shim thought to himself, "Strange! I wonder what this is all about?"

The side dishes, moreover, were quite unusual. By the time he finished enjoying his rice, the day had ended and it was dusk. The woman reappeared.

"Please heed me, blind man. Please follow me into the inner parlor."

Blindman Shim answered, "I don't know whether or not there is a master in this house. Why! How could I enter the inner parlor of someone else's house?"

"I understand. Please don't see fault in it. Please just follow me."

"Please heed me. Is it that there is an illness here that you act thus? I don't even know how to recite a mystic text."[236]

"Here, now. Please be done with this empty talk. Please go in."

His cane dragging, he was led away. His suspicions were aroused.

"Oh, dear! Maybe I'm being dragged into a trap! This is dangerous!"

Mumbling like this, he went up into the parlor. When he had sat in [2:31a] the seat of honor, a woman to his left asked him a question.

"You're Blindman Shim, aren't you?"

"How did you know?"

"I have ways of knowing. After your long journey, I hope you are comfortable.

"My family name is An.   *chung n*
We have lived in the capital for generations;
But my parents unfortunately are dead,
And now I take care of this house alone.

"My age is twenty-five
And I have not yet been able to marry.
Having early learned the art of augury,
I divined the identity of the man
Who is to be my spouse
And then, some days ago, had a dream.

"The sun and moon fell into a well
And were submerged in the water.
I pulled them out
And hugged them to my breast.

"The sun and moon of the sky are man's eyes.
Since the sun and moon fell,
I knew he would be blind like myself.
Since they were submerged in water,
I knew his family name was Shim.[237]

"I immediately had my servant
Wait at the gate for several days
To query every passing blind man.
With the help of heaven and the gods
You and I have now met.
Is this not a destined match?"

Blindman Shim chuckled.
"What you say is well and good, but would it be easy to carry out?"   [2:3
Blindwoman An called her servant for tea and offered it. After urging
him to drink,

"Where do you live and what sort of family do you have?"

Blindman Shim told her of his situation from beginning to end in its every detail. His tears flowed and Blindwoman An consoled him.

That night they slept in each other's arms. After a while, at a happy climax, both their eyes seemed to flutter and jerk but what could they see of each other? Though these two had four eyes between them, they could not see so much as a tobacco seed.[238] Helpless to do anything about it, they went to sleep.

They rose in the morning. Being their first night, and after he had hankered so long, how happy he should have been. But Blindman Shim sat deep in worry.

Blindwoman An asked, "For what reason are you not in a pleasant mood? Indeed, I feel shamed."

Blindman Shim answered, "Basically, it is my destiny to be wretched and my whole life has been a fulfillment of that. Whenever something good occurs, it is always followed by something unpleasant. Now again. Last night I had a dream. It was a sign that my whole life is to be unfortunate. My [2:32a] body seemed to enter a fire where my skin was taken off and used to cover a drum. Then leaves seemed to fall from a tree and cover its roots. Was it not probably a dream foretelling my death?"

Blindwoman An listened and then responded, "That was a good dream. The unlucky is lucky. Let me try to explain your dream."

She washed her hands again, lit incense, and knelt formally. After lifting her box of divining sticks up high and reciting a spell, she interpreted the divination signs and wrote some words.

Body enters fire: can look forward to a return.
Skin makes drum: the drum's sound is called kung, which means "palace,"
   a sign he will enter the palace.
Fallen leaves return to roots: can meet his progeny.

"I am so very glad it is an auspicious dream," she said.

Blindman Shim laughed and spoke.

"That's impossible, there's no connection at all! A total invention! I have no progeny, so whom will I meet? When I attend the feast, I'll only be going into the palace for a rice handout."

Blindwoman An spoke again.

"Though you don't believe me now, wait and see how things end up." [2:32b]

Having eaten his morning rice,   *chung mo*
He arrives outside the palace gate:
They already have called
The blind men in to feast.

He goes inside the palace
Which is very fine within:
The tone is dark and somber
And the sound of blind men fills the air.

At this time, the Empress Shim had held the feast for several days.   *an*
Whenever she opened and examined the register of names there was no
blind man with the name of Shim. She lamented.

"This feast was held   *chinyang c*
With hopes of seeing Father,
But I've not been able to see him.

"Could he have died in deep lament
Believing I had died at the Indang Sea?
Did the Buddha of Mongun Temple
Work a miracle to open up his eyes,
So that he sees all heaven and earth
And is gone now from blind men's ranks?

"Today is the last day of the feast;
Shall I go and look myself?"

She took her seat in the back gardens and supervised the blind men's   *a*
feast. Court music was scattered here and there and food was served in
abundance. After the feast had ended, she ordered the register of blind   [2:3
men's names be presented, then gave each a suit of clothing. The blind men
all offered their congratulations to her. Then one blind man, who was not
listed in the register of names, stood up conspicuously.

The Empress asked, "Which blind man are you?"

Since it was a lady of the court who asked him, Blindman Shim was
struck with awe.

"In truth, I have neither home nor family. I take heaven and earth for
my house; I plant my feet on the ground and wander about the world. Since

I clearly lack any village for a residence, I could not enter myself in the register of names and just walked in on my own."

The Empress was pleased.

"Bring him into audience!"

The ladies of the court, receiving this order, took Blindman Shim by the hand to lead him into a detached palace. Blindman Shim was quite unaware. He entered the detached palace, frightened and unable to control his steps, and stood at the foot of the stairs.

She did not recognize Blindman Shim's face. His white hair had grown thin and the Empress, having spent three years in the Dragon's Palace, only dimly remembered her father's face. She asked, "Do you have a wife [2:33b] and children?"

He prostrated himself and answered as his tears flowed.

아무연분에상처

"In a certain year I lost my wife *chung mori*
And was left with just my daughter,
Who was motherless in her first seven days.
Even though my eyes were dim,
I held the little baby in my arms
And begged her mother's milk to drink.
With difficulty I brought her up;
But steadily she grew apace.
Her filiality was native,
Surpassing people of the past.

"There came a wicked monk, who said
My eyes would open and I would see
If I offered up three hundred sacks
Of sacrificial rice.
Your servant's daughter heard this talk.
Unable to sit calmly by
Without another course to take,
She sold herself to Nanking sailors—
While your servant never knew—
For three hundred sacks of rice.
As a sacrifice at the Indang Sea
She drowned and died,
At fifteen years of age.

"Not only are my eyes not opened
But I have also lost my daughter.
There is no place in this world
For a man to live who sells his child.
I pray you take my life!"

[2:3

The Empress listened tearfully. From the details of what she heard, she   a
knew he was indeed her father. But, with the bond between father and
child, how could she have waited for him to finish speaking? Actually, such
is done to fashion a story.

He has barely finished speaking   *chajin n*
When the Empress leaps to stocking feet
And dashes down to embrace her father.

"Father! I am really
Your daughter Shim Ch'ŏng
Who was drowned at the Indang Sea!"

Blindman Shim is astounded.
"What talk is this?"

How glad he is!
Suddenly, his two eyes—
With a sound like a falling rain-hat—
His two eyes are suddenly bright!
The many blind men there assembled,
At the sound of Blindman Shim's eyes opening,
All at once roll their eyes
With a crackling sound like
Magpie chicks being fed.

All blind men's eyes are bright.
Blind men who are in their homes,
And eyes of blind women, too, are bright.
Those blind before or after birth,
Those half-blind
And even those whose clear eyes cannot see,

The eyes of every one of them grows bright.
For blind men,
It is the dawning of a world.

[2:34b]

Blindman Shim was glad, indeed he was glad. But when he opened his   *aniri*
eyes to see, this was, actually, a stranger. She said she was his daughter and,
hence, he knew it to be so; but it was a face he had never known at all.
Could he know her? Nearly expiring for joy, he danced and sang.

"Joyful! Joyful!   *chung chung mori*
All sing praise!

"However well Hsiang Chuang
May have done his dance
At the high feast in Hung-men,[239]
How could he match my dance?
When Han Kao-tsu on horseback
Gained control of the world
They say he did a sword dance well,
But, oh-ho! Could that touch my dance?

"Ah, lo! People of the world!
More precious the birth of a girl than a boy![240]
To see once more
My daughter Shim Ch'ŏng who had died—
Has Yang Kuei-fei, who died,
Been born again?
Has the beauty Yü
Returned to life again?

"No matter how you look at it,
She's my daughter, Shim Ch'ŏng!
Thanks to her, my eyes are opened—
Again I can enjoy the brightness of
The sun and the moon.
As an auspicious star appears
And portentous clouds arise:
The officials all respond in song.[241]
I see again the world of Yao and Shun.

"Joyful! Joyful!
More precious the birth of a girl than a boy   [2:35a]
Was said with me in mind!"

Innumerable other blind men also danced their dances, as innocent as   *aniri*
newborns!

"Joyful! Joyful!   *chung chung mori*
All sing praise!

"Oh, time! Oh, time! Do not move on!
Springtime that has gone
Can also come again;
But, when you and I grow old,
It's difficult to be young once more.

"It is said in texts of yore that
Time evades our grasp.
These words of wise and ancient
Mencius and Confucius.
What is there for us to do?"

He sang again, "Long life! Long life to Her Majesty!"   *anir*
That same day, Blindman Shim was dressed in court robes and, following court etiquette, attended the morning reception. The Empress called
him into audience again at the inner palace, where he expressed the lonely
thoughts that he had harbored and told her every detail of Blindwoman An.
Hearing of this, the Empress dispatched a palanquin to have An-ssi escorted
thither and caused to be together with her father.

The Emperor commanded that Shim Hak-kyu be given the title, Father
of the Empress, and that An-ssi be ennobled as Lady Chŏngnyŏl. Further-   [2:35b]
more, he presented Lady Chang especially with much gold and silver, suspended labor duties for the people of Tohwa Ward, and presented much
gold and silver to them to help others who might be in trouble. Thus were
his commands. The whole world resounded with his benevolence, which
the people of Tohwa regarded as great as the skies and seas. He recalled the
Prefect of Mujang and had him promoted to duty as the Magistrate of Yeju.[242]

He instructed the magistrate immediately to apprehend Blindman Hwang and Ppaengdŏk's mother. His orders were strict. The Magistrate of Yeju sent out an order to the three hundred and six jurisdictions for the capture and dispatch of Blindman Hwang and Ppaengdŏk's mother.

With the Father of the Empress sitting in judgment at Ch'ŏnch'ŏng Hall, Blindman Hwang and Ppaengdŏk's mother were brought in. The Father of the Empress interrogated them on the spot.

"You heartless wretch! What did you mean by leaving—in the depth of the night and in the midst of endless mountain ranges—a blind man who was unable to distinguish heaven from earth, only to take up with Blindman Hwang?"

"I was led astray by the woman of a man named Chŏngyŏn, who keeps an inn at the post-station."

The Father of the Empress, in a heightening rage, had Ppaengdŏk's [2:36a] mother drawn and quartered. He then called for Blindman Hwang and spoke to him.

"You merciless fellow! Are you not a blind man, too? You may enjoy luring away another man's wife—but the man who has been left, is he not to be pitied? Even though you would be what they call a 'butterfly mad for the flowers,' how could you have done this? It would be appropriate to kill you but, since I only send you into exile, bear me no resentment! I am doing this to forestall bad behavior and to prevent men of later generations from modeling themselves after such an improper affair as this."

Thus he spoke and gave his instructions. All the officials of the court and the people of the realm sang praises of such virtuous influence.

Our progeny·are prosperous and the world is at peace;
Empress Shim's virtuous influence o'erspreads the Four Seas.
We pray for a dynasty linking generations over many myriad years
And humbly pray that it be, indeed, an eternity.[243]

The Empress addressed the Emperor.

"There has never been such happiness before; let us hold a Feast of Great Peace!"

The Emperor approved and let it be known throughout the realm. All [2:36b] the best dancers and singers were summoned, a place was set for the Emperor in the Hwanggŭk Palace, and all the officials of the court were gathered to celebrate. The kings of the various countries obediently presented the treasures of the world; and the best singers and the best dancers, sum-

moned from across the realm, almost all appeared. Embarked on an age of
wisdom and peace, the people in every locality danced and sang.

> "The lofty virtue of   *chung mor*
> Our heaven-sent filial Empress
> O'erspreads the Four Seas!
> Under the sun and moon of Yao
> And within the heaven and earth of Shun,
> The song of a boy at the crossroads meant such joy[244]
> That the vast oceans were fermented
> To make Great Peace Wine
> And both sovereign and people were drunk together,
> Joyful for many generations.
> At a Feast of Great Peace like this,
> Who would not be joyful?"

While they sang thus, the Emperor and the Father of the Empress took   *anir*
their places in the Hwanggŭk Palace and called forth famous dancers and
singers. After they had feasted for three days to the pleasure of high and
low alike with songs, dances, plays, jests, and the music of harps and lutes,
the Emperor, Empress, and the Father of the Empress all returned to the
palace.

The story changes.   [2:37a]

각
설
이
때
에
항
후

At this time, the Empress and An-ssi, now Lady Chŏngnyŏl, both
became pregnant in the same month of the same year and then both
bore sons in the same month. When she heard that her father had
gained a son, the gentle-hearted Empress announced it to the Emperor
even before her own. The Emperor, too, was glad and made presents
of much fabric, gold, silver, and silk. He then dispatched an official of
ceremonies to ask after their comfort.

The Father of the Empress could not measure the overwhelming joy in
his happy heart at having produced a son in his declining years facing eighty.
In addition, the Emperor had sent him gold, silver, silk, and fabrics and an
important official to inquire! Awed and grateful, he prostrated himself with
reverence and endlessly acclaimed the Imperial Blessing to the official of
ceremonies.

And the Empress, further pleased, also conferred gold, silver, and treasures upon him and sent an official of ceremonies to inquire. The Father of

the Empress, even further gladdened, prepared himself in court robes and followed the official of ceremonies into the detached palace where he presented himself to the Empress. But while the Empress, too, had borne a son, how could he ever reckon the joy within his heart? The Empress took [2:37b] her father's hand and, thinking of past events, was both happy and sad. At this, the Father of the Empress, too, was saddened.

At this time, the Father of the Empress, following the official of ceremonies, was returning to his residence when he came to the foot of the Jade Steps. The Emperor praised him greatly.

"From what I hear, you have received a precious child in old age. He is, furthermore, of the same root and born in the same month and year as my prince. Is this not a happy thing? On another day, when he has become a clear and bright youth, I shall discuss the affairs of state with him."

To this the courtier replied, "In ancient times, Confucius said, 'To bear a son is not difficult, to raise him is; to raise a son is not difficult, to teach him is.' Let us wait and see."

He finished speaking and withdrew. He looked on his baby's face. It had a generous look and a handsome physiognomy that was truly modeled on men of yore.

Named T'ae-dong, he grew little by little and reached the age of ten.[245] He was without peer in his intelligence and prudence and was skilled in literature and music. Could the love of his mother and father have been [2:38a] compared to holding treasured jade in hand? Pitiless time flowed like the waters and he reached the age of thirteen.

At this time, the Empress was intent on sending the Crown Prince off in marriage and proposed to the Emperor that the nephew and uncle born on the same day of the same month be married. The Emperor was pleased and ordered a wide search.

At this time, it happened that the Secretary of State, Kwŏn Sŏng-un, had a daughter with the virtue of a T'ai Jen, the talent of a Pan Chao and, in her person, surpassed the beauty Yü.[246]

At this time, the King of Yŏn had a princess named Princess Anyang. The Emperor heard that she was of surpassing virtue and adept at every task. He ordered the King of Yŏn and Secretary of State Kwŏn to appear in audience and, when they were in his presence, proposed marriages to them. The princess and the maiden were the same age of sixteen. Permission was happily given and the Emperor spoke to his court.

"How would it be for the maiden Kwŏn to be made the spouse of the

Crown Prince and for the princess of the King of Yŏn to be taken for the spouse of T'ae-dong?"

All answered him, saying, "That is proper."

The Empress, the Father of the Empress, and the imperial court were [2:38b] all pleased. The Emperor ordered the Court Astrologer to select a day: it was the fifteenth day of the third month of spring.

As a felicitous court event, the day was auspicious and a great feast was prepared. Lords from every locality and all the officials of the court stood as imperial guard in order of rank and the two ladies, escorted by three thousand ladies of the court who assisted on all sides, took their places at the nuptial dais.

The two grooms, like the sun and moon, were escorted by officers of the court. It was as if they were ushered by the attendants of Ursa Major. The brides were fair as May in red and green garments adorned with the seven jewels, every kind of ornatment hanging at their waists, and flowered crowns on their heads.

First-rate beauties were selected from among the assembled three thousand women of the court to serve as escorts to the left and right of the two brides. Even Heng-o of the Lunar Palace could not have been more dazzling than this.

They met at the nuptial dais, where splendid, brilliantly embroidered curtains rose high into the void. The brilliance of the interior of the palace would be difficult to describe in a single word.

After the two grooms had each presented his mandarin duck[247] and [2:39a] given silks, they both retired to take their places in their residences. On their first night in the bridal chamber by nuptial candlelight, they passed the night quietly in high spirits like mandarin ducks meeting on blue waters.

Emerging, it was the Crown Prince who first met the Secretary of State. The joy of the Secretary and his lady was quite beyond reckoning.

At this time, T'ae-dong, for his part, presented himself to the King and Queen of Yŏn. Both the King and Queen were pleased and boundlessly glad.

Soon thereafter, T'ae-dong, together with the Crown Prince, went forth to prostrate themselves at the morning court. The Emperor was pleased and called the Father of the Empress into audience to sit together and receive the first greetings of the newlyweds. After the court officials finished their morning audience, the Emperor spoke to them.

"Previously I had expressed my intent that T'ae-dong enter the court but that was before his marriage. Until now, he has had no official rank. What is your opinion on this?"

The civil and military officials all replied, "The man is excellent; we pray you instruct us immediately."

Hence, the Emperor forthwith called T'ae-dong before him and bestowed rank, conferring upon him the title of Hallim Scholar, Royal Tutor, and the honorary office of Third Minister of Personnel. The Emperor ennobled his wife as Lady Wangyŏl and presented them with much gold, silver, and fabric. [2:39b]

"You were earlier a student of classic texts and so had not helped in the governance of the realm. But from this day forward, as a remunerated state official, assist in the governance of the realm, as exhaustive in loyalty as in effort!"

The groom prostrated himself, then withdrew and went to see his mother. With what words could one describe her happy, joyful heart? Then, going into the detached palace, he expressed his gratitude before the Empress. Though overcome with happiness, the Empress asked, "How do you find your wife?"

T'ae-dong modestly shifted in his seat.

"I have found her chaste and pure."

The Empress asked further, "What rank was given you when you attended court this morning?"

"I received thus and such."[248]

The Empress, even further pleased, passed the day enjoying the company of the Crown Prince and the groom but, as the sun was setting, ended the feast.

"You must quickly proceed to your new homes!"

T'ae-dong replied to her, "I shall take her quickly and bring glory to my parents." [2:40a]

The Empress was very happy.

"That is what I would ask of you."

And so, for this day, the Crown Prince and the Hallim Scholar withdrew.

Several days later, the Father of the Empress selected a date and had Lady Wangyŏl move into her husband's home. The lady went before her parents-in-law and presented herself according to etiquette. The Father of the Empress and Lady Chŏngnyŏl loved and prized her like gold and jade.

A new detached palace was built where Lady Wangnyŏl was caused to take up residence.

The story changes.

At this time, the Hallim Scholar by day made plans for affairs of state and at night devoted himself to studying the Way. There was no one who did not praise him, not to mention the grand and lesser officials and the common people.

In this way and that, the Hallim Scholar's age reached twenty.

At this time, the Emperor inquired into the Hallim Scholar's reputation and moral character through the court officials. One day he called the Scholar Shim into court and spoke.

"I have heard that your reputation and moral character are known throughout the realm. How could I begrudge you rank?"

He promoted him to high rank, making him President of the Board of Personnel and a member of the National Academy.

"Be a comrade to the Crown Prince!"   [2:40b]

Furthermore, the Emperor elevated his father's rank, entitling him as King Namp'yŏng; he gave Lady Chŏngnyŏl An-ssi the title of Queen Insŏng; he further added the title Lady Kongnyŏl to that of Lady Wangnyŏl, held by the President's lady.[249] King Namp'yŏng, the President's lady, and Queen Insŏng all acclaimed the imperial benevolence.

"What good works have we done to be given such rank as this?" they said, singing praises of the Emperor for his generosity day and night.

At this time, King Namp'yŏng had reached the age of eighty[250] and happened to fall ill but even one hundred medicines were ineffective. At this point, no matter how the gentle and filial Empress and his good-hearted lady tried to cure the illness, a man to die cannot be called back. In just seven days he departed the world. The whole family was deeply grieved and the Empress, lamenting, also notified the Emperor. The Emperor spoke.

"It has been rare from days of yore for men to reach eighty. Please do not grieve overly."

The Emperor ordered that he be laid to rest in the Myŏngnŭng Gardens with the rites due a king and also instructed the Empress to enter mourning for three years.

When we think of the hardships the Father of the Empress faced when [2:41a] he was young, what lingering regrets can we have?

Ah! People of the world!   *chante*

Is there a difference between then and now?

Think not lightly of men
By speaking of riches and glory!
Sadness follows the greatest joy
And sweetness follows the greatest pain!
Of all humankind this is true.
The fair name of Empress Shim
Has been passed over the years.

NOTES
BIBLIOGRAPHY
INDICES

NOTES

Introduction: Of Singers and Tales

1. Traditional epigram quoted in Cho Dong-il, "P'ansori ŭi chŏnbanjŏk sŏnggyŏk," p. 20.

2. Such an opening song is known variously as *tan'ga* (short song), *hŏduga* (head song), *ch'oduga* (head song), and *mok p'unŭn sori* (throat-clearing song).

3. Interview tape-recorded on March 29, 1972. For more on Kim So-hŭi, see Chapter Six.

4. Lee Ki-baik, *Han'guk sa shillon,* pp. 236–237.

5. Yi Pyŏng-do, et al., eds., *Han'guk tae paekkwa sajŏn,* I, 54.

6. In its earliest use, in the late-Koryŏ and early-Chosŏn periods, the word *kwang-dae* meant either "mask" or "puppet" without distinction. Though it continued in these uses, *kwangdae* was also applied to the actor who performed in a mask-drama, beginning as early as the Koryŏ period. See Lee Duhyŏn, *Han'guk kamyŏn kŭk,* pp. 39–43, 124.

7. Lee Duhyŏn, *Han'guk yŏn'gŭk sa,* p. 105.

8. Ibid., pp. 93, 105; Pak Hŏn-bong, *Ch'angak taegang,* p. 47; and Cho Dong-il, *Han'guk munhak t'ongsa,* II, p. 474.

9. Some seminal research on the shaman connection: Kim Dong-uk, "P'ansori pal-saeng ko," I and II, passim; Pak Hŏn-bong, pp. 45–48; Kim T'ae-gon, " 'Shim Ch'ŏng chŏn' ŭi kŭnwŏn sŏlhwa: muga rŭl t'ong-han koch'al," pp. 86–101; Cho Dong-il, "P'an-sori ŭi chŏnbanjŏk sŏnggyŏk," pp. 16–17; Seo Dae-seok, "P'ansori wa sŏsa muga ŭi taebi yŏn'gu," pp. 7–44; Im Chin-t'aek, "Sarainnŭn p'ansori," pp. 306–318; and B. C. A. Walraven, *Muga: The Songs of Korean Shamanism,* pp. 96–101.

10. Cho Dong-il, "P'ansori ŭi chŏnbanjŏk sŏnggyŏk," p. 16.

11. Chŏng No-sik, *Chosŏn ch'anggŭk sa,* p. 184.

1. Where Did the Kwangdae Come From?

1. Patrick D. Hanan, "The Development of Fiction and Drama," p. 119. Hanan develops the question of borrowing between Chinese literatures at greater length throughout *The Chinese Short Story.*

2. The early Shilla word used to designate the king, *ch'ach'aung,* meant "shaman." The eighth-century scholar Kim Tae-mun is quoted in the *Samguk sagi* as defining *ch'ach'aung* in the following words: "This means shaman. The shaman waits upon the spirits and gods and conducts religious services. Therefore, the people respect him with awe. Accordingly, they call their chief a shaman." See Kim Pu-shik, *Samguk sagi,* pp. 4, 18.

3. Although the *Samguk sagi* reports establishment of the *hwarang* order in the thirty-seventh year of King Chinhŭng (576), it is widely assumed that this was no more than the nationalization of a communal organization that had already been in existence before then.

4. Richard Rutt, "Flower Boys of Silla," p. 23. The only thorough and scholarly treatment of the *hwarang* in English, Rutt cites the major sources in Korean and Japanese. On pp. 30–46, he shows that members of the *hwarang* order were chosen and enrolled, and that membership was not hereditary. He also emphasizes that they were not members for life, a fact which would distinguish them from professional shamans.

5. Lee Ki-baik, p. 84.

6. Ibid., p. 82.

7. Ichiro Hori, *Folk Religion in Japan,* pp. 141–179. Hori relates Japanese mountain worship to that of other cultures and concludes, "Japanese mountain worship . . . has preserved many features of ancient shamanism which can be traced to the prehistoric period."

8. For names of famous *hwarang* of high birth and their selection, see Rutt, "Flower Boys," pp. 30–46.

9. An Kye-hyŏn, "P'algwanhoe ko," as cited in Rutt, "Flower Boys," p. 54.

10. Lee Duhyŏn, *Han'guk yŏn'gŭk sa,* p. 27.

11. Cho Dong-il, *T'ongsa,* I, 40.

12. Kim Dong-uk, "P'ansori palsaeng ko," I and II; and Pak Hŏn-bong, p. 45ff.

13. Cho Dong-il, *T'ongsa,* II, 171; Lee Duhyŏn, *Han'guk yŏn'gŭk sa,* p. 69.

14. Lee Duhyŏn, *Han'guk yŏn'gŭk sa,* p. 65.

15. Ibid., p. 79–81.

16. Ibid., p. 61.

17. The two poems are "Sandae chapkŭk" (Stage theatricals) and "Kunahaeng" (Visiting an exorcism), preserved in the 25-book *Mogŭn chip* (Mogŭn's collection), Yi Saek's collected papers, which were published posthumously by his descendants.

18. Lee Duhyŏn, *Han'guk yŏn'gŭk sa,* p. 63.

19. Kim Dong-uk, "P'ansori palsaeng ko," I, 177ff; Pak Hŏn-bong, pp. 45ff.

20. Kim T'ae-gon, "Han'guk musok ŭi chiyŏk chŏk t'ŭkching," pp. 35–38.

21. Han'guk munhwa illyuhak-hoe, *Han'guk minsok chonghap chosa pogosŏ, chŏnnam-p'yŏn,* p. 189–219. This is one small part of a massive report on popular culture sponsored by the Korean government.

22. Ibid., p. 207.

23. For the development of Japanese narrative, see Barbara Ruch, "Medieval Jon-

gleurs and the Making of a National Literature." In Japan, religious establishments—both Buddhist monasteries and Shinto shrines—emerged as major cultural centers with the decline of central authority during the 400-year medieval epoch that followed the end of the Heian period in 1185. During the comparatively tranquil middle years of that epoch, a time known as the Muromachi period (1336–1573), a popular literary tradition emerged and was carried along the highways and into the villages by a variety of jongleurs: both secular professionals in search of a livelihood and proselytizing priests and nuns in search of converts. Barbara Ruch says that these medieval entertainers "did more than probably any other groups to build what can be called Japan's first body of a truly national literature and to spread it throughout the country." In a manner reminiscent of the Chinese experience, the rise of these jongleurs was facilitated by the powerful monasteries and shrines that afforded them home, audience, protection, and patronage.

24. Kim Dong-uk, "P'ansori palsaeng ko," I, 185.

25. Cho Dong-il, *T'ongsa*, II, 469.

26. Lee Duhyŏn, *Han'guk Kamyŏn kŭk*, pp. 129–132; Lee Duhyŏn, *Han'guk yŏn'gŭk sa*, p. 71; and Kim Dong-uk, *Han'guk kayo ŭi yŏn'gu*, pp. 288–292. The English terminology is taken from Lee Duhyŏn, *Kamyŏn kŭk*, pp. 443–444.

27. The Sino-Korean terms used in the *Shillok* (Veritable records) are *kyushik chihŭi* for spectacle show, *sohak chihŭi* for farce, and *ŭmak* for music. See Lee Duhyŏn, *Han'guk yŏn'gŭk sa*, p. 71.

28. Yang Chae-yŏn, "Sandaehŭi e ch'wi-hayŏ," pp. 191–200. Yang describes and documents eleven types of occasions which called for a *sandaehŭi* performance.

29. Lee Duhyŏn, *Kamyŏn kŭk*, p. 130; and Yang Chae-yŏn, p. 200.

Tung Yueh's "Ch'ao-hsien fu" has been translated by Richard Rutt in *Transactions of the Royal Asiatic Society Korea Branch* 49:29–73 (1973). Rutt, however, does not render into English the explicit comparison Tung Yueh makes between the size of the stage and the main palace gate, Kwanghwa-mun.

A later description of the visit of a Chinese ambassador comes from the pen of the Dutch shipwreck survivor, Hendrick Hamel, who lived thirteen years in Korea (1653–1666) and reported a visit of the Ch'ing envoy in the 1650s in which *sandaehŭi* performers took part: "When the *Tartar's* Embassador comes, the King goes in Person with all his Court out of Town to receive him, waits upon him to his Lodging, and in all places everybody does him as much or more honour than to the King. All sorts of Musicians, Dancers, and Vaulters, go before him, striving who shall divert him most." From Gari Ledyard, *The Dutch Come to Korea*, p. 225

30. Yang Chae-yŏn, pp. 199–202, provides a physical description of the *sandaehŭi* stage that testifies to the importance and scale of these undertakings. At its largest, the outdoor stage was a raised platform of about thirty by forty feet; at the back and on two sides were curtains of about forty feet in height, held up by many vertical bamboo poles. Smaller stages, built for lesser occasions, had the same relative proportions. A passage in the *Kwanghaegun ilgi* describes the structure erected on the occasion of the visit of a Chinese embassy in 1582. Two groups of four stages were built, facing each other, that required the labors of 1,300 to 1,400 soldiers (*Kwanghaegun* 156:1b, quoted in Yang Chae-yŏn, p. 199). Such heights made the work dangerous enough that a safety net was sometimes needed (*Chungjong shillok* 43:37b–38a, as quoted in Yang Chae-yŏn p. 200).

Many workers were crushed to death when one of these structures collapsed in 1623 (*Injong shillok* 2:51b, as quoted in Yang Chae-yŏn p. 200).

31. Yang Chae-yŏn, p. 210.

32. Cho Dong-il, *T'ongsa*, II, 470.

33. For an example, see Lee Duhyŏn, *Han'guk yŏn'gŭk sa*, p. 99.

34. Pak Hŏn-bong, p. 49.

35. Kim Dong-uk, *Han'guk kayo ŭi yŏn'gu*, pp. 351–352; and Lee Duhyŏn, *Kamyŏn kŭk*, p. 134. Ch'oe Nam-sŏn, *Chosŏn sangsik mundap sokp'yŏn*, p. 335, remarks on the professional lives of these wandering performers: "They did not enjoy any special patronage of a positive sort and barely managed to survive in their position at the lowest levels of society. And there they simply languished without development; their worth could only fall and they knew no improvement. But this, actually, was only to be expected. Under such conditions as these, a thousand years may as well have been a day, for they never went beyond some facile talent and humorous sketches. In the end, they never achieved the birth and growth of the pure drama found elsewhere. This, too, was impossible for them."

36. Lee Duhyŏn, *Han'guk yŏn'gŭk sa*, p. 87.

37. Cho Dong-il, *T'ongsa*, II, 470.

38. *Myŏngjong shillok* 27:69b, as quoted in Yang Chae-yŏn, p. 210.

39. Yang Chae-yŏn, p. 209.

40. *Sejong shillok* 53:7a, as quoted in Yang Chae-yŏn, p. 209.

41. *Chungjong shillok* 83:66b, as quoted in Yang Chae-yŏn, p. 210.

42. *Sŏnjo shillok* 198:11b, as quoted in Yang Chae-yŏn, p. 209.

43. *Sukchong shillok* 38a:7a–13b, as quoted in Yang Chae-yŏn, p. 209.

44. An 1824 document (*Kapshin wanmun*) regarding the "Chaein of the Eight Provinces" states that "stages of the left and right were not erected for performance after the year of *kapchin* [1784]."

45. Yang Chae-yŏn, p. 210.

46. Yi Ik, *Sŏngho sasŏl*, as quoted in Yang Chae-yŏn, p. 210.

47. Lee Duhyŏn, *Han'guk yŏn'gŭk sa*, p. 73.

48. Cho Dong-il, *T'ongsa*, II, 472.

49. Ibid., II, 473.

50. Peter H. Lee, *A Korean Storyteller's Miscellany*, p. 124.

51. Cho Dong-il, *T'ongsa*, II, 473–474; Lee Duhyŏn, *Han'guk yŏn'gŭk sa*, p. 96.

52. Peter H. Lee, *A Korean Storyteller's Miscellany*, p. 124.

53. Cho Dong-il, *T'ongsa*, II, 477.

54. Lee Ki-baik, pp. 299–302.

55. Yi Ik, *Sŏngho sasŏl*, as quoted in Yang Chae-yŏn, p. 211.

56. Yu Tŭk-kong, *Kyŏngdo chapki*, vol. 1, *yuga*, as quoted in Yang Chae-yŏn, p. 211.

57. This translation is based on Donald N. Clark, "Hanyang ka."

58. Ch'oe Nam-sŏn, p. 334.

59. Yi Hye-gu, "Song Man-jae ŭi 'Kwanuhŭi,'" pp. 112, 119.

60. Ibid., p. 112.

61. Although I have been unable to identify this Pang Ŭng-gyo, there is a possibility that he was related to the Pang Ŭng-gyu mentioned in Pak Hŏn-bong, Explanatory

Notes (pŏmnye), p. 2. Pak identifies the latter Pang as grand-nephew of the early-nineteenth-century master singer Pang Man-ch'un (fl. ca. 1830).

62. Ibid.

63. Akamatsu Chijō and Akiba Takashi, *Chōsen fuzoku no kenkyū*, II, 134, 142.

64. In the terminology of Korean shamanism, as described by Akamatsu and Akiba, a *ch'angbu* is the musician-husband of a shaman who serves as her accompanist on the drum and can also perform as a singer in his own right (II, 31, 33, 209, 234, 281). The "Ch'angbu" section of the *ch'ŏnsin kut* consists of three parts. The first is an invocation addressed to the spirit of a dead *ch'angbu*, and the second is a first-person promise of protection by the spirit who sings through the medium of the shaman. The third part is an account by the shaman (again in the third person) of Creation and ancestral beginnings, followed by a narration of the journeys of *ch'angbu* to the capital where they meet the new licentiates and accompany them back home to perform the *tŏktam* (I, 107–115).

65. Yi Hye-gu, "Song Man-jae ŭi 'Kwanuhŭi,'" p. 111.

2. The Kwangdae's Nineteenth-Century Heyday

1. This text is a translation into Chinese poetry of the content of a performance of the "Song of Ch'un-hyang," which Yu Chin-han of Ch'ungch'ŏng Province witnessed during a visit to Chŏlla Province in 1753. It is found in his literary collection, *Manhwa chip* (Manhwa collection; 1754), which was titled after his pen name. Hence the expression, "Manhwa text." For further detail on Yu Chin-han and the circumstances of his poem, see Chŏng Pyŏng-hŏn, "P'ansori ŭi hyŏngsŏng kwa pyŏnmo," p. 259.

2. Chŏng Pyŏng-hŏn, "P'ansori ŭi hyŏngsŏng kwa pyŏnmo," p. 248.

3. Chŏng No-sik, p. 17.

4. Vena Hrdlickova, "Some Observations on the Chinese Art of Story-telling," p. 59n26, notes that there is a common tendency in oral literatures for later performers to attribute origins of their art to specific earlier individuals or incidents, rather than accept gradual evolution.

5. Pak Hwang, *P'ansori ibaengnyŏn sa*, pp. 82–84.

6. Cho Dong-il, *T'ongsa*, III, 178.

7. Song Bang-song, *Han'guk ŭmak t'ongsa*, p. 454.

8. Chŏng No-shik, pp. 30–31. In relating the same story, Pak Hwang (*P'ansori ibaengnyŏn sa*, p. 105) adds the unique and intriguing but quite undeveloped comment, "It is said that the Shim Ch'ŏng shaman rite was made into p'ansori by Pang Man-ch'un."

9. Cho Dong-il, *T'ongsa*, III, 179.

10. Ibid., III, 180.

11. Lee Ki-baik, pp. 236–237.

12. Pak Hŏn-bong, p. 47, divides entertainers into three categories of ascending difficulty: physical performers (acrobats, rope-walkers, fire-eaters, etc.), instrumentalists, and singers. The performers' strong sense of group identity discouraged participation by outsiders.

13. Chŏng No-sik, pp. 35–36.

14. In that the two lines of descent were identified with two different schools of singing technique, we see that school affiliation was an artistic rather than a political matter. In other cases, marriage across school lines can be cited in Chŏng's study.

15. Kim Dong-uk, *Han'guk kayo ŭi yŏn'gu*, p. 300.

16. Akamatsu and Akiba, II, 31, 33, 209, 234, 281. "The shamans of the south intermarry within their class with a *mubu*, who is also called a *chaein, kongin, kwangdae*, or *hwarang.* . . . He assists the shaman in the invocation of spirits mainly by providing the musical accompaniment. He is an artist specializing in music; and the association of such musically skilled *mubu* is called a *mubu-gye*" (Ibid., II, 131).

17. Ibid., II, 31, 277.

18. Ibid., II, 277.

19. Ibid., II, 284.

20. For text and discussion, see Yi Hye-gu, "Song Man-jae ŭi 'Kwanuhŭi' "; Kim Dong-uk, "P'ansori palsaeng ko, I"; Pak Hŏn-bong, *Ch'angak taegang;* and Kim Dong-uk, *Han'guk kayo ŭi yŏn'gu.* There is further information in Akamatsu and Akiba, II.

21. Yi Hye-gu, "Song Man-jae ŭi 'Kwanuhŭi,' " p. 23. According to Kim Dong-uk, "P'ansori palsaeng ko," I, 186, nn. 5 and 12, the documents were in the collection of Yi Pyŏng-gi (Karam) in 1955. They have probably since entered the library of Seoul National University.

22. Akamatsu and Akiba, II, 285.

23. Kim Dong-uk, "P'ansori palsaeng ko, I," p. 182.

24. Ch'ŏngyang and Kongju, both located in South Ch'ungch'ŏng Province, are separated by about 21 miles.

25. Sohn Pow-key, et al., *The History of Korea*, p. 170.

26. William E. Henthorn (*A History of Korea*, p. 207) quotes Shikata Hiroshi, *Chō-sen keizai no kenkyū, 3* (A study of the economy of Chosŏn, 3) (1938), p. 386.

27. Chŏng No-sik, p. 75.

28. Ibid., pp. 57–58.

3. **Singers in the Twentieth Century**

1. Pak Hwang, *Ch'anggŭk sa yŏn'gu*, p. 16. Pak bases this statement on remarks that had been made by Song Man-gap and Yi Tong-baek. Predecessors of such variety troupes, of course, had already existed at least since Koryŏ times.

2. Ibid., p. 16. The Chinese pronunciation is *hsieh-lü ch'ang-hsi.*

3. Men could not play the roles of women as was done elsewhere in East Asia. Pak Hwang (*Ch'anggŭk sa yŏn'gu*, p. 64) quotes the drummer Han Sŏng-jun, who traveled the southern provinces in 1908 with a ch'anggŭk touring company organized by Song Man-gap. According to Han, the troupe could not perform complete versions of the "Song of Ch'un-hyang" or "Song of Shim Ch'ŏng" because they had only one female kwangdae in their troupe. Therefore they performed only selected scenes from those works. From this we may infer that women were essential to ch'anggŭk and that men were not acceptable in female roles unless performing in the traditional, solo mode.

4. Chŏng No-shik, p. 233.

5. Ibid., p. 234.

6. Pak Hwang, *P'ansori ibaengnyŏn sa,* pp. 122–125. She moved into the palace and lived there until the Taewŏn'gun fell from power in 1873. There is some suggestion that Shin Chae-hyo also had strong feelings for her. She died in 1901, three years after the Taewŏn'gun.

7. She is also called Kang So-hyang.

8. This "dialogue singing" is described in Pak Hwang, *Ch'anggŭk sa yŏn'gu,* pp. 20–21.

9. Such residential areas of late-nineteenth-century Seoul are described in Yi Hyo-jae, "Life in Urban Korea," pp. 16–17.

10. Horace N. Allen, *Korea: Fact and Fancy,* p. 176. "Ryongsan" is Yongsan. This refers to a foreign settlement site in Yongsan by the Han River that had been requested from the Korean government on August 18, 1884 (Allen, p. 167).

11. The only exceptions were high officials, blind men, foreigners, and people going to and from a druggist. For these and other aspects of Seoul in the late nineteenth century and early twentieth century, see "Sŏul by Night" in Percival Lowell, *Chosŏn: The Land of the Morning Calm,* pp. 226–237; "First Impressions of the Capital" in Isabella Bird Bishop, *Korea and Her Neighbours,* pp. 35–48; and "Seoul, the Capital of Korea" in Burton Holmes, *Burton Holmes Travelogues,* X, 5–112.

12. All Bishop quotes are from Isabella Bird Bishop, pp. 435–436.

13. Ibid., pp. 43 and 60.

14. Yi Kyu-tae, *Modern Transformation of Korea,* p. 221.

15. Isabella Bird Bishop, pp. 43–44. She puts the size of the Japanese settlement at 5,000 but this may be on the large side. The total Japanese throughout Korea in 1894 was 9,354 (Chŏng Sang-ch'ŏn, et al., *Seoul yukpaengnyŏn sa,* p. 1111). The mix of foreigners in Seoul by 1897 is reported as Japanese (2,058), Chinese (1,273), American (95), Russian (57), English (37), French (31), German (9), and one lone Dane (Ibid., p. 1120).

16. Pak Hwang, *Ch'anggŭk sa yŏn'gu,* p. 17. We can assume that Yi Tong-baek spoke with authority regarding Kang Yong-hwan and the theatrical version of the "Song of Ch'un-hyang" because they were close colleagues and also performed together. They played the two leading male roles in that first adaptation of p'ansori for the stage. When considered as a model for the staging of p'ansori, this Chinese opera performed in Seoul is particularly noteworthy in that it used no scenery, equipment, or props and relied solely on gesture; that it combined singing with spoken dialogue; and that, while several performers appeared at the same time, each performer was assigned only one role. (Pak Hwang, *P'ansori ibaengnyŏn sa,* p. 136–138).

17. Quoted in Yu Ik-sŏ, *Myŏngin myŏngch'ang,* p. 28. But Ch'oe Wŏn-shik, " 'Ŭn-segye' yŏn'gu," p. 282, gives the year as 1906 instead of 1904.

18. Ibid.

19. Two theaters were located along Chongno (one was the Tansŏngsa) and two in Yongsan. Others were near the East Gate street car barns, outside West Gate, and in Sadong. See Ch'oe Wŏn-shik, p. 283.

20. The theater did not become widely known as the Hŭidae. Rather, it soon became known by the name of its administrative organ, Hyŏmnyulsa, and then, later on, was named after the famous Wŏngaksa company that used it in 1908–1909 and produced a ch'anggŭk there called "Silver World."

21. Ch'oe Wŏn-shik, p. 284.

22. Ch'oe Nam-sŏn, pp. 344–346. The translation is abridged and tightened.

23. The case for this origin and sequence of the play and novel, "Silver World," has been made persuasively in Ch'oe Wŏn-shik, "Ŭnsegye yŏn'gu."

24. On the antipathy between the performers and the pro-Japanese establishment, see Pak Hwang, *Ch'anggŭk sa yŏn'gu*, pp. 45–46; Pak Hwang, *P'ansori ibaengnyŏn sa*, pp. 147–149; and Cho Dong-il, *T'ongsa*, IV, 385–387.

25. This person, called the *toch'ang* (lead singer), took a position to one side of the action that was unfolding on the stage, according to Ch'oe Chong-min of the Academy of Korean Studies Music Department (in conversation, summer 1990).

26. Pak Hwang, *Ch'anggŭk sa yŏn'gu*, pp. 22–24.

27. Quoted by Pak Hwang, *P'ansori ibaengnyŏn sa*, pp. 142–144.

28. Ibid., pp. 149–150. The following description of the touring company is drawn from this source.

29. Ibid.

30. Ibid., p. 150.

31. These resurrected works included "Tale of the Maiden Sug-yŏng" (*Sug-yŏng nangja chŏn*; 1936), "Tale of Chief Aide Pae" (*Pae-bijang chŏn*; 1937), and "Tale of Ong Ko-jip" (*Ong Ko-jip chŏn*; 1938). See the next chapter for more detail on the forms in which p'ansori survived.

32. This survey is based upon tabular materials in Pak Hwang, *Ch'anggŭk sa yŏn'gu*, pp. 243–245.

33. Chang Duk-soon, et al., eds., *Han'guk kubi munhak sŏnjip*, pp. 269–270.

34. Pak Hwang, *Ch'anggŭk sa yŏn'gu*, pp. 115–118.

35. Ibid., pp. 119–120.

36. For a list, see Pak Hwang, *Ch'anggŭk sa yŏn'gu*, p. 111.

37. Ibid., pp. 269–270.

38. Hyun's Western-style opera, composed in the spring of 1950, was given seventy-six performances in four productions during the decade of the 1950s. In addition to Hyun's adaptation, critic James Wade reports in the *Korea Journal* (December 1966, p. 45) "there was a little-known grand opera on the same subject by a Japanese composer, very much in the Italianate manner, printed in Japan in the early 1940s." In the same article, Wade reviews yet another grand opera treatment of Ch'un-hyang which was mounted in October 1966. If one also includes Father William Quiery's 1965 musical comedy version in English for his Sŏgang University students, that makes four Westernized treatments.

39. The "Song of Ch'un-hyang" in 1987, "Tale of Chief Aide Pae" in 1988, and "Song of Shim Ch'ŏng" in April and May of 1989.

4. How Did P'ansori Evolve?

1. The rise of Buddhist monastic establishments often coincided with periods of political disunion and weakened central authority: during the Six Dynasties period in China (third to sixth centuries); from late Shilla through the Koryŏ period in Korea

(ninth to fourteenth centuries); and from late Kamakura through the Muromachi period in Japan (thirteenth to sixteenth centuries).

2. John L. Bishop, *The Colloquial Short Story in China,* p. 3. Many of the stories with which Chinese Buddhist monks illustrated the meaning of their religion to an illiterate audience had a content and structure derived directly from intermediate versions of Indian tales that were later to constitute the stuff of such Pali collections as the *Jātaka Book* (Buddha birth stories; ca. A.D. 440).

3. Edwin O. Reischauer, *Ennin's Travels in T'ang China,* pp. 183–187.

4. Ibid., pp. 165, 282.

5. Ibid., pp. 281–283.

6. Ruch, p. 288.

7. Kenneth D. Butler, Jr., "Textual Evolution of the *Heike monogatari,*" pp. 5–6. This article is drawn from his unpublished dissertation, "The Birth of an Epic."

8. Peter H. Lee, "Introduction to the Chang'ga," p. 98.

9. Yi Pyŏng-do et al., eds., I, 568, 597.

10. Lee Ki-baik, p. 185.

11. Yi Man-yŏl, *Han'guk sa yŏnp'yo,* p. 51.

12. Lee Ki-baik, p. 186.

13. Ibid., p. 191.

14. Cho Dong-il, "P'ansori ŭi chŏnbanjŏk sŏnggyŏk," p. 17.

15. Cho Dong-il, *T'ongsa,* III, 506.

16. The spirit of the shrine, whose history is narrated in song by a shaman in the context of ritual, has the attributes of a mythic hero. Like the hero of a foundation myth, this spirit is born in hardship, survives difficult trials, demonstrates surpassing powers, achieves a position of glory, and leads a hero's life. This biographical pattern is discussed in detail in Kim Yŏl-gyu, *Han'guk minsok gwa munhak yŭon'gu,* pp. 53–74.

17. This summary of the narrative folk song is based on Cho Dong-il, *T'ongsa,* III, 512–513.

18. This point of view can be found early in Yi Hye-gu, "Song Man-jae ŭi 'Kwanuhŭi' "; Chang Chu-gŭn, "Han'guk kubi munhak sa"; and Cho Sŏng, "Miji ŭi kut kwa muga." It was carried forward by Seo Dae-seok in "P'ansori hyŏngsŏng ŭi sabŭi" and "P'ansori wa sŏsa muga."

19. Cho Dong-il, *T'ongsa,* III, 515.

20. Seo Dae-seok "P'ansori hyŏngsŏng ŭi sabŭi."

21. In comparing performance forms, Seo Dae-seok finds several striking similarities: public attitude toward the singing as a festive event, supportive function of the accompanist and his cries of encouragement, alternation between speech and song and the function of the speech, and the use of dramatic gesture to supplement the content of the narrative song ("P'ansori wa sŏsa muga," pp. 13–15).

22. Self-accompaniment can be found among shamans and student singers of p'ansori. See Seo Dae-seok, "P'ansori wa sŏsa muga," pp. 11 and 15.

23. Kim Dong-uk, *Han'guk kayo ŭi yŏn'gu,* p. 322.

24. Cho Dong-il, *T'ongsa,* III, 516.

25. Song Man-jae's Chinese poem was thoroughly annotated in Yi Hye-gu, "Song Man-jae ŭi kwanuhŭi." Yi Hye-gu's seminal work has been reprinted in Yi Hye-gu,

Han'guk ŭmak yŏn'gu; Cho Dong-il et al., *P'ansori ŭi ihae;* and Hŏ Kyu et al., *P'ansori yŏn'gu.*

26. Kim Dong-uk, "P'ansori sa yŏng'gu ŭi che munje," p. 20.

27. Yi Hye-gu, "Song Man-jae ŭi 'Kwanuhŭi,' " p. 114.

28. Chŏng No-shik, pp. 11–12.

29. Kang Han-yŏng, ed., *Shin Chae-hyo p'ansori sasŏl chip.*

30. Originally published in 1933, later reprinted in Yi Ch'ang-bae, *Kayo chipsŏng,* pp. 467–522.

31. Kang Han-yŏng, "Shin Chae-hyo ŭi p'ansori sasŏl yŏn'gu," p. 29, gives estimated dates when Shin may have been working on each of his six manuscripts.

32. Yu Ik-sŏ, *Myŏngin myŏngch'ang,* p. 40.

33. Quoted by Ch'oe Wŏn-shik, p. 277.

34. Ch'oe Wŏn-shik, pp. 275–279; and Yu Ik-sŏ, *Myŏngin myŏngch'ang,* pp. 40–41. See also Cho Dong-il, *T'ongsa,* IV, 385–386.

35. Cho Dong-il, *T'ongsa,* III, 522. Cho remarks that, in particular, considerable skill is displayed when it describes male and female genitalia in a section called "The Ballad of the Utensils."

36. Cho Dong-il, *T'ongsa,* IV, 52–53.

37. For an introduction to the Parry-Lord theory, see "Structural Organization" in Chapter Five below.

38. Pak Hŏn-bong, *Ch'anggŭk taegang,* Explanatory Notes (pŏmnye), pp. 2–3. Of passing interest is a remark made by Yu Yŏng-dae (*"Shim Ch'ŏng chŏn" yŏn'gu,* p. 33) that "Hyŏn Ch'ŏl's son is now living in the United States and so it is a question whether that singer's text survives or not."

39. Cho Dong-il (*T'ongsa,* III, 522) observes that the libretti can be distinguished from the novels only because descriptive passages using literary language were relatively longer in the novels.

5. *The Nature of the Text*

1. Cho Dong-il, *T'ongsa,* III, 521.

2. Kim Dong-uk, "P'ansori palsaeng ko," I, 201; and Seo Dae-seok, "P'ansori wa sŏsa muga," pp. 28–29.

3. Ibid., p. 30.

4. Ibid., pp. 28–29.

5. Cho Dong-il, "Hŭngbu chŏn ŭi yangmyŏnsŏng," p. 107.

6. The first comprehensive description of this wide distribution was made in Kim T'ae-jun (*Chosŏn sosŏl sa,* pp. 108–115) and is still being quoted.

7. Kim Pu-shik, pp. 750–751, 756; Iryŏn, *Samguk yusa,* pp. 174, 466–467.

8. Ch'oe Sang-su, *Han'guk min'gan chŏnsŏ chip,* pp. 100–101.

9. Kim T'ae-gon, *Hwangch'ŏn muga yŏn'gu.* "Princess Paridegi" is drawn from a ceremony called *ogu kut* (a rite for the recently dead), which Kim T'ae-gon discusses on pp. 35–43. The tale itself is discussed on pp. 124–155 and the full texts of four variants are appended to his work.

10. See Chŏng Pyŏng-uk, "Koshiga ŭmnyullon sŏsŏl," on natural word length and prosody, esp. p. 390. The Korean four-foot line is comparable to the verse form that prevailed in the English language before the time of Chaucer, which was alliterative verse with four stresses per line—a verse rhythm that may be inherent in other Germanic languages as well.

11. See David McCann, *Form and Freedom in Korean Poetry,* pp. 24–46.

12. This question of rhythm and its effect is discussed in Yi Hye-gu, "P'ansori ŭi ŭmakchŏk t'ŭksŏng," esp. pp. 164–166.

13. Albert B. Lord, *The Singer of Tales.*

14. Milman Parry, "Studies in the Epic Technique of Oral Verse-Making," p. 80.

15. Lord, p. 47.

16. Lord, ch. 4, esp. pp. 94–98. Robert Scholes and Robert Kellogg, *The Nature of Narrative,* pp. 26–28, call a theme a *topos,* defining it as a traditional image having two elements: its *motif,* which refers to disembodied concepts and ideas (e.g., the meaning), and its *theme,* which refers to the external world (e.g., the action). In a given traditional *topos,* the same theme and motif are consistently associated with each other—a certain action always has the same meaning. For example, in Shim Ch'ŏng's elaborate visit to the Dragon King's Crystal Palace, we have the *topos* of a journey to another world: the sacred thematic content of shamanistic ritual is associated with this particular journey motif.

17. Lord, pp. 99, 100, 101, respectively.

18. Note the Yugoslav singer's inability to name his song in the interview quoted in Lord, p. 286n2.

19. Almost every biographical entry in Chŏng No-sik, *Ch'angguk sa,* gives selections from the singer's most famous sequences. So closely is wording associated with certain kwangdae that Pak Hŏn-bong (in his *Ch'angak taegang*) is able to attribute systematically the passages of his conflated p'ansori texts to famous kwangdae, both living and dead.

20. In the Wanp'an text of the "Song of Shim Ch'ŏng," the Pledge Episode appears on ff. 1:17a–1:19a and the Crystal Palace Episode, on ff. 2:8a–2:9b. For the convenience of readers, the folios are marked in the translation given in Chapter Eight.

21. Yi Sŏn-yu, *Oga chŏnjip,* pp. 1–55. This was recently reprinted without date by the Korean National Music Research Society, as no. 6 in their series of materials on Korean music.

22. The only substantial example in a major p'ansori work where three characters (two major, one secondary) engage in a three-way exchange of *ch'ang* on equal footing is the Confrontation Episode in the "Song of Ch'un-hyang," involving Ch'un-hyang (the heroine), Yi Mong-nyong (her lover), and Wŏlmae (the heroine's mother).

6. Music, Theory, and Transmission

1. The following comments summarize information which is common knowledge among Korean p'ansori specialists and is available, with only minor variations, in numerous published works. This presentation is based upon the following sources: Cho

Dong-il, *P'ansori ŭi ihae,* pp. 131–197; Chŏng Pyŏng-uk, *Han'guk ŭi p'ansori,* pp. 36–84; Pak Hŏn-bong, *Ch'anggŭk taegang,* pp. 58–73; Song Bang-song, *Han'guk ŭmak t'ongsa,* pp. 453–461; and Yi Po-hyŏng, "P'ansori ran muŏshinya?," pp. 7–16.

2. This is *imyŏn ŭl kŭrinda* (depict the interior) in Korean, a common term in p'ansori criticism.

3. Chŏng Pyŏng-uk, *Han'guk ŭi p'ansori,* p. 38.

4. The song cataloguing flowers in the emperor's garden is found on ff. 2:15b–2:16b of the Wanp'an text of the "Song of Shim Ch'ŏng."

5. Chŏng Pyŏng-uk, *Han'guk ŭi p'ansori,* p. 48.

6. See ff. 2:1a–2:3b of the Wanp'an text.

7. See ff. 1:5b–1:8a of the Wanp'an text.

8. Yi Po-hyŏng, "P'ansori ran muŏshinya?," pp. 14, 36.

9. Yi Po-hyŏng, "P'ansori sasŏl," p. 197.

10. Song Bang-song, *Ŭmak t'ongsa,* p. 454; and Kang Han-yŏng, *P'ansori,* pp. 69–75.

11. Chŏng Pyŏng-uk, "Haesŏl," p. 8.

12. The complete original text is reprinted in Kim Dong-uk, *Ch'un-hyang chŏn yŏn'gu,* pp. 167–193.

13. Kim Dong-uk (" 'Ch'un-hyang chŏn' ibon ko," p. 5) refers to this as "a new document" in 1955.

14. Kim Dong-uk, *Ch'un-hyang chŏn yŏn'gu,* p. 165.

15. Catalpa wood was favored for carving movable wooden type.

16. I am grateful to my colleague in Chinese literature, David McCraw, for his help in interpreting these lines. The originals appear in Kim Dong-uk, *Ch'un-hyang chŏn yŏn'gu,* p. 192.

17. Yu Chin-han was the sixth-generation descendant of a brother of the great Yu Mong-in (Ŏudang; 1559–1623), noted official, and author of the miscellany, *Ŏu yadam* (Ŏu's anecdotes; 1621).

18. For more on this, see Kim Dong-uk, *"Ch'un-hyang chŏn" yŏn'gu,* p. 12; and Kim Dong-uk, "P'ansori sa yŏng'gu ŭi che munje," p. 15.

19. Only four stanzas survive in Chŏng No-shik, p. 6.

20. The four poets referred to are Ko Su-gwan, Song Hŭng-nok, Yŏm Kye-dal, and Mo Hŭng-gap.

21. Yi Hye-gu, "Song Man-jae ŭi Kwanuhŭi," pp. 114–115.

22. Excerpts from the introductions are given in Chŏng No-shik, p. 7; and Kim Dong-uk, *"Ch'un-hyang chŏn" yŏn'gu,* p. 104. Kwanghan Pavilion is where the hero and heroine of the "Song of Ch'un-hyang" meet for the first time. *Akpu* is the Korean pronunciation of *yueh-fu,* a classical Chinese poetic style. The term, meaning "music bureau," designates songs associated with the Han-dynasty Bureau of Music and also poems written in imitation of those songs.

23. Cho Dong-il, *T'ongsa,* III, 247.

24. Kang Han-yŏng, *P'ansori,* p. 86.

25. The original text of the "Song of the Kwangdae" appears in Pak Hŏn-bong, *Ch'angak taegang,* pp. 538–543 (annotated); and Kang Han-yŏng, *Shin Chae-hyo p'ansori sasŏl chip,* pp. 669–670. The translation here is by Marshall R. Pihl. Song Bang-song, *"Kwangdae ka,"* is an annotated English translation.

26. Kang Han-yŏng, "Kwangdae ka haesŏl," p. 147.
27. Kang Han-yŏng, "P'ansori ŭi iron," pp. 10–11.
28. Cho Dong-il, "P'ansori ŭi chŏnbanjŏk sŏnggyŏk," p. 22.
29. These two texts can be found in Kang Han-yŏng, "P'ansori ŭi iron," pp. 9–16; and in Ch'oe Tong-hyŏn, "P'ansori yŏn'gu sa," pp. 392–393. Cho Dong-il (*T'ongsa*, III, 242) gives Chŏng Hyŏn-sŏk's birth and death dates as 1864–1906 but this does not make good sense. It would have him being appointed to high office, writing books, and pontificating to Shin Chae-hyo as a pre-adolescent. Since Kang Han-yŏng ("Ingan Shin Chae-hyo ŭi chaejomyŏn," p. 24) mentions in passing that Chŏng Hyŏn-sŏk was one year older than Shin Chae-hyo, I give his birth as 1811.
30. Kang Han-yŏng, "P'ansori ŭi iron," p. 13.
31. The three bonds (*samgang*) are those of prince and minister, father and son, and husband and wife. The five moral rules that govern the cardinal human relationships (*oryun*) are righteousness between prince and minister, love between father and son, distinction between husband and wife, precedence between older and younger, and fidelity between friend and friend.
32. These remarks refer to the songs of Ch'un-hyang, Shim Ch'ŏng, Hŭng-bu, Maehwa of Kangnŭng, the Water Palace, and the Red Cliff, respectively.
33. Cho Dong-il, "P'ansori ŭi chŏnbanjŏk sŏnggyŏk," p. 26.
34. Kang Han-yŏng, "Ingan Shin Chae-hyo ŭi chaejomyŏn," p. 24.
35. Kang Han-yŏng, "P'ansori ŭi iron," p. 13.
36. Ibid., p. 12–13.
37. Chŏng No-shik, p. 70.
38. All the quotations in this paragraph are from Chŏng No-shik. See under entry for the singer quoted: Mo Hŭng-gap (p. 28), Pang Man-ch'un (p. 31), Yi Nal-ch'i (pp. 69–70), Chŏn To-sŏng (p. 195), Kwŏn Sam-dŭk (p. 18), Song Hŭng-nok (p. 23), and Pak Man-sun (p. 59).
39. Yu Ik-sŏ, et al., *Myŏngin myŏngch'ang,* pp. 323–338.
40. Chŏng No-shik, p. 63.
41. Ibid., p. 63–64. Kim Se-jong's advice brings to mind Hamlet's instruction to his players: "Suit the action to the word, the word to the action; with this special observance, that you o'erstep not the modesty of nature" (*Hamlet* III.ii.20).
42. Unattributed biographical information and quotations from Kim So-hŭi are taken from taped interviews conducted by the author on March 10 and 29, 1972.
43. Han Myŏng-hŭi, "Ajik to ch'angch'anghan sorikkun," pp. 19–20. Han implies here that the common name "Sun-ok" lacks the theatrical elegance of "So-hŭi."
44. She never finished high school formally and made the following comment to Han Myŏng-hŭi ("Ajik to ch'angch'anghan sorikkun," p. 21): "Even today it's a matter of lasting regret that I really couldn't study. Even after achieving some success through p'ansori, I still continued to lament about my schooling while touring around giving my performances. Then, one day, an educator who heard me said I should look into correspondence lessons. And so, with those lessons, I finished my high school studies."
45. Even today, Kim lowers her voice with respect when referring to her first master, whom she describes as having been "the highest-ranked p'ansori singer in the country, the King of P'ansori."
46. Chŏng Pyŏng-uk, "Haesŏl," p. 9.

47. Learning from several masters is not the norm. Indeed, among contemporary scholars and aficionados, there are those who take exception to Kim So-hŭi's mixed training.

48. Chŏng Pyŏng-uk, "Haesŏl," p. 8.

49. Pak Hŏn-bong, *Ch'angak taegang,* pp. 258–259.

50. Kim So-hŭi, *P'ansori "Shim Ch'ŏng chŏn"* and *"Shim Ch'ŏng ka."*

7. P'ansori on Paper

1. Yi Sŏn-yu, *Oga chŏnjip* (1933), contains very early transcriptions of performance.

2. Yu Yŏng-dae, pp. 57, 84–89, 92, 101, 149; Chŏng Pyŏng-hŏn, "Yi Nal-ch'i p'an Shim Ch'ŏng ka," p. 247; and Ch'oe Un-shik, *Shim Ch'ŏng chŏn yŏn'gu,* pp. 69–71.

3. Ch'oe Un-shik, *Shim Ch'ŏng chŏn yŏn'gu,* pp. 18–45.

4. This count, which does not include inaccessible kwangdae materials, is based upon Ch'oe Un-shik (*Shim Ch'ŏng chŏn yŏn'gu*), pp. 18–20; Yu Yŏng-dae, pp. 229–232; and the author's own, more recent research.

5. O Se-ha, "Shim Ch'ŏng chŏn ibon ko," p. 110.

6. Shin Chae-hyo, *P'ansori sasŏl chip,* pp. 156–249.

7. Han'guk munhwa yŏn'gu wŏn, *Han'guk kodae sosŏl chongsŏ.* The Seoul text of the "Song of Shim Ch'ŏng" is included in vol. 1, pp. 229–276.

8. Yun Se-p'yŏng (p. 10) identifies his basic text as the Hŭidong Sŏgwan edition, one which I have not seen mentioned elsewhere.

9. Later reprinted in Yi Ch'ang-bae, pp. 467–522.

10. Pak Hŏn-bong, *Ch'angak taegang.*

11. For example: Munhwajae kwalliguk, *P'ansori Shim Ch'ŏng ka;* Kim Ki-su, pp. 238–369; and Chŏng Pyŏng-uk, *Han'guk ŭi p'ansori,* pp. 313–357.

12. Allen, pp. 109–120.

13. Hong Tjyong-ou [Hong Chong-u], *Le Bois Sec Refleuri* (Paris: Ernest Leroux, 1893).

14. *Winning Buddha's Smile,* tr. Charles M. Taylor (Boston: Richard G. Bedger, the Gorham Press, 1919).

15. "The Story of Shim Ch'ŏng," tr. Alan C. Heyman, *Korea Journal* 30.3:50–67 and 30.4:57–67 (March and April 1990).

16. The Wanp'an edition from the Kim Dong-uk collection was reproduced in *Inmun kwahak charyo ch'ongsŏ* (Cultural science materials), no. 8 (Seoul, Yonsei University, 1972) and also appears in Kim Dong-uk, *Kososŏl p'an'gakpon chŏnjip,* pp. 179–214.

17. Kim Dong-uk, *Kososŏl p'an'gakpon chŏnjip,* p. 4.

8. The Song of Shim Ch'ŏng

1. This woodblock-printed Wanp'an version of the "Song of Shim Ch'ŏng" was labeled a "tale" by its 1916 publisher in imitation of titling conventions long observed by classic written fiction in Korea. While such use of the word *tale* erroneously implies written origins for the oral art of p'ansori, this Wanp'an edition was actually derived

from performances of the "Song of Shim Ch'ŏng" by singers of the River and Mountain School.

2. The Sung dynasty ruled China from 960 to 1126 and is one the major sources of the East Asian cultural tradition. Korea believed itself exemplary among China's tributary states and based much of its formal culture on the Chinese model, which meant that it officially reckoned time in terms of the Chinese calendar. A Korean story, therefore, could open as easily with a reference to a Chinese historical landmark as with one that was Korean.

3. This character's name varies from text to text, being Shim Hyŏn in the Seoul woodblock edition, and Shim Soe in the Hashimoto 1894 manuscript.

4. "A career of advancement to the capital with official rank" translates *naksu ch'ŏngun ŭi pyŏsŭl*, an allusion to lines by the T'ang poet Sung Chih-wen (?–710):

Green trees on the road to the capital of Ch'in;
Clouds in the blue at the bridge over the River Lo.

"Clouds in the blue" (*ch'ŏngun*) is a common metaphor which speaks of high official position; and the Lo River (*Naksu*), which flowed through Lo-yang, an ancient Chinese capital, alludes to the national capital.

5. This common figure, which occurs in the poetry of the T'ang poets Po Chü-i (772–846), Tu Fu (712–770), and Li Po (?705–762), symbolizes ministerial rank, since high ministers of their era tied their seals of office to their belts by purple ribbons.

6. Shim's wife was of the Kwak family and, following custom, did not adopt her husband's family name but remained Kwak-ssi, Mme. Kwak. She is called Chŏng-ssi in the Seoul woodblock edition. This same convention is used in the case of Blindwoman An (ff. 2:35a, 2:36b, 2:39b), who is sometimes called An-ssi.

7. These are classic paragons among Chinese women. T'ai Jen and T'ai Ssu were, respectively, the mother and wife of ancient China's King Wen (the Duke of Chou) and are remembered for their virtue and chastity. Chuang Chiang, wife of Minister Chuang of Wei during the Warring States period, was famous for her beauty. Mu Lan was a filial heroine of the fifth century A.D., who went to war disguised as a man and fought in place of her father.

8. The names of these four Chinese classical works are expressed in fourteen characters that scan nicely as two parallel seven-character lines:

Li-chi, Chia-li, Nei-tse-p'ien;
Chou-nan, Chao-nan, kuan-chü-shih.

The *Li-chi* (Book of rites) is a lengthy work from the first century B.C. on such topics as government, home management, etiquette, music, and ceremonies. It incorporates the *Nei-tse-p'ien* (Home rules), which bears on customs and rites within the family and was meant especially for the training of women. A later work on courtesy and rites within the family was the *Chia-li* (Family rituals) by the twelfth-century philosopher Chu Hsi. "Chou-nan" and "Chao-nan" are the titles of the first two chapters of the famous anthology of poetry, *Shih ching* (Book of songs; sixth century B.C.); the phrase *kuan-chü-shih* (the *kuan-chü* poem) refers to the opening verse of the anthology.

9. Yen Hui was the favorite disciple of Confucius and took great pleasure in learning even though he lived in dire poverty. In the same context, the Shin Chae-hyo manuscript gives Yuan Hsien, another disciple of Confucius, who lived in voluntary poverty as he studied the Way.

10. These two paragons of Confucian loyalty chose to flee to Mount Shou-yang and there starve to death rather than transfer their allegiance to a conquering ruler.

11. In several texts (e.g., Shin, Ansŏng, Chŏng Kwŏn-jin) the dyeing is a task separate from the preparation of food and is treated as one more source of income.

12. The value of these units of money cannot be estimated because the story is not set in a specific period and, worse, some episodes were developed and embellished in the course of transmission by different singers who lived at different times.

13. This is a slight corruption of a line from Mencius: "Mencius said, 'There are three things which are unfilial, and to have no posterity is the greatest of them.'" James Legge, *The Works of Mencius,* p. 313. The "three thousand unfilial acts" might be traced to a line in the *Hsiao ching* (Classic of filial piety): "There are five punishments for three thousand offences, and of these none is greater than unfiliality." (*Kambun taikei,* V, 12 ["Hsiao ching"]).

14. "With every effort made" translates "having sold my labor and ground my bones."

15. Ursa Major, the Big Dipper, is regarded as an auspicious constellation and is taken as an object of worship by some sects of esoteric Buddhism in Korea. Altars and temples for this purpose, called *ch'ilsŏng-dan* and *ch'ilsŏng-gak,* are found in the hills behind some Korean Buddhist temples. The bodhisattva Miao Chien, identified by some with Kuan-yin, is said to rule in Ursa Major and can grant long life and other wishes. Kim Dong-uk suggested in conversation that Korean worship of Ursa Major has origins in shamanism.

16. The eighth day of the fourth month is the traditional birthday of the Buddha, an auspicious date. *Kapcha,* furthermore, is the first year of the Chinese sixty-year cycle, another felicitous choice.

17. The Queen Mother of the West (Hsi-wang-mu) is a mythical Taoist character, first mentioned by the fifth- or fourth-century B.C. Chinese philosopher Lieh-tzu. The fruit of the sacred peach tree, which she is said to have planted, ripens only once in three thousand years and is eaten by the immortals when they gather for their feast at Yao Lake, the abode of the Queen Mother of the West. The use of the past tense ("I was the daughter of the Queen Mother of the West") suggests that the fairy's banishment on earth marks the beginning of a new existence as Kwak-ssi's daughter, Shim Ch'ŏng.

18. The concubine's name, Yü-chen fei-tzu, recalls the beautiful and famous concubine of the T'ang Emperor Ming Huang (Hsuan Tsung), Yang Kuei-fei, whose personal name was Yü-huan and who was also known as Chen-fei. Kwak-ssi, after her death, becomes "Lady Yü-chen of the Kuang-han (lunar) Palace." See f. 2:11a.

19. The Jade Emperor is the supreme being of the Taoist pantheon and figures into the "Song of Shim Ch'ŏng" several times, intervening on the heroine's behalf.

20. In the Chang Chi-yŏng text, this is "Tai-shang lao-chün," a title was given to the philosopher Lao-tzu by the Emperor Chen Tsung of the Sung dynasty. The present text appears to give us yet another pseudonym for Lao-tzu, drawn from the fact that he was said to have left the world through Han-ku Pass, which is located near the southern end of the T'ai-hang Mountains.

21. This "passing dream" refers to the T'ang-dynasty tale, "A Lifetime in a Dream" by Li Kung-tso (fl. early eighth century): "Nan-k'o t'ai-shou chuan," in Lu Hsun, ed.,

T'ang Sung ch'uan-chi chi, pp. 77–84. Also Wolfgang Bauer and Herbert Franke, trs., *The Golden Casket,* pp. 93–107. A dream foretelling the birth of a child is a common device in traditional Korean fiction.

22. Chang Chi-yŏng, *Hong Kil-tong chŏn—Shim Ch'ŏng chŏn,* p. 97n1, says that these five precautions to be observed during pregnancy are found in the Han dynasty *Lieh-nü-chuan* (Biographies of women). The first two also appear in the *Analects,* Book X, as precautions observed by a gentleman. See James Legge, *The Confucian Analects,* pp. 232–233.

23. The text does not specify where the straw is placed but, on the strength of the implications of other texts, I have let it appear to serve as a kneeling-mat. The "pure water," is *chŏnghwasu,* well water drawn at early dawn for use in devotions or decocting medicines.

24. "I pray. Lo, I pray" is a formulaic opening for prayers.

25. According to some traditional Korean folk-beliefs, the three gods, Hwanin, Hwanung, and Hwangŏm, created mankind and all things. They also oversee childbirth, at which time they are commonly invoked in prayer. The text reads only *samshin che-wang,* their collective title. Ch'oe Un-shik (*Shim Ch'ŏng chŏn yŏn'gu,* p. 27n7) explains them as "the three gods who oversee conception, birth, and rearing."

26. Kim Dong-uk suggested in conversation that Blindman Shim is using an earthy simile here to describe the quick and easy birth of the baby. With the cucumber symbolic of the clitoris, we have: "as easily as the clitoris pops out through a ragged skirt." Kim also offered a parallel traditional expression regarding the male organ: "as a cock pops out of torn pants."

27. This expression, *kŏdong poso* ("see the behavior"), is a rhetorical device used by the kwangdae, directly addressing his audience, usually introducing a passage describing behavior.

28. Clam, in this metaphor, stands for vulva, or girl. Some annotators have the blind man beginning to speak from the earlier words, "felt between . . . ." My interpretation follows Kim Dong-uk.

29. This allusive passage draws heavily on the *Book of Songs.* Like so many other such Chinese borrowings in p'ansori literature, these are from the opening songs of the work, more easily accessible and widely known than the later, less widely studied sections. The allusions here are to the first and fifth songs of the *Book of Songs* (*Mao Concordance,* nos. 1, 5; Arthur Waley, *The Book of Songs,* nos. 87, 164). Blindman Shim is here making the point that, even though women may not conduct memorial services for ancestors, their menfolk may do so.

30. The first food Kwak-ssi is to take after childbirth, seaweed soup and boiled white rice, is here being consecrated before the same three gods whom Blindman Shim invoked in his prayer just before the birth.

31. This month-by-month recitation of the stages of pregnancy varies according to the text, particularly after the sixth month. While the Wanp'an and Ansŏng woodblock editions seem to stick to a natural, physiological course, the Pak Hŏn-bong, Yi Sŏn-yu, and Chŏng Kwŏn-jin texts correlate the number of the month and the phenomenon involved (e.g., six viscera in the sixth month, seven openings of the head in the seventh month, nine bodily openings in the ninth month).

Fourth month: Kim Dong-uk commented in conversation that, according to premodern Korean legal concepts, miscarriage after this point where the fetus has "taken on human form" was considered manslaughter.

Fifth month: the Wanp'an text has *oep'o* which seems an error for *op'o* "five sacks" (i.e., organs) in view of the Ansŏng woodblock edition's *ojang* "five viscera."

Sixth month: the "six feelings" are joy, anger, sorrow, pleasure, love, and hatred.

Seventh month: "forty-eight thousand hairs" sounds like there is something behind it, perhaps something felicitous or an association with Buddhism.

Eighth month: the "full burden" here is *ch'im cham* in the Wanp'an woodblock edition, which makes no sense. However, I find *ch'an chim* in a manuscript in Kim Dong-uk's collection and in the Ansŏng woodblock edition. Without doing violence to the context or syntax, *ch'an* could be regarded the perfect modifier of the verb *ch'a-,* "to be full," and *chim* as the noun, "burden." This interpretation, however, did not satisfy all the Korean informants I consulted, though they, too, were puzzled.

Diamond Gate is the Buddhist "diamond door of the *garbhadhatu mandala,*" according to Soothill and Hodous (*A Dictionary of Chinese Buddhist Terms,* p. 283). The *garbhadhatu,* they add (p. 312), is "the womb treasury, the universal source from which all things are produced."

32. *Tung-fang Shuo,* a Chinese of the Former Han Dynasty, figures into much legend and, having wisdom and supernatural powers, is said to have thrice stolen from Hsi-wang-mu the famous peaches of immortality. (For Hsi-wang-mu, see n. 17.)

T'ai Jen is introduced in n. 7.

Shun, one of the legendary founding emperors of China, was noted for his exemplary filial piety even in the face of his father's great enmity toward him.

Tseng Ts'an, a disciple of Confucius, is regarded, along with the Emperor Shun, as one of the twenty-four exemplars of filial piety.

Ch'i Liang's wife defended her husband's honor when he was accused of an offense against the state: see James Legge, *The Ch'un Ts'ew,* pp. 499, 504.

Pan Chao, sister of the historian Pan Ku, took over and completed her brother's work on the *Han shu* (History of the Former Han dynasty) upon his death.

Shih Ch'ung, famous for his vast wealth and ostentatious use of it, is said even to have used wax for fuel in order to out-do others in the conspicuous display of his wealth.

33. Sukhyang of the P'yojin River is the heroine of the traditional and anonymous Korean novel, *Sukhyang chŏn* (Tale of Sukhyang), who attempts to commit suicide by jumping into the P'yojin River but is saved from drowning by ladies-in-waiting from the Dragon's Palace. This reference is a parallel to Shim Ch'ŏng's own fate.

34. The Weaving Girl is the star Vega in the constellation Lyra. According to myth, she and the Herding Boy (the star Altair in the constellation Aquila) meet on the Magpie Bridge, formed for them across the Milky Way by massed magpies once a year, on the seventh day of the seventh lunar month.

35. These are the first seven days of a twenty-one-day period during which various percautions are taken and outsiders are traditionally excluded from a house where a child has been born.

36. *Saengwŏn* was the title given a man who had passed the lower-level national civil-service examination. The title was also used as a title of respect for an old scholar.

The latter use probably applies here, in view of his knowledge of Chinese herbal medicine—the province of an elder.

37. Shen Nung is a legendary Chinese emperor, said to have taught the people the art of agriculture and to have discovered the therapeutic value of herbs, hence becoming the father of Chinese herbal medicine.

38. Yellow Springs is the Taoist and shamanistic world after death.

39. This is drawn from a line in Tu Fu's poem, "Wen Kuan-chün shou Ho-nan-Ho-pei" (On learning of the recovery of Honan and Hopei by the imperial army). See David Hawkes, *A Little Primer of Tu Fu,* no. 19. The couplet in question reads,

> In broad daylight I must sing and give way to wine;
> I must make a friend of green spring and return home happily!

40. This incorporates a line from Li Po's poem "Pa-chiu wen-yueh" (Holding wine and questioning the moon) which reads, "How long has the moon been in blue heaven?"

41. Heng-o resides in the Lunar Palace of the moon and, according to one story, maintains her immortality by eating a medicine ground for her by the rabbit that can be seen on the surface of the moon. Instead of an old man's face, Koreans see a rabbit on its haunches (right), facing a cassia tree (left) on the surface of the moon.

42. Nü Ying and O Huang, the two daughters of the legendary sage Emperor Yao who are honored at the Huang-Ling shrine (named after its location). As wives of the Emperor Shun, these two are said to have cried so bitterly at the death of their husband that their tears became blood and stained young bamboo shoots, producing a strain of spotted bamboo that can be found growing even today.

43. Hoesa Pavilion is a reference to *Sa-ssi namjŏng ki* (Record of Lady Sa's journey to the south), a Korean novel by Kim Man-jung (1637–1692).

44. Traditionally, both an inner coffin (*kwan*) and an outer coffin (*kwak*) were used. The expression, *kwan-kwak,* is also used today to refer to a single coffin.

45. Burials occur an odd number of days after death. Here, the third day was chosen.

46. The refrain *wŏnŏ wŏnŏ* and other, similar, refrains in this dirge are meaningless phrases traditionally sung as part of a Korean dirge.

47. Mount Pei-mang, located to the north of the ancient Chinese capital of Lo-yang, is the site of the royal tombs of the Eastern Han dynasty and of the graves of many famous officials of the T'ang and Sung dynasties.

48. Pine and catalpa commonly serve as shade trees surrounding graves in Korea.

49. The Korean for this line does not make sense. The English is guesswork, based only on a recognizable syllable or two and the context (f. 1:9b, line 10).

50. This saying expresses the desolation one feels after an event is over or when one has been abandoned. It is used in a parallel situation in the "Song of Ch'un-hyang" by the heroine's mother when she contemplates losing both her daughter and son-in-law.

51. Although this is a typical opening for a Korean lullaby, the Wanp'an wood-block edition does not continue in this lullaby format. In the Pak Hŏn-bong and Chŏng Kwŏn-jin texts, however, Shim continues with a lullaby essentially the same as the one he sings after the child's birth.

52. The translation expands the original to make it self-explanatory. It reads, literally, "He passed each month's *sak* and *mang* and the lesser and greater *ki*."

53. "Unparalleled beauty" translates *kuksaek* ("a beauty of the nation"), a phrase which recalls the opening line of Po Chü-i's "Song of Unending Sorrow:" "China's emperor, craving beauty that might shake an empire . . . ." See Witter Bynner, tr., *The Jade Mountain,* p. 94.

54. The text reads *ch'il-p'al se,* "seven-eight years." Most texts give Shim Ch'ŏng's age at this point in this sort of hyphenated fashion, in the area of seven or eight years of age. That this is an age of awareness is reflected in the popular dictum, "After the age of seven, boys and girls neither sit nor dine together," which appears in the "Home Rules" section of the *Book of Rites.*

55. Tzu-lu (also called Chung Yu), the oldest of Confucius' disciples, is characterized as his "best friend and severest critic." See H. G. Creel, *Confucius and the Chinese Way,* p. 64. According to a story in the apocryphal *K'ung-tzu chia-yü* (Discourses of the Confucian school), he neglected his own diet while carrying rice to his parents over distances of more than one hundred *li.*

56. This story is found in the *Records of the Historian (Shih chi)* in the section on Emperor Wen. T'i-jung's father had been accused of a crime and sentenced to punishment by mutilation. An only child, she sent a letter to the officials concerned, offering to become a government slave to atone for her father's crime and save him from his punishment. The emperor, hearing of this, was moved to pardon her father. See Burton Watson, tr., *Records of the Grand Historian of China,* pp. 356–357. The Wanp'an woodblock edition errs in saying that her father was imprisoned in Lo-yang. The *Records of the Historian* gives the location as Ch'ang-an, then capital of the Han Empire.

57. "Ten spoons make one meal" is to say, "one spoonful each from ten people will make one person's meal."

58. "Princess" translates the Confucian term *chün-tzu* which, applied to a man, is variously translated "gentleman," "superior man," "man of the higher type," "wise man," "princely man," and so forth. He is the ideal Confucian in conduct and outlook. This is the first time I have seen it used to epitomize the character of a woman.

59. Murŭng, read *wu-ling* in Chinese, recalls T'ao Ch'ien's short prose gem, "Peach Blossom Spring," in which a certain fisherman from the village of Wu-ling one day happens upon a utopian village in the upper waters of the Peach Blossom Spring. In this context, it is worth noting that Blindman Shim lives in Tohwa (peach blossom) Ward.

60. Whereas the narrative perspective here is from the point of view of the Shim household, the Chang Chi-yŏng text shifts to Murŭng Village: "One day Lady Chang of Murŭng Village across the way, having heard rumors of Shim Ch'ŏng, sends a serving girl to fetch her." The visit to Lady Chang's, the subject of this lengthy episode, is truncated in the Shin manuscript and Ansŏng woodblock edition: the character of Lady Chang does not appear and Shim Ch'ŏng goes to her house only to beg food at a feast. Her lateness in returning from the feast (because she is pressed to eat there) sets up the following episode in which her worried father wanders out in search of her. The Seoul and Ansŏng woodblock editions drop all reference to Lady Chang. They say only that Shim Ch'ŏng one day went out to beg and did not come back until late, causing her father anxiety.

61. Ch'ai-sang Village was the home of the Chinese poet T'ao Ch'ien, also known as the Master of Five Willows (because of the trees fronting his house). As indicated in

the two previous notes, the place names Murŭng and Tohwa also bring T'ao Ch'ien and his poetry to mind.

62. This sentence echos a line from a poem in the Chinese *shih* style by the Koryŏ-period scholar Yi Kyu-bo (1168–1241):

> Bamboo roots, bent as a dragon's waist, cleave the soil;
> Plantain leaves, long as a phoenix tail, touch my window.

63. The inner middle gate leads to the secluded women's quarters of a traditional Korean mansion.

64. According to Chang Chi-yŏng (p. 133n26), there is a story that the Sung Emperor Kao Tsung once owned a collection of talking parakeets from the Lung Mountains (Lung-shan) but had them sent back to their home when they asked him to do so. Later on, a passing official is said to have heard them calling their greetings to the emperor. The T'ang-dynasty poet Ts'en Ts'an (fl. ca. 750) picked up the theme of these talking parakeets in his poem, "Fu-Pei-t'ing tu-Lung ssu-chia" (Thoughts of home on Lung-shan while reporting to Pei-t'ing).

> Moving west toward Lun-t'ai, ten thousand leagues or more;
> And knowing well that news of home must daily lessen now;
> Ah, Lung-shan parakeets that speak our words so well—
> Please help me send some letters to the people at my house!

65. That is, her daughters-in-law see only that her bed is prepared in the evening and ask after her in the morning.

66. This passage is typically Chinese in its imagery. Though I can identify no specific source, the conceit is a common one in Chinese poetry.

67. In all texts this monk is designated by the expression *hwaju-sŭng*. Although Chang Chi-yŏng (p. 139n6) describes him as something like an abbot, Unhŏyongha, *Pulgyo sajŏn* (p. 965), and Soothill and Hodous (p. 141a) define the term as "one who collects alms for a temple."

68. That is, "not forget even after death when there is nothing left of me but white, bleached bones."

69. In the Seoul, Chŏng Kwŏn-jin, and Pak Hŏn-bong texts, the following interview between Blindman Shim and the monk occurs at the wayside, not in Shim's house.

70. It has been noted (n. 60) that the Shin Chae-hyo text departs from the Wanp'an text in the Lady Chang Visitation Episode. Now we shall see that it also goes on to handle the pledge of rice differently, too. In the Wanp'an woodblock edition, the pledge is made between Blindman Shim and the monk before Shim Ch'ŏng's return. But, in the Shin Chae-hyo manuscript, Shim Ch'ŏng returns just after the monk has brought her father home and in time for her to make the pledge herself, her father merely overhearing. See also n. 73.

71. The unit of volume translated by "sack" is the *sŏk*, which equals about five U.S. bushels. One tenth of a *sŏk* is a *mal*; and one tenth of a *mal* is a *toe*.

72. This is a line from Su Shih's (1036–1101) rhymeprose work, "The Red Cliff I." See Cyril Birch, ed., *Anthology of Chinese Literature*, p. 382, 1. 28.

73. In the Shin Chae-hyo manuscript, she returns home to find her bedraggled father with the monk who rescued him. She prepares them food and asks the monk about the Buddha in an exchange that reads like a catechism. When the monk tells her that three hundred sacks of rice, earnestly given, would restore her father's sight, Shim

Ch'ŏng makes the pledge, herself. After the monk leaves, she reassures her doubting father in the same terms as the Wanp'an woodblock edition. In her prayers, she explicitly asks that the gods direct her to someone who would buy her for the price of three hundred sacks of rice.

74. The text actually reads, ". . . while stamping her feet, she massages his whole body." This unusual combination appears only in the Wanp'an text. I have resolved the question by making the two acts sequential instead of simultaneous.

75. The firebox refers to the kitchen stove which supplies heat, through its exhaust, to the floors of the interior rooms, as in radiant heating.

76. Wang Hsiang of the ancient Chinese Chin dynasty, one of the twenty-four exemplars of filial piety, is said to have broken through the ice (also said to have melted a hole with the heat of his naked body) in order to catch a carp out of season for his ailing stepmother, who liked fresh fish.

77. Kuo Chü is another of the twenty-four exemplars of filial piety. According to another version of his story, they lacked sufficient food for the family, including his parents. Therefore, he and his wife dug a grave in which to bury their child alive, in the belief that they could always have another child but never regain their parents. At the bottom of the hole, they found a pot of gold, which was heaven's reward for their filial piety.

78. This is likely an interpolated line of *shih* poetry but I cannot identify a source for it. Kim Dong-uk suggested in conversation that it reads like the work of a T'ang poet.

79. Literally, "On a certain day of a certain month of the sexagenary cycle."

80. Here I translate the Chang Chi-yŏng text (p. 147n10) in preference to the Wanp'an woodblock edition, which seems to have become corrupted by an impressionistic use of numbers. See also Soothill and Hodous, p. 35a–b.

81. *Muja* is the twenty-fifth year of the sexagenary cycle.

82. In the opening lines of the Wanp'an text, Blindman Shim is described as becoming blind before he was twenty. This is an example of the sort of inconsistency that can crop up between episodes of p'ansori because of its cumulative authorship.

83. In most texts, days and months pass after Shim Ch'ŏng starts her prayers and before the sailors appear. Some texts, like the Wanp'an woodblock edition, simply mark this passage of time by the expression, "One day . . . ." The shaman text gives the period as one hundred days, while the Shin Chae-hyo manuscript specifies seven nights of prayer. Only in the Seoul woodblock edition and the Pak Hŏn-bong text does she hear the sailors calling out in the streets the very next morning, after only one night of prayer. The treatment in the Seoul woodblock edition is particularly interesting because of the mysterious appearance before her of an "old monk" (probably the alms-gathering monk from Mongun Temple) when she returns to the room after night-long prayers but cannot get to sleep. "Tomorrow there will be some men wanting to buy you," the monk foretells. "Do not avoid this even though you sell yourself and go somewhere to die. Heaven will be moved by your filial piety and you will become ennobled at the place where you would die." (Seoul text, f. 3b, lines 12–14; W. E. Skillend, "The Story of Sim Ch'ŏng," p. 117).

84. In the Shin Chae-hyo text (p. 185), however, Blindman Shim does not receive this news with such uncritical pleasure, as the following dialogue from that text suggests:

"If that is so, child, will you stay at that house?"

"Oh, I'll come and go."

"Child. If I end up with my eyes unopened and my daughter gone, I will suffer two losses!"

"The resolution of every matter rests with Heaven. Let us wait and see."

85. Su T'ung-ch'ien (also called Su T'ung-kuo), a son of the Han-dynasty envoy Su Wu, was born to a second wife whom the envoy married while a prisoner of the Hsiung-nu. When Su Wu, after having been repatriated himself, sent for his son, the boy was forced to leave his mother behind. Although no source identifies the poet whose line is quoted here, Chang Chi-yŏng (p. 155n8) suggests that it takes off on a line from a poem addressed to Su Wu by his fellow prisoner, Li Ling. See Arthur Waley, *Chinese Poems*, p. 44.

86. Other texts give Shantung instead of Lung Mountain (Lung-shan), which is more accurate because the T'ang-dynasty poet being quoted, Wang Wei (699–759), is speaking of friends (he calls them "brothers"), whom he has left behind in his home province of Shantung. He is recalling their custom of climbing the mountains to pick dogwood blossoms and drink wine each year on the ninth day of the ninth month.

I live alone in a foreign place where I am a stranger.
Every time it comes to festival, I think again of kin;
I cast my thoughts afar to brothers as they climb the heights;
They all put dogwood in their hair but there's one less with them now.

87. This allusion is drawn from another poem by Wang Wei, which calls for a toast to an official just before his departure to a new post, where he will be beyond the reach of his friends. It has been effectively translated by C. H. Kwock and Vincent McHugh as "Seeing Master Yuan off on his Mission to Kucha" in Cyril Birch, *Anthology of Chinese Literature*. p. 224.

88. This line is drawn from a poem by the T'ang poet Wang Po, "Ts'ai-lien-ch'ü" (Picking the lotus).

89. This reference to the Water Palace does not imply Shim Ch'ŏng's foreknowledge of her coming sojourn at the Crystal Palace (also called the Water Palace) before being returned to this world. The expression "go to the water palace" is a metaphor for death by drowning. The Ansŏng woodblock edition has "go to the water kingdom" for this. There is an irony in the question Shim Ch'ŏng poses here. Since the "Yellow Springs" refers to death while living on the surface of the earth and "watery palace," refers to death under water by drowning, Shim Ch'ŏng would be eternally separated from her mother.

90. According to the *Huai-nan tzu*, an eclectic Taoist text compiled under the patronage of Liu An, Prince of Huai-nan (?–122 B.C.), Hsien Lake in the West is the place where the sun spends the night. The same text also says that the sun rises through the branches of the mythical Fu-sang Tree, which is situated in the Eastern Sea. Kwŏn Sang-no and Chang To-bin, *Kosa sŏngŏ sajŏn*, p. 1154, *ham chi*.

91. Meng Ch'ang-chün, a native of the ancient state of Ch'i, had been imprisoned in Ch'in on charges of treason. When he escaped with the help of the King's favorite concubine, he made straight for the frontier gates to get out of the country but reached there while it was still dark and the gates, hence, were still closed. He would have been

recaptured had not his clever retainer imitated the rooster's crow and tricked the gate-keeper into believing it was already dawn and time to open the gates.

92. When a person appears riding a cart in a dream, it is usually interpreted as foretelling death. However, it is also common to interpret dreams in reverse of their apparent meaning, as is done by Blindwoman An in a later episode of the "Song of Shim Ch'ŏng."

93. This should read "two hundred sacks" to agree with the amount brought into the village.

94. Shim Ch'ŏng expresses this idea by a four-character reference to the story of Wei K'o, an ancient Chinese whose favor to a dying man was repaid when that old man appeared as a spirit on the battlefield and caused grass to bind the legs of Wei K'o's enemy.

95. This poem and Lady Chang's responding poem are given twice, once in Chinese and again in Korean translation. I give them only once in English.

96. "Older daughter of the house" is literally, "big maiden of So-and-so's house." All other texts use a plausible name instead of "So-and-so."

97. Tano Day festival, celebrated annually on the fifth day of the fifth month, is passed in feasting, rituals, and games. In keeping with traditional Chinese cosmology, double-odd numbers of the yearly calendar are marked by celebration, like third month–third day, seventh month–seventh day, ninth month–ninth day, and so forth.

98. The seventh night of the seventh month is the night on which the Weaver Girl and Shepherd Boy meet in heaven. On this night, young girls pray to the weaver and shepherd for skills in weaving and needlework. See n. 34.

99. "Oh! To go home!" refers to the soul of Tu Yü, ruler of the ancient Chinese kingdom of Shu, who had relinquished his throne to one of his ministers but then found himself unable to reclaim it after a change of heart. He died in exile and his soul became a cuckoo that cried, spitting blood, "Oh! To go home! Oh! To go home!"

100. These are the closing lines of a poem by Wang Wei, "Hsi-t'i-p'an-shih," which is beautifully translated as "Light Lines on a Flat Rock" in G. W. Robinson, tr., *Poems of Wang Wei,* p. 103.

101. "Passengers' tent" is guesswork. The text reads *paetchang,* which might be the ship's hold, a large chest on board, or a large tent pitched on deck for passengers.

102. Phrases like "the story changes" and "at this time" are used to mark major breaks in the narrative where there has been a change in the locale, character, or time (though not at every such change).

103. "Move into the mainstream waters" alludes to the opening line of the "Odes of Yung" in the *Book of Songs (Mao Concordance,* no. 45), which James Legge translates as, "It floats about, that boat of cypress wood, there in the middle of the Ho." In his analysis, Legge notes that the image of a boat cut adrift refers to a woman who has lost her husband, an appropriate image here. See James Legge, *The She King,* p. 73.

104. Here (f. 2:1a) begins a lengthy sequence of allusive passages that ends with Shim Ch'ŏng's arrival at the Indang Sea (f. 2:4b), where she is to sacrifice herself. Her progress is at first marked by allusions to Chinese poems that are associated with famous sights along the way and then, later, by encounters with famous Chinese who had died unfortunate deaths.

105. According to Chang Chi-yŏng (p. 180n17), this line comes from a poem by the T'ang poet Ch'ien Ch'i (eighth century), "Hsiang-ling ku-se shih" (Song of the Hsiang spirits):

Upon the song's end, no man is seen;
Above the river, countless peaks are green.

106. Although this scans like *shih* poetry and is treated as a quotation by the text, I have not yet been able to find a source for it.

107. Chia I held the post of Royal Tutor under the Prince of Ch'ang-sha in the second century A.D. He later served in the same capacity under the Prince of Liang, for whom he cared so deeply that he died of grief when the prince was killed in an accident. This may seem an odd reference to introduce here but is probably chosen because Ch'ang-sha is located on the Hsiang River in Hunan and near Tung-t'ing Lake, the general locale of this passage.

108. Ch'ü Yuan, a Chinese of the fourth century B.C., is the archetype of the loyal minister and is also well remembered for his lengthy poem, "Li Sao" (On encountering sorrow). Compounded frustrations and disappointments in official life led him to commit suicide by jumping into the Mi-lo River. He is said to have ended up in the stomach of a fish, still loyal to his prince. See n. 131.

109. These are the last two lines of "Huang-ho lou" (The Yellow Crane Terrace) by Ts'ui Hao (fl. ca. 750). For a full translation, see Bynner, p. 114. There is a tradition that the master poet Li Po had intended to write of the Yellow Crane Pavilion himself until he saw Ts'ui's work and gave up. The pavilion is located on the Yangtze River to the north of Tung-t'ing Lake.

110. Here are two lines from Li Po's poem, "Teng Chin-ling Feng-huang-t'ai" (Climbing to Phoenix Terrace at Chin-ling). For a full translation, see Obata Shigeyoshi, tr., *The Works of Li Po*, no. 76. The terrace is located near Nanking in Kiangsu Province.

111. It was on the Hsin-yang River, near Chiu-chiang on the Yangtze, that Po Chü-i (772–846) wrote his "P'i-p'a hsing" (Song of a lute), which recalls his encounter with a former dancing-girl of the capital, who played the lute and sang for him.

112. These references to the Red Cliff, Su Shih, and Ts'ao Ts'ao allude to Su's rhymeprose, "Ch'ih-pi fu" (The Red Cliff). This short piece recalls the exploits of Ts'ao Ts'ao, bold minister and cunning rebel, who had suffered defeat in a naval battle 800 years before at a spot on the Yangtze River thereafter known as the Red Cliff because of the red discolorations said to have been left by the burning of Ts'ao's armada.

113. This paraphrases the well-known poem by Chang Chi (eighth century), "Feng-ch'iao yeh-po" (A night mooring at Maple Bridge):

The moon falls, a crow cries, and frost fills the heavens.
Fishermen's fires between the river maples meet our anxious eyes.
From Cold Mountain Temple outside Ku-su Fort
The sound of a midnight bell reaches the traveler's boat.

Ku-su Fort is located in the area of Soochow in Kiangsu Province near the mouth of the Yangtze River.

114. The incident to which this alludes is the fall of the sixth-century kingdom of Ch'en as its last ruler, the wastrel Ch'en Shu-pao, caroused and sang his favorite air, "Courtyard Flowers" (Hou-t'ing-hua). The event took place near the Ch'in-huai River, which enters the Yangtze near Nanking. The quotation preceding this reference consists

of the first and third lines of "Po Ch'in-huai" (Mooring on the Ch'in-huai) by Tu Mu (803–852), but they are given in the reverse of their proper order:

> Smoke veils the cold waters and moonlight covers the sands:
> We make a night mooring near a tavern on the Ch'in-huai.
> Wine-selling women do not know the sorrow of a kingdom's ruin:
> Still across the river they sing of Courtyard Flowers.

The incident in question is a common referent in Chinese and Korean poetry and also appears in poems by the Chinese Liu Yü-hsi (772–842) and Li Shang-yin (813–858). The Korean poet Ko Kyŏng-myŏng (1533–1592) reworked Tu Mu's poem as a *shijo* in a reference to Hideyoshi's devastating sixteenth-century invasion of Korea:

> We moor our boat on the Ch'in-huai and go in search of a tavern;
> Wine-selling women across the stream know not the sorrow of a kingdom's ruin:
> As smoke veils the water and moonlight mantles the sand, they sing of Courtyard Flowers.

115. Where the Hsiao and the Hsiang Rivers enter Tung-t'ing Lake are Eight Sights that have figured as motifs in traditional Chinese painting and poetry. The eight sights appearing in the subsequent stanzas of the text differ in part from those given in standard reference works. In the list below, the standard Eight Sights are followed by the sights given in our text, where different.

1 Night Rain on the Hsiao and Hsiang
2 Autumn Moon over Tung-t'ing Lake
3 Returning Sails from Distant Shores
4 Twilight at the Fishing Village (Sunset at Wu-shan)
5 Evening Snow in the River Skies (Evening Clouds at Ts'ang-wu)
6 Wild Geese Lighting at P'ing-sha
7 Mountain Mists of Shan-shih (Double Shrine at Huang-ling)
8 Evening Bell at Yen Temple (Evening Bell at Han Temple)

116. See n. 42.

117. These two lines are suggestive of a *shijo* poem by the sixteenth-century Korean poet Yi Hu-baek, who was probably responding to a Chinese precedent. See Chŏng Pyŏng-uk, *Shijo munhak sajŏn*, no. 670.

> Bright Tung-t'ing moon, the soul of Prince Huai,
> Shines over seven hundred leagues of water;
> Does he, perhaps, bend down to see his faithful Ch'u Yüan's spirit in the stomach of a fish?

The immediate reference here is to one of the Eight Sights of the Hsiao and Hsiang, "Autumn Moon over Tung-t'ing Lake."

118. This vision was made famous in a prose introduction by Wang Po (648–676), "T'eng-wang-ko hsu" (Introduction to T'eng-wang Pavilion), which was appended to a poem he had written on the occasion of the rebuilding of the T'eng-wang Pavilion (located near Po-yang Lake). The two most famous lines of this work provide the reference here: "Thinning mists and a lonely ibis take flight together; autumn waters and endless skies together are one color."

119. This alludes to Tu Fu's poem, "Teng Yo-yang-lou" (Climbing Yo-yang Pavilion). Yo-yang Pavilion is introduced four stanzas before this point, where the narration reads, "Entering the Hsiao and Hsiang Rivers— / The towering structure of the Yo-yang Pavilion."

Having heard of old Tung-t'ing's waters,
Today I climb to Yo-yang Pavilion.
Wu to the East and Ch'u to the South,
The world floats before me day or night.
With no word of friends or family,
I am old and ill in a solitary boat.
In the north, war horses at the mountain passes:
And I lean on the railing and cry.

120. This may be a quotation but I have not yet been able to identify it.

121. This line, which appears again on f. 2:18b, is from "Returning Geese," by the T'ang-dynasty poet Ch'ien Ch'i:

For what reason must you leave, estranged, these rivers Hsiao and Hsiang?
Blue waters and bright sand, moss upon both banks.
When we strike the twenty-five-string lute one moonlit night,
You will come flying, unable to endure our pure sorrow.

The conceit seems to be a commonplace in Korean poetry, appearing also in a *shijo* by Yi Chŏng-bo (1693–1766). See Chŏng Pyŏng-uk, *Shijo munhak sajŏn*, no. 1197.

You there! Wild geese returning to the moonbright Hsiao and Hsiang!
Was the lute of the Hsiang Spirit so sad
That now you cry so, unable to endure pure sorrow?

122. Double Shrine of Huang-ling is the shrine to O Huang and Nü Ying. See n. 42.

123. This is the end of Li Po's poem about O Huang and Nü Ying, "Yuan-pieh-li" (The parting). For a full translation, see Arthur Waley, *The Poetry and Career of Li Po*, pp. 36–37. A similar conceit opens the modern Korean national anthem:

Until the East Sea is dry and Paektu Mountain wears away,
With God's protection may our land survive evermore!

124. The Emperor Shun, a legendary sage emperor of China and husband of O Huang and Nü Ying (who appear before Shim Ch'ŏng here), is said to have invented the five-stringed harp and composed a song for it about the south wind which brought peace and harmony to the lives of all the people. The song refers to the conduct of filial piety, the south wind symbolizing one's parents.

125. Wu Tzu-hsu, a model of loyalty who served the state of Wu, fell into disrepute when rivals at court turned to their advantage his warning that the state of Yueh was not to be trusted, a statement that contradicted policy. He committed suicide with a sword given him by the king, who had his body wrapped in leather and thrown into the river. Nine years later, the armies of Yueh did, in fact, destroy the state of Wu.

126. This phrase, drawn from an anecdote which appears in the *Tso chuan* (Tso commentary), refers to a good man in difficult straits. See James Legge, *The Ch'un Ts'ew*, p. 3.

127. The speaker, Prince Huai of Ch'u, had been invited to visit the state of Ch'in by its reigning Prince Chao, only to be deceived and imprisoned by Ch'in soldiers at the Wu Barrier Gate. He died in exile. See Chang Chi-yŏng, p. 188n4.

128. The lonely cuckoo is the soul of the ruler Tu Yü. See n. 99.

129. The expression, "sound of the bludgeon at Po-lang," refers to an unsuccessful

attempt to assassinate Ch'in Shih-huang-ti (the powerful emperor of Ch'in who unified China in the third century B.C.) at Po-lang (on the banks of the Yellow River in Honan south of Sinsiang).

130. "Whose expression is dejected / And whose features are emaciated" are a direct quote, set in Korean syntax, from the third line of "Yü-fu" (The fisherman), an anonymous work in rhyming prose from the third century B.C. about the rejected but still loyal minister Ch'ü Yuan. See next note.

131. "Li Sao" (On encountering sorrow) is the major poetical work of the third century B.C. Chinese statesman and poet, Ch'ü Yuan, who had served Prince Huai of Ch'u well, only to fall victim to court intrigue. The work is an expression of his despair at being so misunderstood by his prince. See n. 108.

132. Though only the first and tenth lines of the 187-line "Li Sao" are quoted here, they are sufficient to identify the poet and to express his innocent sincerity. The translation comes from David Hawkes, *Ch'u Tz'u*, p. 22.

133. These two lines are from the "Ch'ilsŏk-pu" (Seven night fu) by the Korean poet Kim In-hu (1510–1560), which appears in the collection of his works, *Hasŏ chip*.

134. These two lines by Wang Po come from his "Appreciation on T'eng-wang Pavilion." See n. 118.

135. These are the third and fourth lines of Tu Fu's poem, "Teng-kao" (From a height), which is thoroughly analyzed in Hawkes, *A Little Primer of Tu Fu*, pp. 203–205.

136. I have set these four lines in italics because they read like lines of poetry but I have not yet found a source for them. Chang Chi-yŏng (p. 189n17) says only that they describe the fall scenery of the Honan area of China.

137. Chang Chi-yŏng (p. 190n18) identifies this couplet as drawn from a poem by the Korean poet Shin Kwang-su (?1711–?1775) which, in turn, is indebted to Tu Fu's "Climbing Yo-yang Pavilion".

138. These are the concluding lines of one of Li Po's poems on the subject of Tung-t'ing Lake (see Obata, p. 171). The Queens of Hsiang are the wives of the Emperor Shun, O Huang and Nü Ying.

139. "Autumn Sorrow" is another name for Sung Yü's fourth-century *Chiu-pien* (Nine arguments). See Hawkes, *Ch'u Tz'u*, p. 92ff.

140. The narrator is comparing Shim Ch'ŏng's merchant boat to the ill-fated boats of legend—sent forth by the first Ch'in emperor and by the first Han emperor—that carried others to their deaths. The Ch'in-dynasty emperor, Shih-huang-ti, hearing that the Elixir of Eternal Life was to be found on an enchanted island in the East Sea, sent the Taoist adept Hsu Shih with three thousand boys and girls to gather herbs for the elixer but they never returned. The Han Emperor Wu-ti, also interested in Taoist alchemy, sent out many expeditions in search of the Elixir of Eternal Life.

141. This description of a storm-tossed ship shares many elements with an anonymous narrative *shijo* poem which appears as no. 224 in Richard Rutt, *Bamboo Grove*. See also Chŏng Pyŏng-uk, *Shijo munhak sajŏn*, no. 330, who reports ten extant versions.

142. *Turidung-duridung* is the sound of drumming.

143. The "Thirty-third Heaven" is given by Soothill and Hodous (p. 60) as Indra's Heaven, centered on Mount Sumeru, where Indra rules. "Mansions of the Sky" here translates the "twenty-eight constellations" of the Chinese zodiac.

144. The Four Sages are Confucius, Mencius, Yen Hui (a disciple of Confucius) and Tseng Ts'an (another disciple of Confucius).

145. The text of the invocation, up to this point, is corrupt in many places (particularly in the first ten lines) and does not appear in variant editions, which would have afforded a comparative basis for analysis. It was probably recited purely for its impressionistic value with little concern for its literal content. From this point on, however, the text grows more specific with boat lore, and variant texts offer useful guidance to the translator.

146. This is the Yellow Emperor, famous among China's legendary founding rulers. His name, Hsien Yuan, may be a village near his home or it may refer to wheeled vehicles, which he is said to have invented.

147. Hsia Yü, first ruler of the Hsia dynasty, is said by the *Book of Documents* (*Shu ching*) to have organized the territory of the realm according to its use and, on the basis of distance from the capital, established Five Domains: 1) the Imperial Domain, 2) the Domain of the Nobles, 3) the Peace-securing Domain, 4) the Domain of Restraint, and 5) the Wild Domain. For detailed discussion, see James Legge, *The Shoo King*, pp. 142–147.

148. Wu Tzu-hsu, a native of the Ch'u state, fled to the Wu state as a result of political adversity. While he was in flight to Wu, a fisherman is said to have aided the fugitive by ferrying him across a river. Hence, the rowing song. For more on Wu Tzu-hsu, see n. 125.

149. "The general who fell at Kai-hsia" refers to the rout of Hsiang Yü in 202 B.C. by the forces of his great rival Liu Pang at the battle of Kai-hsia. Liu Pang then founded the Han dynasty.

150. This incident occurs in *San-kuo-chih yen-i* (Romance of the Three Kingdoms). See C. H. Brewitt-Taylor, tr., *San Kuo or Romance of the Three Kingdoms*, I, 508–518. It is also retold in Su Shih's rhymeprose, "The Red Cliff."

151. T'ao Ch'ien (365–427), a Chinese poet of the Six Dynasties period, quit his government post after only eighty-three days with the complaint that he could not "crook the hinges of my back for five pecks of rice a day." Chang Han, a third-century poet, also quit his post to go home one day in autumn when his nostalgia grew to be too much for him.

152. These two lines are adapted from the opening section of Su Shih's "The Red Cliff." The year *jen-hsu* is the fifty-ninth year in the Chinese sexagenary cycle, which is used to number years in sixty-year cycles.

153. Since this line stubbornly resists decipherment, I have substituted what appears in its place in many other texts: two lines from a hymn of praise to Buddha in the *Diamond Sutra*. They appear in the Korean *Kŭmgang-gyŏng samgahae* (Thrice-annotated Diamond Sutra) (Seoul: Han'gŭl hakhoe reprint, 1961), vol. 5, pp. 50–52. The metaphorical poem speaks of the search for compassion and enlightenment, using the symbols of fishing. The moonlight is symbolic of the Buddha's infinite wisdom. The relevant passage reads:

He drops a thousand-foot line straight down;
If one wave barely stirs, ten thousand more follow.

The night is quiet, water cold, and the fish do not eat;
The boat returns, filled only with the brightness of the moon.

154. These two lines are drawn from Wang Po's (648–676) poem, "T'sai-lien-ch'ü" (Picking the lotus).

155. I have dropped an indecipherable line referring to a fisherman.

156. Emerald-land (*yuri-guk*) often implies a fairyland but here seems to substitute for an explicit reference to Korea.

157. Water and rice is a self-deprecating request since such ceremonies involve a hearty feast, like the one the sailors had prepared earlier.

158. This is a line from Su Shih's prose gem "The Red Cliff," where the poet compares himself with a hero of old: "And what are you and I compared with him? Fishermen and woodcutters on the river's isles, with fish and shrimps and deer for mates, riding a boat as shallow as a leaf, pouring each other drinks from battlegourds; mayflies visiting between heaven and earth, infinitesimal grains in the vast sea, mourning the passing of our instant of life, envying the long river which never ends!" (Birch, p. 382.)

159. "Wild goose" is a reference to the tradition that the Chinese envoy Su Wu, while held prisoner in the far north by the barbarian Hsiung-nu, sent an appeal back to his emperor in a letter tied to the leg of a wild goose. See n. 85.

160. See n. 19 for the Jade Emperor.

161. Although Shim Ch'ŏng has already jumped into the water, the text here uses the word, "tomorrow" and employs a prospective verb form. This apparent "flashback" is not unique to the Wanp'an text.

162. Originally a Chinese metaphysical concept translated as "Great Unity" or "Great Monad," T'ai-i was personified as a Supreme Being of popular Taoism. This Korean text treats T'ai-i as a fairy ranking below the Jade Emperor.

163. Ch'ih Sung-tzu is an immortal of the Chinese Taoist pantheon who is said to have controlled the wind and rain in the legendary age.

164. Ko Hsien-weng is another legendary Taoist figure.

165. Ma Ku was a Taoist fairy of ancient China and an adept in the black art. Fu Fei, the daughter of the legendary Chinese Emperor Fu Hsi, drowned in the Lo River (a tributary of the Yellow River).

166. The Lady of Nan-yueh is a legendary Chinese Taoist adept who lived on Mount Nan-yueh, one of the five sacred mountains of China. She and her Eight Fairies also figure into the late-seventeenth-century Korean novel by Kim Man-jung, *Kuun-mong* (The nine cloud dream).

167. These six lines seem to be a conventional catalogue. They also constitute most of the body of a lengthy *shijo* by Kim Su-jang (1690–?). See Chŏng Pyŏng-uk, *Shijo munhak sajŏn,* no. 253. There are traditional anecdotes relating to each of these people and their particular musical talents.

168. These six titles are the names of traditional Chinese tunes to which *tz'u* poetry was conventionally set.

169. The Inner Three Thousand and the Outer Eight Hundred refers to a plenary assembly of government officials: the three thousand of the central administration and eight hundred from provincial offices.

170. In a legend dating from the reign of the Chinese Han Emperor Wu, Tung-fang Shou (see n. 32 under entry for "Tung-fang Shou") identifies the *ch'ing-tao* (blue-bird) as a messenger from the Queen Mother of the West (see n. 17). The *ch'ing-tao*, therefore, refers to a welcome messenger or letter.

171. This section, in which Lady Chang notices the changes in the scroll and prays to invoke Shim Ch'ŏng's soul, does not appear in any of the texts which are marked for rhythm. Therefore, the rhythms I have assigned here, beginning with the notation *aniri*, are based on the scansion of the text and the conventions that apply elsewhere in the text.

172. Change in its color. Although poetry scrolls are typically written in black ink on white paper, the reference here to a "change in color" becomes understandable when we note that, in other versions of the "Song of Shim Ch'ŏng," a professional painter is summoned to do her portrait (presumably in color) during the last meeting with Lady Chang.

173. "Kuang-han Palace" is a name for the Lunar Palace. Yü-chen is the name of a concubine referred to by the fairy who appears before Kwak-ssi in a dream foretelling the birth of Shim Ch'ŏng, on f. 1:3b.

174. Shang-lin Park, the hunting preserve of the Chinese Han emperors, was exhaustively described in Ssu-ma Hsiang-ju's (?–117) rhymeprose work "Shang-lin fu" which, among other things, catalogues the flowers abounding there.

175. The Huang-chi Palace was the principal palace of the Ming-dynasty emperors.

176. While nearly every line in this heavily allusive passage makes a specific reference, I have not yet found an appropriate reference for this opening pair.

177. This couplet incorporates a line from the Sung-dynasty poet Lin Pu's (?965–1026) "Shan-yuan hsiao-mei" (Plums in a mountain garden), which tells of his love for the cultivation of plum trees (instead of taking a wife).

178. A line from the T'ang poet Liu Yü-hsi (772–842), this refers to Liu Lang, a Chinese Rip van Winkle, who returned from herb-gathering on Mount T'ien-t'ai with his friend Yuan Chao to find that seven generations had passed in what seemed only six months.

179. The periodic redness of the moon is explained as the flowering of the cassia that is said to be visible there. See n. 41.

180. This echoes a poetic fragment that is commonly attributed to Li Po. See, for example, Ch'oe Un-shik, *Shim Ch'ŏng chŏn yŏn'gu*, p. 113n20. I have not located the original poem. The fragment reads, "As I drink at Lung-shan on the ninth, / A yellow flower laughs at me."

181. This line is from "Tai pei pai-t'ou weng" (For an old man who regrets white hair) by the T'ang poet Liu T'ing-chih:

I gamboled with young nobles in the shade of flowering trees;
Clear songs, clever dances, and drinking by the falling flowers.

182. The first line of this couplet is the closing line of a poem by Liu Fang-p'ing (fl. ca. 800), "Ch'un-yuan," which tells of a woman abandoned by her lover and is translated by Soame Jenyns as "Spring Bitterness," in *Three Hundred Poems of the T'ang Dynasty*, p. 57.

Ch'ang-hsin was a Han-dynasty palace, occupied by court women in the reign of

Ch'eng-ti. When a favorite of the emperor, Pan Chieh-yü, was replaced by another, she retired from the Ch'ang-hsin Palace, sad and lonely, "Like a summer fan cast aside come autumn."

183. Hsing-t'an, the Apricot Altar, is the name of a place where Confucius and his disciples once gathered to study. It is mentioned in the *Works of Chuang-tzu* as the setting of a famous encounter between Confucius and a sage-like fisherman. See Burton Watson, *The Complete Works of Chuang-tzu*, p. 344.

184. This couplet is another reference to Liu Lang. See n. 178.

185. The azalea is also called the "cuckoo flower." For the connection between cuckoo and blood, see n. 99.

186. The "Shu chrysanthemum" is named after the ancient Chinese state of Shu, also called Minor Han, or Shu Han (221–263).

187. See n. 17 for jade peach of Yao Lake and n. 32 for Tung-fang Shuo.

188. Literally "from country of the Western frontier" but indicating India, the source of Buddhism, and its symbol, the lotus.

189. This recalls an early scene in Po Chü-i's "Ch'ang-hen-ko" (A song of enduring sorrow) in which the T'ang Emperor Hsuan Tsung (also known as Ming Huang) observes Yang Kuei-fei being bathed in the Hua-ch'ing Pool and chooses her for his concubine. Although he only observes in the poem by Po Chü-i, the Korean text clearly has the emperor himself bathe. Yang Kuei-fei also figures into n. 18.

190. The Ansŏng woodblock edition and the Hashimoto manuscript of 1897 both specify, "She sent her maid away," which might make better sense.

191. One word in this line, *naryu,* is unknown. Ch'oe Un-shik, *Shim Ch'ŏng chŏn yŏn'gu,* p. 119, l. 11, gives it as *narae,* which is also unknown.

192. See nn. 85 and 159 for the story of Su Wu and the letter he sent by tying it to the leg of a wild goose.

193. For this allusion, see n. 121.

194. These two sentences are common epistolary formulas used in traditional Korean letter-writing, as is the following "this unfilial daughter."

195. According to traditional Chinese reckoning, each day was divided into twelve two-hour periods, which I translate as "watches."

196. At this point in the text there is an unmarked shift from dialogue to narration, which may have resulted from an engraver's error.

197. A Chinese emperor here appears to be exercising jurisdiction over a Korean blind man, but this was not a conflict in the mind of the Korean p'ansori audience. We know the "Emperor" here to be Chinese because the use of that title was the exclusive prerogative of the Chinese sovereign, because his capital is called "Hwangsŏng" (imperial capital), and because Shim Ch'ŏng had sold herself to "sailors from Nanking," who took her home with them in the lotus. While Koreans traditionally distinguished themselves from Chinese and other East Asian ethnic groups, they also saw themselves, at the same time, as participants in a regional culture based on the common denominator of the Chinese written language. In addition, Koreans belonged to a Chinese tributary state and knew their king to be a vassal of the Chinese emperor, whom they therefore regarded as their emperor, as well.

198. Yao and Shun, two mythical Chinese sovereigns, were exemplars and cultural heroes.

199. "Bedding" is a guess for the unknown word, *kodongmok.*

200. "I am a silly old bastard" translates archaic slang that is clearly self-depreca-tory but, beyond that, unknown today.

201. This sort of patter was called out by the attendants of an official as he moved through the countryside, to warn others of their approach. Some of it given here is incomprehensible and the translation is only an approximation.

202. The following translation of the petition's text is based entirely upon the inter-pretation in Ch'oe Un-shik, *Shim Ch'ŏng chŏn yŏn'gu,* pp. 130–133. The version given in the Wanp'an text is a pastiche of Chinese phrases that are nearly indecipherable.

203. Tseng Tien was a disciple of Confucius and the father of Tseng Ts'an, one of the twenty-four exemplars of filial piety. His relevance here is not known.

204. This following passage in the *chung chung mori* rhythm is an interpolated song long popular in the p'ansori repertoire, called the "Bird Ballad" (*sae-t'aryŏng*). Such bal-lads abound on many subjects.

205. "Heaven-in-a-vessel" refers to a world inside a hollow gourd into which the legendary Chinese magician Ku Kung would disappear at night. The story is related in Pan Ku's *Han shu* (History of the Former Han dynasty).

206. This, and following lines which are marked by an asterisk at the end, involve some degree of guesswork.

207. This pair turns on puns involving the names of two Chinese poets, Huang T'ing-chien (1050–1110), whose pen name was Yellow Mountain Valley, and T'ao Ch'ien, who was also called the Master of Five Willows. T'ao's village was known, after him, as the Village of the Five Willows. See n. 61.

208. Ning Ch'i, a poor man of ancient China, was riding an ox when discovered by a high official and elevated to high rank. Meng Hao-jan (689–740), a poet of the T'ang dynasty, is said to have sought inspiration while riding a donkey over the snow.

209. The phrase "Po-lo River" is a play on "Po Lo-t'ien," a secondary name of the T'ang-dynasty poet Po Chü-i. The play works only in Korean pronunciation, where the words are homophonous.

210. Chang Ch'ien was a Han-dynasty minister who is celebrated for having been the first official to make China aware of the east-west trade route. There is a poem about him by Li Tsai-wu of the Former Han dynasty which ends, "He took a raft with thoughts of home, did Chang Ch'ien of the Han." (Kwŏn Sang-no and Chang To-bin, *Kosa sŏngŏ sajŏn,* p. 888). Lü Yen, who has already made an appearance on his white heron in the Crystal Palace Episode (f. 2:9a), is ranked among the legendary Taoist immortals.

211. "Broad fields" is a gloss on the secondary name, "Tung-yeh," of the T'ang poet Meng Chiao (751–814). Wo-lung is another name for the hero of the Chinese novel *Romance of the Three Kingdoms,* Chu-ko K'ung-ming, who appears in the next line. Wo-lung comes from the name of a range of hills on his family's land.

212. This line refers to the action of chapter 84 of the *Romance of Three Kingdoms* in which "K'ung-ming Plans the Eight Arrays."

213. The "Four Grayheads of Mount Shang" were four senior officials of ancient China who withdrew from the chaos of the world to seek refuge at Mount Shang.

214. "The Seven Sages of the Bamboo Grove" were a group of wealthy recluses

who frequently debated, composed poetry, and drank together in China of the third century A.D.

215. These two lines are quoted from a poem by the T'ang poet Chang Chi, already mentioned above. See n. 113.

216. *Amit'a-bul, Kwanseum-bosal* is chanted by adherents to the Pure Land sect of Buddhism: "(I submit myself) to the Amita Buddha and to the Goddess of Mercy, Kuan-yin."

217. Chiang Tzu-ya, a wise counselor to King Wen of the Chou dynasty of ancient China, was discovered originally by the king while fishing one day.

218. These two lines refer to the events of chapters 36–38 of the *Romance of Three Kingdoms,* in which Liu Pei visits the clever Chu-ko Liang at his farm in Nan-yang to seek his help.

219. The two lines dropped here because they are too corrupt to yield translation refer to Chang Fei, a major character in the *Romance of the Three Kingdoms.*

220. This sentence incorporates elements of a line from a poem by the T'ang poet Sung Chih-wen. See n. 4.

221. Although the text is unclear, a sexual interpretation seems quite appropriate to this scene.

222. The "meat" he refers to is his male organ.

223. He is toying with a pun: in Korean, the expression "we'll see" can sound like the word for "vulva."

224. *Oyua pangayo* is a refrain equivalent to the English, "O, mill!"

225. "This wood" is the massive, Y-shaped lever of the huge pestle that Blindman Shim is working by treading and shifting his weight. See n. 228.

226. Yu Ch'ao, the legendary Chinese sage, taught men to build houses on the model of the bird's nest.

227. Shen Nung, one of the legendary Sage Rulers who are said to have founded China, taught the people the arts of agriculture. See n. 37.

228. The long, Y-shaped lever on which Blindman Shim is rocking up and down to work the rice-pestle is being treated as a phallic symbol, compared to the "fleshy pestle," or male organ. In the following lines, the shape of the pestle and lever is the basis of his song.

229. For Counselor Chiang, see n. 217 on Chiang Tzu-ya.

230. "The beauty Yü" is the famous beauty Yü Chi, concubine of Hsiang Chi, who was a fierce hegemon of the ancient Chinese state of Ch'u.

231. Literally, "with the footwork used for a swinging song." Since swinging was a woman's sport and was done only standing, he is suggesting that he steps on and off the lever like a girl mounting a swing.

232. King Wen of the ancient Chinese kingdom of Chu, out hunting one day, met the high-principled elder statesman Lü Shang, who was fishing. King Wen, bowing low, successfully prevailed upon the good man to serve as his chief counselor.

233. Po-li Hsi, a minister of the ancient Chinese state of Chin, was so beloved that when he died the land was gripped by sadness; there were neither songs nor games and even the rice mill pounders were silent.

234. The mortar into which the pestle descends during the process of pounding is here called a "clam," a common symbol for the vulva. See n. 28.

235. That is, having been born through the vagina, he would know all about such things in detail.

236. Blindman Shim guesses that he is being taken to an ill person to read mystical texts to promote recovery, a stock-in-trade of many blind men.

237. The Chinese character for the name Shim means "submerged."

238. "Tobacco seed" here refers ironically to a folk-song from the Tongnae area of South Kyŏngsang Province. In the excerpt below, the water-dropper referred to is the size of an orange and the tobacco seed is exceedingly small. The fragment is a dialogue:

"Inside the bodice of a linen jacket,
    See the water-dropper breasts!"
"Have a tobacco-seed's look and go:
    If you look too much you'll strain yourself!"

239. Hsiang Chuang, a loyal follower of the Chinese Han-dynasty ruler Kao Tsu, did a sword dance at a state dinner attended by the king of Ch'u with the intention of assassinating the latter. The famous "Hsiang-chuang Dance" has been modeled on this event.

240. This line is taken from Po Chü-i's lengthy poem on the story of the T'ang imperial concubine Yang Kuei-fei, "Ch'ang-hen ko" (A song of enduring sorrow). See n. 189 and Bynner, p. 95. Yang Kuei-fei's birth so glorified her clan that, in Bynner's translation:

She brought to every father, every mother through the empire
Happiness when a girl was born rather than a boy.

241. According to the *Shih-pa-shih-lueh* (Selections from the eighteen histories), the legendary Chinese Emperor Shun composed the "Nan-feng shih" (Poem of the south wind), which brought peace and harmony to his people. See n. 124. Blindman Shim's three lines here are drawn from the *Shih-pa-shih-lueh* where it describes the reaction of Emperor Shun's court officials upon hearing this "Poem of the South Wind." (*Kambun taikei*, vol. 5, *Shih-pa-shih-lueh*, p. 10).

242. The text gives "Much'ang," which is probably an engraving error for Prefect of Mujang, the official appointment given to the captain of the trading ship from Nan-king.

243. The English can only suggest the style of this high-flown, formulaic paean.

244. This is drawn from an anecdote about the ancient ruler Yao, which appears at the end of the chapter about Confucius in *The Book of Lieh-tzu*. "Yao had ruled the realm for fifty years but did not know whether the realm was in order or not. So then he wandered about the crossroads in disguise and heard the ballad of a boy." The song told Yao that all was in order; and, with satisfaction, he turned the realm over to his successor, Shun. See A. C. Graham, tr., *The Book of Lieh-tzu*, p. 90.

245. This makes Blindman Shim's new son, T'ae-dong, the uncle of the Crown Prince. From this point on, several characters are known by differing names. A chart of names and relationships will help clarify the situation.

```
Kwak-ssi ───────┬─── Blindman Shim Hak-kyu ──────┬──── Blindwoman An
                │      "Father of the Empress"     │      "Lady Chŏngnyŏl"
                │      "King Namp'yŏng"            │      "Queen Insŏng"
                │                                  │
Emperor ──┬─── Shim Ch'ŏng              T'ae-dong ──────── Princess of Yŏn
          │      "Empress"                "Hallim Scholar"   "Lady Wangnyŏl"
Crown Prince ──────── Daughter of         "Scholar Shim"     "Lady Kongnyŏl"
                      Kwŏn Sŏng-un        "President"
                      (Sec'y of State)    "Minister"
```

246. For T'ai Jen, see n. 7. Pan Chao completed the work of Pan Ku, her brother, on his *History of the Former Han Dynasty*. See n. 32, under "Pan Chao."

247. In a traditional Korean wedding ceremony, the groom presents the bride with a carved, wooden mandarin duck as a symbol of conjugal faithfulness.

248. "Thus and such," "so and so" and other such vague terms are sometimes used in p'ansori libretti, perhaps to avoid unwanted repetition.

249. "The President's lady" refers to the wife of T'ae-dong, who has just received appointment to President of the Board of Personnel. See the chart of titles and relationships in n. 245.

250. When his son was born, King Namp'yŏng (Blindman Shim) was "in the declining years facing eighty." Since the son is here twenty, the father should now be "facing one hundred."

BIBLIOGRAPHY
OF SOURCES CITED

Akamatsu Chijō and Akiba Takashi. *Chōsen fuzoku no kenkyū* (A study of Korean shaman practices). 2 vols. Keijō, Ōsaka yagō shoten, 1938.

Allen, Horace N. *Korea: Fact and Fancy.* Seoul, Methodist Publishing House, 1904. Originally published as *Korean Tales:* New York, Putnam, 1889.

An Kye-hyŏn. "P'algwanhoe ko" (A study of the *p'algwanhoe*), in *Tongguk sahak* 4:31–54 (1956).

Bauer, Wolfgang, and Herbert Franke, trs. and eds. *The Golden Casket.* New York, Harcourt, Brace and World, 1964.

Birch, Cyril, ed. *Anthology of Chinese Literature.* New York, Grove Press, 1965.

Bishop, Isabella Bird. *Korea and Her Neighbours.* London, John Murray, 1898.

Bishop, John L. *The Colloquial Short Story in China.* Cambridge, Harvard University Press, 1956.

Brewitt-Taylor, C. H., tr. *San Kuo or Romance of the Three Kingdoms.* 2 vols. Shanghai, Kelly and Walsh, 1925.

Butler, Kenneth D., Jr. "Textual Evolution of the *Heike monogatari*," *Harvard Journal of Asiatic Studies* 26:5–51 (1966).

Bynner, Witter, tr. *The Jade Mountain.* Garden City, Doubleday Anchor Books, 1964.

Chang Chi-yŏng, ed. *Hong Kil-tong chŏn – Shim Ch'ŏng chŏn* (The "Tale of Hong Kil-tong" [and the] "Tale of Shim Ch'ŏng"). Seoul, Chŏngŭm sa, 1964.

Chang Chu-gŭn. "Han'guk kubi munhak sa, sang" (History of Korean oral literature, I), in *Han'guk munhwa sa taegye IV, ŏnŏ munhak sa* (Outline of Korean cultural history IV, history of language and literature). Seoul, Koryŏ taehakkyo, minjok munhwa yŏn'gu so, 1967.

Chang Duk-soon (Chang Tŏk-sun) et al., eds. *Han'guk kubi munhak sŏnjip* (Selection of Korean oral literature). 2nd ed. Seoul, Ilchogak, 1984.

Cho Dong-il (Cho Tong-il). "Hŭngbu chŏn ŭi yangmyŏnsŏng" (The two aspects of the "Tale of Hŭngbu"), in *Nonmun chip* (Thesis Collection), no. 5. Taegu, Kyemyŏng University, 1969.

———. "P'ansori ŭi chŏnbanjŏk sŏnggyŏk" (The general nature of p'ansori), in Cho Dong-il et al., eds., *P'ansori ŭi ihae* (q.v.).

———. *Han'guk munhak t'ongsa* (Comprehensive history of Korean literature). Rev. ed. 5 vols. Seoul, Chishik sanŏp sa, 1989.

——— et al., eds. *P'ansori ŭi ihae* (Understanding p'ansori). Seoul, Ch'angjak kwa pip'yŏng sa, 1978.

Cho Sŏng. "Miji ŭi kut kwa muga" (Rites and songs of the hereditary shamans). Presented at the 42nd monthly meeting of the Korean Cultural Anthropology Society. Seoul, Seoul National University College of Liberal Arts and Sciences, April 4, 1968.

Ch'oe Nam-sŏn. *Chosŏn sangsik mundap sokp'yŏn* (Common sense questions and answers on Korea, II). Seoul, Tongmyŏng sa, 1947.

Ch'oe Sang-su. *Han'guk min'gan chŏnsŏl chip* (Collected popular Korean legends). Seoul, T'ongmungwan, 1958.

Ch'oe Tong-hyŏn. "P'ansori yŏn'gu sa" (History of p'ansori research), in Kang Han-yŏng et al., eds., *P'ansori* (q.v.)

Ch'oe Un-shik. *Shim Ch'ŏng chŏn yŏn'gu* (A study of the "Tale of Shim Ch'ŏng"). Seoul, Chimmun tang, 1982.

———. *Shim Ch'ŏng chŏn* (The "Tale of Shim Ch'ŏng"). Seoul, Shiin sa, 1984.

Ch'oe Wŏn-shik. "Ŭnsegye yŏn'gu" (A study on "Silver World"), in *Ch'angjak kwa pip'yŏng* 13.2:271–297 (no. 48, 1978).

Chŏng Kwŏn-jin. *P'ansori Shim Ch'ŏng ka* (P'ansori "Song of Shim Ch'ŏng"). Seoul, Bureau of Cultural Properties, 1968.

Chŏng No-shik. *Chosŏn ch'anggŭk sa* (History of Korean singing drama). Seoul, Chosŏn ilbo sa, 1940.

Chŏng Pyŏng-hŏn. "Yi Nal-ch'i p'an Shim Ch'ŏng ka ŭi sŏnggyŏk kwa p'ansori sachŏk wich'i" (The nature of and position in p'ansori history of Yi Nal-ch'i's "Song of Shim Ch'ŏng"), *Kugŏ kyoyuk* 53/54:231–247 (December 1985).

———. "P'ansori ŭi hyŏngsŏng kwa pyŏnmo" (Formation and change in p'ansori), in Kang Han-yŏng et al., eds., *P'ansori* (q.v.).

Chŏng Pyŏng-uk. "Koshiga ŭmnyullon sŏsŏl" (An introduction to a theory of prosody for old poetry), in *Ch'oe Hyŏn-bae sŏnsaeng hwan'gap kinyŏm nonmun chip* (Commemorative theses for the sixtieth birthday of Ch'oe Hyŏn-bae). Seoul, Sasanggye sa, 1954.

———. *Shijo munhak sajŏn* (Dictionary of *shijo* literature). Seoul, Sin'gu munhwa sa, 1966.

———. "Haesŏl" (Explanatory note), in Kim So-hŭi, *Shim Ch'ŏng ka* (q.v.).

———. *Han'guk ŭi p'ansori* (Korea's p'ansori). Seoul, Chimmun tang, 1981.

Chŏng Sang-ch'ŏn, et al. *Seoul yukpaengnyŏn sa* (Six-hundred-year history of Seoul). 3 vols. Seoul, City of Seoul, 1979.

Clark, Donald N. "Hanyang ka" ("Song of the capital"), in David McCann, ed., *Black Crane*. Ithaca, Cornell University East Asian Papers, no. 14, 1977.

Creel, H. G. *Confucius and the Chinese Way*. New York, Harper and Row, 1960.

Graham, A. C., tr. *The Book of Lieh-tzu*. London, John Murray, 1960.

Han Myŏng-hŭi. "Ajik to ch'angch'anghan sorikkun" (A still-great singer), in Yu Ik-sŏ et al., *Myŏngin myŏngch'ang* (q.v.).

Hanan, Patrick D. "The Development of Fiction and Drama," in Raymond Dawson, ed., *The Legacy of China*. Oxford, The Clarendon Press, 1964.

———. *The Chinese Short Story*. Cambridge, Harvard University Press, 1973.

Han'guk munhwa illyuhak-hoe (Korean cultural anthropology society), ed. *Han'guk minsok chonghap chosa pogosŏ, chŏnnam-p'yŏn* (Consolidated research report on Korean popular culture, South Chŏlla). Seoul, Munhwa kongbobu munhwajae kwalli kuk, 1969.

Han'guk munhwa yŏn'gu wŏn. *Han'guk kodae sosŏl chongsŏ* (Korean old novels series). 4 vols. Seoul, Ewha Women's University, 1958–1961.

Hawkes, David. *Ch'u Tz'u: The Songs of the South*. Boston, Beacon Press, 1962.

———. *A Little Primer of Tu Fu*. Oxford, The Clarendon Press, 1967.

Henthorn, William E. "The Early Days of Western-Inspired Drama in Korea," in *Yearbook of Comparative and General Literature*, no. 15, Supplement Section. Bloomington, Indiana, 1966.

———. *A History of Korea*. New York, The Free Press, 1971.

Heyman, Alan C., tr. "The Story of Shim Ch'ŏng," in *Korea Journal*, 30.3:50–67 and 30.4:57–67 (March and April 1990).

Hŏ Kyu et al., eds. *P'ansori yŏn'gu* (P'ansori studies). Seoul, P'ansori hakhoe, 1989.

Holmes, Burton, ed. "Seoul, the Capital City of Korea," in *Burton Holmes Travelogues*, vol. 10. New York, The Travelogue Bureau, 1920.

Hong, Tjyong-ou [Hong Chong-u]. *Le Bois Sec Refleuri*. Paris, Ernest Leroux, 1893.

Hori, Ichiro. *Folk Religion in Japan*. Chicago, University of Chicago Press, 1968.

Howard, Keith. *Bands, Songs, and Shamanistic Rituals: Folk Music in Korean Society*. Seoul, Royal Asiatic Society, Korea Branch, 1989.

Hrdlickova, Vena. "Some Observations on the Chinese Art of Story-telling," in *Acta Universitatis Carolinae—Philologica 3: Orientalia Praegensia* (University Karlova) 3:53–77 (1964).

Im Chin-t'aek. "Sarainnŭn p'ansori" (Living p'ansori), in Paek Nak-ch'ŏng et al., eds., *Han'guk munhak ŭi hyŏndangye, II* (The present stage of Korean literature, II). Seoul, Ch'angjak kwa pip'yŏng sa, 1983.

Iryŏn. *Samguk yusa* (Memorabilia of the Three Kingdoms; 1285), tr. Yi Pyŏng-do. Seoul, Tongguk munhwa sa, 1962.

Jenyns, Soame, tr. *Three Hundred Poems of the T'ang Dynasty*. London, John Murray, 1944.

Kambun taikei (Survey of the Chinese classics). 20 vols. Tokyo, 1914.

Kang Han-yŏng. "Kwangdae ka haesŏl" (Commentary on the "Song of the Kwangdae"), *Hyŏndae munhak* 2.8:146–157 (1956).

———. "Shin Chae-hyo ŭi p'ansori sasŏl yŏn'gu" (A study of Shin Chae-hyo's p'ansori libretti), in Cho Ŭi-sŏl et al., eds, *Shin Chae-hyo p'ansori chŏnjip* (Complete p'ansori of Shin Chae-hyo), charyo ch'ongsŏ, No. 5. Seoul, Yonsei University inmun kwahak yŏn'gu so, 1969.

———. "P'ansori ŭi iron" (The theory of p'ansori), *Kugŏ kungmun hak* 49/50:9–16 (September 1970).

———. *P'ansori*. Seoul, Sejong taewang kinyŏm saŏp hoe, 1977.

————. "Ingan Shin Chae-hyo ŭi chaejomyŏn" (A re-illumination of the man Shin Chae-hyo), in Kang Han-yŏng et al., eds., *P'ansori* (q.v.).

———— ed. *Shin Chae-hyo p'ansori sasŏl chip* (Collected p'ansori libretti of Shin Chae-hyo). Seoul, Minjung sŏgwan, 1971.

———— et. al., eds. *P'ansori*. Chŏnju, Chŏnbuk aehyang undong ponbu, 1988.

Kim Dong-uk (Kim Tong-uk). "Ch'un-hyang chŏn ibon ko" (A study of the variant editions of the "Tale of Ch'un-hyang), in *Samship chunyŏn kinyŏm nonmun chip* (Thirtieth anniversary commemorative thesis collection). Seoul, Chungang University, 1955.

————. "P'ansori palsaeng ko, I" (An inquiry into the origins of p'ansori, I), in *Nonmun chip* (Collected theses), no. 2. Seoul, Seoul National University, 1955.

————. "P'ansori palsaeng ko, II" (An inquiry into the origins of p'ansori, II), in *Nonmun chip* (Collected theses), no. 3. Seoul, Seoul National University, 1956.

————. "Han'gŭl sosŏl panggakpon ŭi sŏngnip e tae-hayŏ" (On the advent of commercial editions of vernacular novels), in *Hyangt'o Sŏul* 8:38–67 (July 1960).

————. *Han'guk kayo ŭi yŏn'gu* (A study of Korean songs). Seoul, Ŭryu munhwa sa, 1961.

————. *Ch'un-hyang chŏn yŏn'gu* (A Study of the "Tale of Ch'un-hyang"). Seoul, Yonsei University, 1965.

————. "P'ansori sa yŏng'gu ŭi che munje" (Several questions in the study of p'ansori history), *Inmun kwahak* 20:1–28 (1968).

————, ed. "Wanp'an Shim Ch'ŏng chŏn," *Inmun kwahak charyo ch'ongsŏ* (Cultural science materials), no. 8. Seoul, Yonsei University, 1972.

————. *Kososŏl p'an'gakpon chŏnjip* (Collection of woodblock editions of old novels). Seoul, Yonsei University, 1973.

Kim Ki-su. *Han'guk ŭmak: Sugung ka, Hŭngbu ka, Shim Ch'ŏng ka* (Korean music: "Song of the Water Palace," "Song of Hŭngbu," and "Song of Shim Ch'ŏng"). Seoul, Chŏnt'ong ŭmak yŏn'gu hoe, 1981.

Kim Pu-sik. *Samguk sagi* (History of the three kingdoms; 1145), tr. Kim Chong-gwŏn. Seoul, Sŏnjin munhwa sa, 1960.

Kim So-hŭi. *P'ansori Shim Ch'ŏng chŏn* (P'ansori "Tale of Shim Ch'ŏng"). Seoul, Sinsegye Record Company, 1969.

————. *Shim Ch'ŏng ka* ("Song of Shim Ch'ŏng"). Seoul, Sŏngŭm Record Company, 1974.

Kim T'ae-gon. *Hwangch'ŏn muga yŏn'gu* (A study of Hwangch'ŏn shaman chants). Seoul, Ch'angu sa, 1966.

————. "Shim Ch'ŏng chŏn ŭi kŭnwŏn sŏlhwa: muga rŭl t'ong-han koch'al" (Source tale of the "Tale of Shim Ch'ŏng": an investigation through shaman songs), *Mulli hakch'ong* 4:86–101 (1967). Seoul, Kyung Hee University.

————. "Han'guk musok ŭi chiyŏk chŏk t'ŭkching" (Regional characteristics of Korean shaman culture), in Kim In-hoe et al., eds. *Han'guk musok ŭi chonghap chŏk koch'al* (Comprehensive study of Korean shaman culture). Seoul, Kodae minsok munhwa yŏn'gu so, 1982.

Kim T'ae-jun. *Chosŏn sosŏl sa* (History of Korean novels). Seoul, Ch'ŏngjin sŏgwan, 1933.

Kim Yŏl-gyu. *Han'guk minsok kwa munhak yŏn'gu* (Studies on Korean folklore and literature). 2nd ed. Seoul, Ilchogak, 1989.

Kwŏn Sang-no and Chang To-bin. *Kosa sŏngŏ sajŏn* (Dictionary of allusions and phrases). Seoul, Hagwŏn sa, 1961.

Kwanghaegun ilgi (Records of Kwanghaegun), 3 vols. Seoul, Kuksa p'yŏnch'an wiwŏnhoe, 1991.

Ledyard, Gari. *The Dutch Come to Korea.* Seoul, Royal Asiatic Society, 1971.

Lee Duhyŏn (Yi Tu-hyŏn). "History of Korean Drama," *Korea Journal* 4.6:4–7 (June 1964).

————. *Han'guk kamyŏn kŭk* (Korean mask drama). Seoul, Han'guk kamyŏn kŭk yŏn'gu hoe, 1969.

————. *Han'guk yŏn'gŭk sa* (History of Korean drama). Rev. ed. Seoul, Hagyŏn sa, 1987.

Lee Ki-baik (Yi Ki-baek). *Han'guk sa shillon* (A new history of Korea). Rev. ed. Seoul, Ilchogak, 1990.

Lee, Peter H. "Introduction to the Chang'ga: The Long Poem," *Oriens Extremus* 3:94–115 (1956).

————. *A Korean Storyteller's Miscellany: The P'aegwan chapki of Ŏ Sukkwŏn.* Princeton, Princeton University Press, 1989.

Legge, James, tr. *The Shoo King.* Vol. 3 of *The Chinese Classics.* London, 1865.

————. *The She King.* Vol. 4 of *The Chinese Classics.* London, 1872.

————. *The Ch'un Ts'ew.* Vol. 5 of *The Chinese Classics.* London, 1872.

————. *The Confucian Analects.* Vol. 1 of *The Chinese Classics.* London, 1892.

————. *The Works of Mencius.* Vol. 2 of *The Chinese Classics.* London, 1895.

Lord, Albert B. *The Singer of Tales.* New York, Atheneum, 1970. Originally published in 1960 by Harvard University Press.

Lowell, Percival. *Chosŏn: The Land of the Morning Calm.* Boston, Ticknor and Company, 1886.

Lu Hsun, ed. *T'ang Sung ch'uan-ch'i chi* (Collected tales of the T'ang and Sung). Peking, Jen-min wen-hsueh ch'u-pan-she, 1952.

Mao Concordance to Shih Ching. Harvard-Yenching Institute Sinological Index Series, Supplement No. 9. Cambridge, Harvard-Yenching Institute, 1962.

McCann, David. *Form and Freedom in Korean Poetry.* Leiden, E.J. Brill, 1988.

O Se-ha. "Shim Ch'ŏng chŏn ibon ko" (An examination of variant texts of the "Tale of Shim Ch'ŏng"), *Kungmunhak* 6:109–119 (November 1962).

Obata, Shigeyoshi, tr. *The Works of Li Po.* New York, Paragon Reprint Corp, 1965.

Pak Hŏn-bong. *Ch'angak taegang* (Survey of vocal music). Seoul, Kugak yesul hakkyo, 1966.

Pak Hwang. *P'ansori sosa* (Short history of p'ansori). Seoul, Sin'gu munhwa sa, 1974.

————. *Ch'anggŭk sa yŏn'gu* (A study of the history of singing drama). Seoul, Paengnok ch'ulp'an sa, 1976.

————. *P'ansori ibaengnyŏn sa* (Two-hundred-year history of p'ansori). Seoul, Sasang sahoe yŏn'gu so, 1987.

Parry, Milman. "Studies in the Epic Technique of Oral Verse-Making, I, Homer and Homeric Style," *Harvard Studies in Classical Philology* 41:73–147 (1930).

Pihl, Marshall R. "Korea in the Bardic Tradition: P'ansori as an Oral Art," in *Korean*

Studies Forum, no. 2 (Spring–Summer 1977), Korean-American Educational Commission (Seoul).

Reischauer, Edwin O. *Ennin's Travels in T'ang China*. New York, The Ronald Press, 1955.

Robinson, G. W., tr. *Poems of Wang Wei*. Baltimore, Penguin, 1973.

Ruch, Barbara. "Medieval Jongleurs and the Making of a National Literature," in John W. Hall and Toyoda Takeshi, eds., *Japan in the Muromachi Age*. Berkeley, University of California Press, 1977.

Rutt, Richard. "Flower Boys of Silla," *Transactions of the Korea Branch of the Royal Asiatic Society* 38:1–66 (1961).

———. *The Bamboo Grove*. Berkeley, University of California Press, 1971.

Samship chunyŏn kinyŏm nonmun chip (Thirtieth anniversary commemorative thesis collection). Seoul, Chungang University, 1955.

Scholes, Robert, and Robert Kellogg. *The Nature of Narrative*. London, Oxford University Press, 1966.

Seo Dae-seok (Sŏ Tae-sŏk). "P'ansori hyŏngsŏng ŭi sabŭi" (Raising questions about the formation of p'ansori), in *Uri munhwa*, no. 3. Seoul, Uri munhwa yŏn'gu hoe, 1969.

———. "P'ansori wa sŏsa muga ŭi taebi yŏn'gu" (A comparative study of p'ansori and narrative shaman songs), in *Han'guk munhwa yŏn'gu wŏn nonch'ong* (Collected theses of the Institute for Korean cultural research), no. 34. Seoul, Ewha Women's University, 1979.

———. "Pari kongju yŏn'gu" (A study of "Princess Pari"), in Chang Duk-soon et al., eds., *Han'guk kubi munhak sŏnjip* (Selection of Korean oral literature). 2nd ed. Seoul, Ilchogak, 1984.

Shin Chae-hyo. *P'ansori sasŏl chip* (Collected p'ansori libretti [of Shin Chae-hyo]), ed. Kang Han-yŏng. Seoul, Minjung sŏgwan, 1971.

Skillend, W. E. "The Story of Sim Ch'ŏng," in Chung Chong-wha, ed., *Korean Classical Literature*. London, Kegan Paul International, 1989.

Sohn Pow-key, et al. *The History of Korea*. Seoul, Korean National Commission for UNESCO, 1970.

Song Bang-song (Song Pang-song). "*Kwangdae ka*: A Source Material for the P'ansori Tradition," *Korean Journal* 16.8:24–32 (August 1976).

———. *Han'guk ŭmak t'ongsa* (Comprehensive history of Korean music). Seoul, Ilchogak, 1988.

Soothill, William Edward, and Lewis Hodous. *A Dictionary of Chinese Buddhist Terms*. London, Kegan Paul, Trench, Trubner, 1937.

Taylor, Charles M., tr. *Winning Buddha's Smile*. Boston, Richard G. Bedger, the Gorham Press, 1919.

Unhŏyongha, ed. *Pulgyo sajŏn* (Dictionary of Buddhism). Seoul, Pŏpt'ong sa, 1962.

Waley, Arthur. *Chinese Poems*. London, George Allen and Unwin, 1946.

———. *The Poetry and Career of Li Po*. London, George Allen and Unwin, 1950.

———. *Ballads and Stories from Tunhuang*. London, George Allen and Unwin, 1960.

———. *The Book of Songs*. New York, Grove Press, 1960.

Walraven, B. C. A. *Muga: The Songs of Korean Shamanism*. Leiden, by the author, 1985.

Watson, Burton, tr. *Records of the Grand Historian of China*. New York, Columbia University Press, 1961.

———. *The Complete Works of Chuang-tzu*. New York, Columbia University Press, 1968.

Yang Chae-yŏn. "Sandaehŭi e ch'wi-hayŏ" (Concerning the *sandaehŭi*)," in *Samship chu-nyŏn kinyŏm nonmun chip* (q.v.).

Yi Ch'ang-bae, ed. *Kayo chipsŏng* (Collection of songs). Rev. ed. Mimeo. Seoul, Ch'ŏnggu kojŏn sŏngak hagwŏn, 1961. The *Oga chŏnjip* (Complete five songs) of Yi Sŏn-yu is appended to only the revised edition. Neither the original 1955 mimeo imprint nor the 1976 typeset edition (Seoul, Hongin munhwa sa) incorporates it.

Yi cho shillok (Veritable records of the Yi dynasty). 56 vols. Tokyo, Gakushūin, 1964.

Yi Hae-jo. *Kangsangnyŏn* (Lotus on the river). Seoul, Shin'gu sorim, 1912.

Yi Hye-gu. "Song Man-jae ŭi 'Kwanuhŭi'" (Song Man-jae's "Viewing a performance of actors"), in *Samship chunyŏn kinyŏm nonmun chip* (q.v.).

———. *Han'guk ŭmak yŏn'gu* (Studies in Korean music). Seoul, Kungmin ŭmak yŏn'gu hoe, 1957.

———. "P'ansori ŭi ŭmakchŏk t'ŭksŏng" (Characteristics of p'ansori music), in Cho Dong-il et al., eds., *P'ansori ŭi ihae* (q.v.).

Yi Hyo-jae et al. "Life in Urban Korea," in *Transactions of the Korea Branch of the Royal Asiatic Society* 46:1–92 (1971).

Yi Kyu-tae. *Modern Transformation of Korea*. Seoul, Sejong Publishing Company, 1970.

Yi Man-yŏl. *Han'guk sa yŏnp'yo* (Chronological table of Korean history). Seoul, Yŏngmin sa, 1989.

Yi Po-hyŏng. "P'ansori ran muŏshinya?" (What is p'ansori?), in Yi Chae-sŏng, ed., *P'an-sori tasŏt madang* (P'ansori's five songs). Seoul, Han'guk pŭrit'aenik'ŏ hoesa, 1982.

———. "P'ansori sasŏl ŭi kŭkchŏk sanghwang e ttarŭn changdanjo ŭi kusŏng" (Formulation of p'ansori rhythms and modes according to dramatic context of the libretto), in Cho Dong-il et al., eds., *P'ansori ŭi ihae* (q.v.).

Yi Pyŏng-do et al., eds. *Han'guk tae paekkwa sajŏn* (Great encyclopedia of Korean studies). 3 vols. Seoul, Ūryu munhwa sa, 1989.

Yi Sŏn-yu. *Oga chŏnjip* (The five songs). Seoul, Taedong insoe so, 1933.

Yu Ik-sŏ, et al. *Myŏngin myŏngch'ang* (Great people, great singing). Seoul, Tonga ilbo sa, 1987.

Yu Min-yŏng. *Han'guk kaehwagi yŏn'gŭk sahoe sa* (Social history of Korean enlightenment-period theater). Seoul, Saemun sa, 1987.

Yu Yŏng-dae. *Shim Ch'ŏng chŏn yŏn'gu* (A study of the "Tale of Shim Ch'ŏng"). Seoul, Munhak ak'ademi, 1989.

Yun Se-p'yŏng. *Shim Ch'ŏng chŏn* (Tale of Shim Ch'ŏng). Tokyo, Hagu sŏbang, 1955.

GENERAL INDEX

INDEX TO THE TRANSLATION

This listing provides access to the allusive materials that abound in the "Song of Shim Ch'ŏng." Major scenes and episodes are listed under characters' names (Kwak-ssi, Blindman Shim, and Shim Ch'ŏng). Interpolated songs are listed as such in a group.